Mel White's

Readers Theatre Anthology

Twenty-Eight
all-occasion readings
for storytellers

Melvin R. White

MERIWETHER PUBLISHIN
Colorado Springs, Colora

Meriwether Publishing Ltd., Publisher
Box 7710
Colorado Springs, CO 80933

Editor: Arthur L. Zapel
Typesetting: Sharon E. Garlock
Cover design: Tom Myers

© Copyright MCMXCIII Meriwether Publishing Ltd.
Printed in the United States of America
First Edition

Library of Congress Cataloging-in-Publication Data

White, Melvin Robert, 1911-
    Mel White's readers theatre anthology : 28 all-occasion readings for storytellers / by Melvin R. White.
      p.   cm.
   ISBN 0-916260-86-0
   1. Reader's theater.   2. Drama--Collections.   I. Title.
  II. Title: Readers theatre anthology.
PN2081.R4W47   1992
808.8'54--dc20
                                       92-40058
                                           CIP

TABLE OF CONTENTS

NOTE: *The numerals running vertically down the left margin of each page of dialog are for the convenience of the director. With these, he/she may easily direct attention to a specific passage.*

INTRODUCTION

Readers Theatre began for me in the early '60s when I taught the first of several summer sessions at Southwest Missouri State College, and met Dr. Leslie Irene Coger. We had both seen and been excited by the celebrity-filled Drama Quartet, and decided to see what we could do with scripts, stands, and stools. The result was a condensed version of "Romeo and Juliet." Soon we were teaching classes in Readers Theatre, as we chose to call this dramatic approach to literature. We experimented with literature other than plays — newspaper columns, short stories, poetry, essays, letters, radio scripts, and even comic strips. What fun we had, and how quickly this oral interpretation activity spread!

A textbook was needed for our classes, so in 1963, Dr. Coger and I published one at our own expense: "Studies in Readers Theatre." A few years later we were asked to do a workshop at the Chicago convention of the Speech Communication Association. An editor approached us there, and asked if we'd work with him on a textbook, warning us that it would probably be a "prestige publication" with small sales. Three editions of *Readers Theatre Handbook: A Dramatic Approach to Literature* followed. They were published by Scott, Foresman and Company. The first copyright was in 1967.

Readers Theatre had caught on! I was asked to do workshops and/or give lectures at state, regional, and national speech and theatre conventions. The United States Army discovered Readers Theatre, bought 375 copies of our book, one for each Army base around the world that had a producing theatre — and throughout the years has sent me to judge plays, lecture, direct plays and Readers Theatre productions all over the United States, Europe, the Pacific, and the Caribbean. Churches discovered Readers Theatre and began to use it. Secondary schools and junior colleges became interested, and it was found that Readers Theatre is for children, too.

Doing "The Mikado" without music at the University of Arkansas, and later at Brooklyn College, City of New York, at The Banff School of Fine Arts in Canada, and the University of Hawaii was one of most challenging uses I made of Readers Theatre.

1

Introducing Readers Theatre at Brooklyn College in a student lounge with a reading of John Steinbeck's "The Promise," and introducing Readers Theatre into Canada with Stephen Leacock's "Behind the Beyond" were two other noteworthy occasions. Adapting and directing Thornton Wilder's "Skin of Our Teeth" in the Canal Zone at the Army's Surfside Theatre, with other stagings of it at Hawaii and at Banff was much fun for me. In recent years, writing for and performing with the Bay Area Readers Quartet in such varied works as Dorothy Parker's "Glory in the Afternoon," "A New Look at Shakespeare," and Twain's "Adam and Eve" have been very rewarding. Adapting and performing for children's audiences has been exciting, too.

Throughout the years I took pleasure in finding materials to adapt for performance, and did so for my students and others. Eventually, we included sample scripts in our textbooks, because there was a demand for unique titles. Contemporary Drama Service, a division of Meriwether Publishing Ltd., became the leading purveyor of Readers Theatre scripts. They have published seven of my *Readers Theatre Sample Packets*, each with four or five scripts. Three volumes of *Stories for Children* each include three, four or five scripts.

My favorite scripts include "Christmas Comes But Once a Year," "Now Christmas Has Come," "While Shepherds Watched Their Flocks," "Let Us Give Thanks," "Wind in the Willows," and "The Wizard of Oz." These have proved useful to busy teachers and directors who do not have time to work up scripts on their own.

So this theatre professor who liked to work in radio and television slid into oral interpretation with Readers Theatre, and spent most of the last 30 years before retirement in this rewarding speech activity. Now an octogenarian, I find myself teaching Readers Theatre to an occasional ELDERHOSTEL class, and the older students in those classes still seem to find that literature performed orally becomes an exciting, enjoyable, personalized experience.

I have never regretted the years of my life dedicated to the work and pleasure of Readers Theatre. Of all theatre forms I have found it to be the most fun. I hope you will, too.

Melvin R. White, Ph.D.

Readers Theatre-
A Performance Art

Readers Theatre — what is it? Simply, a dramatic approach to literature. Not only are plays shared with audiences by this innovation to dramatic production, but all types of literature: short stories, novels, poems, letters, essays, diaries, radio and television scripts, and news columns. This dramatic art form draws from the customs and practices of traditional theatre and from oral interpretation, too, and is so varied in presentation that it has numerous names: Interpreters Theatre, Chamber Theatre, Platform Theatre, Concert Reading, Group Reading, Multiple Reading, Staged Reading, Theatre of the Mind, and Drama of the Living Voice. Our interest is more in how to present Readers Theatre productions than in its name. Suffice it to say, it is called Readers Theatre by most, a medium in which two or more oral interpreters through their oral reading, with their bodies and voices, cause an audience to *experience* literature as they, the interpreters/actors, experience it. Some have called this "putting the human being back into the literature, physically, vocally, intellectually, and emotionally."

What is Readers Theatre then? Simply, it is creative oral reading of any type of literature which contains "theatre," be it a play or otherwise. That means it has characters speaking in order to express their thoughts, viewpoints, and emotions. It has characters interacting with other characters, with situations, or even in conflict with their own inner thoughts. In plays per se, characters are always found. In Readers Theatre, two or more readers/actors use their voices and bodies to reveal the actions and attitudes of the characters created by an author, be he a playwright, novelist, short story writer, essayist, news columnist, or poet. It calls for mental images of characters playing out a scene that exists primarily in the minds of the participants — and these participants are both the readers/actors and the audiences. Depending on the dramatic possibilities of the literature chosen for presentation, Readers Theatre is sometimes oral reading, and sometimes it approaches conventional theatre. Both ask audiences to stretch their imaginations, but Readers Theatre requires more use of the imagination on the part of both the readers/actors and the audiences.

5

What we are after, then, in Readers Theatre is to make that voice-body connection that makes the audience "see" things without resorting to scenery, props, costumes, make-up, or any of the other devices with which audiences are assisted in a conventional theatrical production.

The choice of the word "readers" to label this style of presentation has produced problems, and many feel it is an unfortunate choice. Much of the controversy centers around the matter of memorization. Many conclude that "readers" means that the interpreter must have a script in his hand or on a stand and must read from it. This is not true. He may work with a script, simply familiarizing himself with his lines. Or he may memorize completely. Often a narrator — the story-teller almost always found in Readers Theatre performances — reads from the script, with the rest of the cast, the dialog interpreters, memorizing their lines. It should be noted, however, that it is more usual to use the script, to keep it in hand or at least readily available. To many, the script is the symbol of the Readers Theatre medium, and even though the material is memorized, it usually is present, establishing the authenticity of the words of the literature being shared.

Let us agree also on what Readers Theatre is not. It is not an exercise in sight reading. It is not an under-rehearsed performance of some piece of literature with a cast of readers with their noses buried in their scripts because they are unfamiliar with them. A Readers Theatre presentation takes as much rehearsal time as a play. In fact, it often takes more rehearsal time, since the interpreters do not have the assistance of those theatrical embellishments, as we have emphasized, of settings, properties, wigs and make-up, special costuming, and all. It is not a script-in-hand walk-through of a staged play, looking like a dress rehearsal or performance of a regular theatrical production, but with a cast that did not get its lines learned. It is not a number of people reading expository, factual material in rotation, unless *interaction* is present. An essay divided up among several readers, each interpreting a section of the essay, is not Readers Theatre, lacking as it would, in most cases, that essential ingredient, characters interacting.

6

Use of Stage/Performance Space

In the early years of Readers Theatre, the presentations were usually quite formal, staged with stools and reading stands/ lecterns, often in formal attire, dinner jackets and floor-length dresses, and often could be described more as "reading hours" than Readers Theatre. This is changing. Now "Readers-Theatre-Style" productions are being given, often memorized, and enhanced with special lighting effects, multi-media, sound effects, and increased staging. The main thing to remember is that whether lines are memorized or not, familiarization is important, a well-rehearsed presentation, not sight-reading. Always the literature, *the word,* is the important element. If you allow lights, costumes, and physical movement to take over the production, and an "almost-stage" performance results, the main purpose of Readers Theatre may be defeated. That purpose is to share the literature with an audience through "theatre of the mind, theatre of the imagination." Whether a simple and formal program using only scripts, stools, and stands, or whether you indulge in enhancement of your material with lights, costumes, and staging, *creative imagination* rather than total-theatre production customs is the keynote to Readers Theatre.

"Give me space," the Readers Theatre director says, "and give me a bare stage. Give me the right words, and I'll use the imagination of the audience rather than a painted set." Space of one kind or another is all that is needed. This can be a regular stage in a theatre, the front of a classroom, a living room, a gymnasium, a clearing in the woods, a section of sidewalk, or a street corner. Those who work in Readers Theatre strip their performing areas of sets, properties, curtains, and even lights, preferring a bare stage or platform on which *the word* is all-important. Preferably the space has a raised area, a platform, not because it is necessary, but because the readers can be more easily seen by the spectators if they are elevated. If a stage is available and it has drapes, play in front of them. But the bare back wall will do nicely, too. Or perform in the lobby if the stage is not available.

So to our performance space. Recommended are stools, boxes, chairs, platforms, ladders, benches, crates, stacks of pillows, stands, and other such paraphernalia. These are not to *be* a setting, but to provide varying levels, varying heights, varying focus areas, places to sit, spots on which to stand and to move. They are to *suggest,* not to *be.* They can be used for composition, for relating characters or separating characters, for focusing attention on key readers, or for minimizing the importance of readers at times. A piano bench becomes a settee or a davenport, a car, a bed, or whatever the narration and/or the dialog tells the audience it is. A longer bench becomes a train, a garden wall, or a dinosaur. A stool becomes a chair; a chair, a stool. A ladder becomes a radio tower, an apple tree, a balcony, a windmill, the top of the Empire State Building, a mountain peak in the Alps, or a pile of turtles in Dr. Seuss' "Yertle the Turtle." Your script may become a dish, a cocktail tray, or even a fan or gun.

How do you decide on your staging? First, of course, analyze your material carefully. If you find it calls for settings, costuming, and properties, forget it for Readers Theatre, and do it as theatre per se. Second, where is this production to be performed? In a regular theatre, in some open space, in a classroom, in a gymnasium, in a cafetorium, or on a lawn? Can this script be presented effectively in the space available? Can it be done without props? Can pantomime suffice to help the audience see props needed? Thus it goes. Just take a bare stage. If you want to do a play as a play, as a dramatic production, then do it that way. Give it the theatrical works — make-up, costumes, sets, lights, sound effects, music, and lights. But if you want it to be truly Readers Theatre, dispense with all but the last three. If and when sound effects, music, and lights can be used to support/augment/reinforce the literature you wish to share with your audience, use them, as long as they do not become more important than the word. If employed, keep them simple. If in doubt, do without them. Use your imagination, and so will your audience. Just start with a bare stage.

Costuming for Readers Theatre

Readers Theatre productions are usually costumed in one of four ways or variations thereof: first, the "anything'll do" approach; second, stylized or formalized; third, suggestive or "character-assisting"; and fourth, complete costuming.

The "anything'll do" approach sometimes is satisfactory, a sort of "come as you are" method of dressing a reading. But too often the clothes chosen by the individual readers range from pseudo-yuppie to opera house formal, and may prove a detrimental empathy. Some prefer formal or stylized costumes such as dinner jackets for men and floor-length evening dresses for women. This approach says: "This is an occasion, and we're dressing up for it. But our attire has no significance beyond the respect we show you, our audience, by looking our best for you." Still formal, the stylized costume reflects an element in the literature such as the period: a Greek play suggests costumes with Greek characteristics, but only suggesting the period and not reproducing it. In other words, costumes which give a feeling of the play and the period. This stylization may find its motivation not only in the period, but in the mood of the play, in the "color" of the literature (dark for tragedy, pastel for romance, light for comedy).

Most commonly used are garments appropriate to the "character" in the literature, to his age, to his personality, to his basic characteristics, as well as to the type of play, its period, and other such considerations. Thus those reading younger characters are found in shirts, sweaters, and trousers. Older women tend to wear somewhat longer dresses, plain and dark for serious women, colorful for the frivolous, and scarlet for "sinful" souls. Men of the church (and villains) affect somber black or dark brown suits. A person reading a bird may have one or two feathers in a cap; a cat, white gloves and boots. The possibilities are endless, but these "suggestions" of costumes perforce need to be purposeful without being distracting.

Most dangerous of all approaches is the fourth, complete costuming, as it too often defeats the simplicity which is inherent in Readers Theatre, the "put the human being back into the piece" approach to sharing literature. In such, the scripts may become intrusively obnoxious, as may the bare stage and its benches, stools, boxes, and all. The question is, if the audience is called upon to imagine everything else, why not the costumes, too? Dr. Leslie Irene Coger first referred to Readers Theatre as "theatre of the mind" in her *Quarterly Journal of Speech* article, April 1963. To costume for Readers Theatre it is well to think in terms of "*costume* for the mind" also, and provide only that which will permit the audience to see attire in the mind's eye, and not see characters on a theatre stage in a full-fledged, produced play.

This anthology includes a wide variety of literary-dramatic materials of varying length and difficulty. Some are simple, easy to cast and produce. Others call for more experienced performers and somewhat elaborate staging. Production notes and stage diagrams are included only to suggest how a working manuscript *might* be performed, not how it *must* be developed. Always keep in mind: there is no one way to present literature in Readers Theatre.

Comedy

THE TOOTH FAIRY WHO DIDN'T HAVE ANY TEETH

by John Keefauver
Arranged for Performance by Melvin R. White, Ph.D.

CAST OF CHARACTERS

TOOTH FAIRY: Adult woman, age immaterial; toothless (this may be achieved by holding lips over the teeth); a comic personality, hopefully.

GREGORY: A boy, anywhere from six to ten years of age; all boy, spirited.

MOTHER: Typical motherly type.

This short one-act play calls for the cast of three, one Boy and two adult Women. It can be played on a bare stage with one piece of furniture, a simple cot or bed — or a bench or several chairs lined up to suggest a cot or bed.

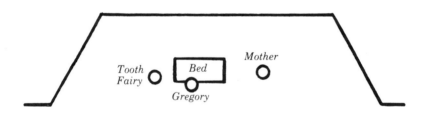

1   **TOOTH FAIRY:** *(May enter from Off-stage to find GREGORY*
2   *sleeping. Shakes him to awaken him.)* **Pardon me. I'm the**
3   **Tooth Fairy. Do you have a tooth under your pillow for**
4   **me?**
5   **GREGORY:** *(Shaking his head and opening his mouth wide)* **No,**
6   **I don't. See, I have every one of my teeth.**
7   **TOOTH FAIRY: Oh my. I can't even find a child's tooth**
8   **tonight. I've been looking and looking. Of course, what I**
9   **really need are some grown-ups' teeth.** *(Opens her mouth*
10   *wide.)* **See? You have every one of your teeth, but I don't**
11   **have any.**
12   **GREGORY:** *(Peering into her mouth)* **You're telling the truth.**
13   **You don't have one single tooth, not one! But if you're**
14   **the Tooth Fairy, why don't you have any teeth?**
15   **TOOTH FAIRY: Because I wouldn't brush my teeth when I**
16   **was a little girl. So, they all fell out — one, two, three,**
17   **four, plop, plop, plop. All of them. Do you brush your**
18   **teeth?**
19   **GREGORY: When my mom and dad make me.**
20   **TOOTH FAIRY: Oh my, Gregory. You'll lose your teeth, too,**
21   **and be a toothless Tooth Fairy like me.**
22   **GREGORY:** *(A bit insulted)* **I'm a** *boy.* **Boys aren't Tooth**
23   **Fairies. I won't be a Tooth Fairy!**
24   **TOOTH FAIRY: Oh yes you will be, when you grow up. There**
25   **are men Tooth Fairies, too. They didn't brush their teeth**
26   **when they were boys.**
27   **GREGORY: What's it like, being a grown-up Tooth Fairy,**
28   **tiptoeing into children's bedrooms to hunt for teeth under**
29   **their pillows? Or waking them up to beg for teeth like**
30   **you did me?**
31   **TOOTH FAIRY: It's exciting.**
32   **GREGORY:** *(Looks again into her mouth.)* **It doesn't sound very**
33   **exciting to me.**
34   **TOOTH FAIRY: We really need teeth.** *(Sighs deeply.)*
35   **GREGORY: I can see that.**

1   TOOTH FAIRY: What we really need are grown-up teeth.
2   Boys' and girls' teeth are much too small for us.
3   GREGORY: *(Giggles.)* Grown-ups don't believe in Tooth
4   Fairies!
5   TOOTH FAIRY: *(Moaning)* Don't you think I know that.
6   Grown-ups never put their teeth under their pillows. No
7   matter how much we need them. All we ever find are
8   children's teeth. We keep hoping that some day we'll find
9   a boy or girl tooth large enough to fit us. Then maybe,
10   someday, we'll find another one and another one until
11   we find a whole mouthful of teeth.
12 GREGORY: Have you ever found a large enough girl or boy
13   tooth?
14 TOOTH FAIRY: No, I've never found a single one.
15 GREGORY: Maybe I could pull out one of my teeth and give
16   it to you — but it'd be too small, I guess.
17 TOOTH FAIRY: I'm afraid so. In fact, Gregory, sometimes we
18   wake up boys and girls, like I did you, to ask them to
19   *please* put their teeth under their pillow when they grow
20   up.
21 GREGORY: Lots of grown-ups have false teeth. Why don't
22   you just get false teeth?
23 TOOTH FAIRY: False teeth cost a lot of money, and Tooth
24   Fairies have hardly any money. It's hard to get a job when
25   you don't have any teeth.
26 GREGORY: But you leave money under the pillow when you
27   take a tooth.
28 TOOTH FAIRY: Just a little bit. That's all we can afford.
29   *(Looking very sad)* A Tooth Fairy, Gregory, needs teeth so
30   bad she — or he — will even use bad teeth.
31 GREGORY: If they have fallen out?
32 TOOTH FAIRY: Oh my, no! Not *if*, Gregory. *When* they fall
33   out!
34 GREGORY: Because kids don't brush them?
35 TOOTH FAIRY: Yes. And when you don't brush yours, yours

1   **will fall out, one, two, three, four, plop, plop, plop. So,**
2   **Gregory, when you get big and your teeth fall out, will**
3   **you please leave them under your pillow for me?**
4   **GREGORY:** *(Yells.)* **No!**
5   **TOOTH FAIRY:** **Not even one?**
6   **GREGORY:** *(Yells even more.)* **No!**
7   **TOOTH FAIRY:** **Not even half a one?**
8   **GREGORY:** *(Even more loudly)* **No-o-o!** *(Runs off-stage, repeating*
9   *"No" several times. TOOTH FAIRY follows him. MOTHER*
10   *enters.)*
11   **MOTHER:** **Gregory!** *(Looks around, sees he is not in his bedroom.)*
12   **Gregory, where are you?**
13   **GREGORY:** *(Calling)* **In here . . . in the bathroom!**
14   **MOTHER:** *(Calling back)* **What're you doing in there?**
15   **GREGORY:** *(Calling)* **Brushing my teeth. Did you brush yours**
16   **before you went to bed?**
17   **MOTHER:** *(Puzzled)* **Why yes, of course I did.**
18   **GREGORY:** **Did Dad?**
19   **MOTHER:** **Yes.**
20   **GREGORY:** **Good, Mom. I don't want to have to ask you again.**
21   **MOTHER:** *(With an "are you kidding?" expression)* **Gregory,**
22   **what are you talking about?**
23   **GREGORY:** **Plop, plop, plop. Good night, Mom.**
24   **MOTHER:** *(Shaking her head with a "that boy" look on her face)*
25   **Good night, Gregory.** *(She exits. Lights out as the curtain*
26   *falls.)*
27
28
29
30
31
32
33
34
35

SOUND AND FURY*

by O. Henry
Arranged by Melvin R. White, Ph.D.
From Ainslee's Magazine, March 1903

CAST OF CHARACTERS

MR. PENNE: An author

MISS LORE: His secretary, an amanuensis

The setting is a simple one, two chairs, or Miss Lore may be seated behind a small table, her pencil and pad in hand, as the scene is the workroom of Mr. Penne's popular novel factory.

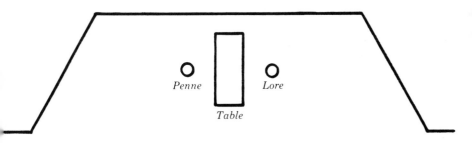

Penne   *Lore*

Table

*Adapted for Readers Theatre by Melvin R. White. Amateur performance rights of this adaptation are granted with the purchase of this book.

1   **MR. PENNE:** *(Entering)* **Good morning, Miss Lore. Glad to see**
2   **you so prompt. We should finish that June installment**
3   **for *Epoch Magazine* today. The editor is crowding me for**
4   **it. Are you quite ready for dictation? We will resume**
5   **where we left off yesterday.** *(May pace as he dictates, off and*
6   *on sitting as he wishes, only to stand and pace again.)* **"Kate,**
7   **with a sigh, rose from his knees, and . . ."**
8   **MISS LORE:** *(Interrupting)* **Excuse me. You mean rose from**
9   *her* **knees instead of** *his,* **don't you?**
10   **MR. PENNE:** **Ah . . . er . . . no, his, if you please. It is the love**
11   **scene in the garden.** *(Dictates.)* **"Rose from his knees**
12   **where, blushing with youth's bewitching coyness, she**
13   **had rested for a moment after Courtland declared his**
14   **love. The hour was one of supreme and tender joy. When**
15   **Kate — scene that Courtland never . . ."**
16   **MISS LORE:** *(Interrupting)* **Excuse me, but wouldn't it be more**
17   **grammatical to say "when Kate** *saw* **instead of** *seen*"?
18   **MR. PENNE:** *(Some slight irritation may show)* **The context will**
19   **explain.** *(Dictates.)* **"When Kate — scene that Cortland**
20   **never forgot . . . and let's spell that C-o-r-t, not C-o-u-r-t-**
21   **l-a-n-d — came tripping across the lawn it seemed to him**
22   **the fairest sight that earth had ever offered to his gaze."**
23   **MISS LORE:** *(Overcome by the beauty of the scene)* **Oh!**
24   **MR. PENNE:** *(Dictates.)* **"Kate had abandoned herself to the**
25   **joy of her new-found love so completely that no shadow**
26   **of her former grief was cast upon it. Cortland, with his**
27   **arm firmly entwined about her waist, knew nothing of**
28   **her sighs . . ."**
29   **MISS LORE:** **Goodness! If he couldn't tell her size with his**
30   **arm around . . .**
31   **MR. PENNE:** *(Frowning)* **"Of her** *sighs* **and tears of the**
32   **previous night.**
33   **MISS LORE:** **Oh!**
34   **MR. PENNE:** *(Dictates.)* **"To Cortland the chief charm of this**
35   **girl was her look of innocence and unworldliness. Never**

1   had nun . . ."
2   MISS LORE: How about changing that to "never had any"?
3   MR. PENNE: *(Emphatically)* "Never had nun in cloistered cell
4   a face more sweet and pure."
5   MISS LORE: Oh!
6   MR. PENNE: "But now Kate must hasten back to the house
7   lest her absence be discovered. After a fond farewell she
8   turned and sped lightly away. Cortland's gaze followed
9   her. He watched her rise . . ."
10 MISS LORE: *(Interrupting)* Excuse me, Mr. Penne, but how
11   could he watch her eyes while her back was turned
12   toward him?
13 MR. PENNE: *(With extreme politeness)* Possibly you would
14   gather my meaning more intelligently if you would wait
15   for the conclusion of the sentence. *(Dictates.)* "Watched
16   her rise as gracefully as a fawn as she mounted the
17   eastern terrace."
18 MISS LORE: Oh!
19 MR. PENNE: "And yet Cortland's position was so far above
20   that of this rustic maiden that he dreaded to consider
21   the social upheaval that would ensue should he marry
22   her. In no uncertain tones the traditional voices of his
23   caste and world cried out loudly to him to let her go.
24   What should follow . . ."
25 MISS LORE: *(Looking up with a start)* I'm sure I can't say, Mr.
26   Penne. Unless *(With a giggle)* you would want to add
27   "Gallagher."
28 MR. PENNE: *(Coldly)* Pardon me. I was not seeking to impose
29   upon you the task of collaborator. Kindly consider the
30   question part of the text.
31 MISS LORE: Oh!
32 MR. PENNE: *(Dictates.)* "On one side was love and Kate; on
33   the other, his heritage of social position and family pride.
34   Would love win? Love, that the poets tell us will last
35   forever!" *(Looks at his watch.)* That's a good long stretch.

1   **Perhaps we'd better knock off a bit.** *(She does not reply.)* **I**
2   **said, Miss Lore, we've been at it quite a long time —**
3   **wouldn't you like to knock off for a while?**
4 **MISS LORE: Oh! Were you addressing me before? I put what**
5   **you said down. I thought it belonged in the story. It**
6   **seemed to fit in all right. Oh, no; I'm not tired.**
7 **MR. PENNE: Very well, then, we'll continue.** *(Dictates.)* **"In**
8   **spite of these doubts, Cortland was a happy man. That**
9   **night at the club he silently toasted Kate's eyes in a**
10   **bumper of the rarest vintage. Afterward he set out for a**
11   **stroll with, as Kate on . . ."**
12 **MISS LORE: Excuse me, Mr. Penne, for venturing a**
13   **suggestion; but don't you think you might state that in**
14   **a less coarse manner?**
15 **MR. PENNE: *(Astounded)* Wh-wh — I'm afraid I fail to**
16   **understand you.**
17 **MISS LORE: His condition. Why not say he was "full" or**
18   **"intoxicated." It would sound much more elegant than**
19   **the way you express it.**
20 **MR. PENNE: *(Still in the dark)* Will you kindly point out, Miss**
21   **Lore, where I have intimated that Cortland was "full," if**
22   **you prefer that word?**
23 **MISS LORE: *(Calmly consulting her stenographic notes)* It is**
24   **right here, word for word.** *(Reads.)* **"Afterward he set out**
25   **for a stroll with a skate on."**
26 **MR. PENNE: *(With peculiar emphasis)* Ah! And now will you**
27   **kindly take down the expurgated phrase?** *(Dictates.)*
28   **"Afterward he set out for a stroll with, as Kate on one**
29   **occasion had fancifully told him, her spirit leaning on**
30   **his arm."**
31 **MISS LORE: Oh!**
32 **MR. PENNE: Chapter Thirty-Four. Heading, "What Kate**
33   **Found in the Garden." "That fragrant summer morning**
34   **brought gracious tasks to all. The bees were at the**
35   **honeysuckle blossoms on the porch. Kate, singing a little**

1	song, was training the riotous branches of her favorite
2	woodbine. The sun, himself, had rows . . ."
3	MISS LORE: Shall I say "had risen"?
4	MR. PENNE: *(Very slowly and with desperate deliberation)*
5	"The — sun — himself — had — rows — of — blushing —
6	pinks and — hollyhocks — and — hyacinths — waiting
7	— that — might — dry — their — dew-drenched cups."
8	MISS LORE: Oh!
9	MR. PENNE: "The earliest trolley, scattering the birds from
10	its pathway like some marauding cat, brought Cortland
11	over from Oldport. He had forgotten his fair . . ."
12	MISS LORE: Hm! I wonder how he got the conductor to . . .
13	MR. PENNE: *(Very loudly)* "Forgotten his fair and roseate
14	visions of the night in the practical light of the sober
15	morn."
16	MISS LORE: Oh!
17	MR. PENNE: "He greeted her with his usual smile and
18	manner. 'See the waves,' he cried, pointing to the heaving
19	waters of the sea, 'ever wooing and returning to the rock-
20	bound shore.' " 'Ready to break,' Kate said, with . . ."
21	MISS LORE: My! One evening he has his arm around her,
22	and the next morning he's ready to break her head! Just
23	like a man!
24	MR. PENNE: *(With suspicious calmness)* There are times, Miss
25	Lore, when a man becomes so exasperated that even a
26	woman — but suppose we finish the sentence. *(Dictates.)*
27	" 'Ready to break,' Kate said, with the thrilling look of a
28	soul-awakened women, 'into foam and spray, destroying
29	themselves upon the shore they love so well.' "
30	MISS LORE: Oh!
31	MR. PENNE: "Cortland, in Kate's presence, heard faintly the
32	voice of caution. Thirty years had not cooled his ardor.
33	It was in his power to bestow great gifts upon this girl.
34	He still retained the beliefs that he had at twenty." *(To MISS*
35	*LORE wearily)* I think that will be enough for the present.

21

1   **MISS LORE:** *(Wisely)* **Well, if he had the twenty that he**
2   **believed he had it might buy her a rather nice one.**
3   **MR. PENNE:** *(Perhaps a double-take; then faintly)* **That last**
4   **sentence was my own. We will discontinue for the day,**
5   **Miss Lore.** *(Sinks into a chair.)*
6   **MISS LORE:**   **Shall I come again tomorrow, Mr. Penne?**
7   **MR. PENNE:** *(Helpless)* **If you will be so good.** *(As MISS LORE*
8   *leaves, closing her book, she smiles and waves cheerily. MR.*
9   *PENNE sinks his head in his hands.)*
10
11
12
13
14
15
16
17
18
19
20
21
22
23
24
25
26
27
28
29
30
31
32
33
34
35

THE TAMING OF THE SHREW*

by William Shakespeare
Arranged for Readers Theatre by Melvin R. White, Ph.D.

CAST OF CHARACTERS
(In order of appearance)

BAPTISTA: A rich gentleman of Padua. An old, fatherly character; has a deep and mature voice.

GREMIO: Suitor to Bianca, Katharina's sister. A juvenile or young lead with vitality.

KATHARINA: The shrew, daughter of Baptista. A vile-tempered lead, highly emotional. A contralto voice is preferred, as the screaming scenes may be too unpleasant if the voice is too sharp.

HORTENSIO: Suitor to Bianca. A juvenile or young lead; his voice should contrast with that of Gremio.

PETRUCHIO: A gentleman of Verona, a suitor of Katharina. A leading man type some 30-35 years old, a handsome, virile, masculine, dashing, loud, boisterous, robust baritone or bass.

GRUMIO: Servant to Petruchio. Comedy character, any age.

TRANIO: A servant. Age and physical type immaterial.

BIONDELLO: A servant. Age and physical type immaterial.

NATHANIEL:
PHILIP: Servants attending Petruchio, comedy characters,
JOSEPH: any age, any types.
NICHOLAS:

LUCENTIO: In love with Bianca. A juvenile or young lead.

WIDOW: A member of the domestic scene with which the play ends; a bit of a shrew herself.

BIANCA: Younger daughter of Baptista, sister of Katharina. A sweet, mild-mannered ingenue.

If a smaller cast is desirable, minor roles may be distributed so that each reader interprets several of these parts.

This shortened version of "The Taming of the Shrew" concerns itself with the main plot, the story of the wooing, marrying, and taming of Katharina Minola by Petruchio, soldier of fortune and man of the world. Since it is to be performed as "theatre of the mind," no settings, costuming, or special effects are necessary. Stools or benches are suggested for those interpreting the main roles; others, such as Petruchio's servants, and those appearing in the final scene, may enter from Off-stage. Although ordinary chairs may be used, rough stools and benches suggesting the Elizabethan period are preferable.

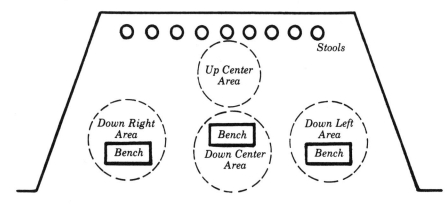

The playing area is divided into four sections: Down Right (DR), Down Left (DL), Up Center (UC), and Down Center (DC).

1   *(As the performance starts, all of the cast with the exception of*
2   *the four servants to PETRUCHIO, the WIDOW, and BIANCA,*
3   *take seats on the stools or benches provided Upstage, and freeze.*
4   *After a moment, BAPTISTA, GREMIO, KATHARINA, and*
5   *HORTENSIO stand and move to the Down Center playing area.)*
6 **BAPTISTA:**   Hortensio, Gremio, importune me no farther,
7   For how I firmly am resolv'd you know;
8   That is, not to bestow my youngest daughter,
9   Before I have a husband for the elder.
10   If either of you both love Katharina,
11   Because I know you well and love you well,
12   Leave shall you have to court her at your pleasure.
13 **GREMIO:**   *(Aside)* To cart her rather. She's too rough for me.
14   There, there, Hortensio, will you any wife?
15 **KATHARINA:**   I pray you, father, is it your will
16   To make a stale of me amongst these mates?
17 **HORTENSIO:**   Mates, maid! How mean you that? No mates
18   for you,
19   Unless you were of gentler, milder mould.
20 **KATHARINA:**   I' faith, sir, you shall never need to fear;
21   I wis it is not half way to her heart;
22   But if it were, doubt not her care should be
23   To comb your noddle with a three-legg'd stool,
24   And paint your face, and use you like a fool. *(Returns to her*
25   *seat.)*
26 **HORTENSIO:**   From all such devils, good Lord, deliver us!
27 **GREMIO:**   And me too, good Lord!
28 **HORTENSIO:**   But a word, I pray. Know now upon advice, it
29   toucheth us both — that we may yet again have access
30   to our fair mistress, and be happy rivals in Bianca's
31   love — to labor and effect one thing 'specially.
32 **GREMIO:**   What's that, I pray?
33 **HORTENSIO:**   Marry, sir, to get a husband for her sister.
34 **GREMIO:**   A husband? A devil!
35 **HORTENSIO:**   I say a husband.

1   GREMIO: I say, a devil. Think'st, Hortensio, though her
2   father be very rich, any man is so very a fool to be married
3   to hell?
4   HORTENSIO: Tush, Gremio! Though it pass your patience,
5   and mine, to endure her loud alarums, why, man, there
6   be good fellows in the world, and a man could light on
7   them, would take her with all faults, and money enough.
8   GREMIO: I cannot tell, but I had as lief take her dowry with
9   this condition, — to be whipped at the high-cross every
10   morning.
11   HORTENSIO: Faith, as you say, there's small choice in
12   rotten apples. But, come; since this bar in law makes us
13   friends, it shall be so far forth friendly maintained, till
14   by helping Baptista's eldest daughter to a husband, we
15   set his youngest free for a husband, and then have to't
16   afresh! Sweet Bianca! Happy man be his dole! He that
17   runs fastest gets the ring. How say you, Signior Gremio?
18   GREMIO: I am agreed; and would I had given him the best
19   horse in Padua to begin his wooing that would
20   thoroughly woo her, wed her, bed her, and rid the house
21   of her! Come!
22   *(The three men return to their seats, as PETRUCHIO and*
23   *GRUMIO move Down Right.)*
24   PETRUCHIO: Verona, for a while I take my leave,
25   To see my friends in Padua; but, of all,
26   My best beloved and approved friend,
27   Hortensio; and, I trow, this is his house.
28   Here, sirrah Grumio; knock, I say.
29   GRUMIO: Knock, sir! Whom should I knock?
30   Is there any man has rebused you, Petruchio?
31   PETRUCHIO: *(Loudly)* Villain, I say, knock me here soundly.
32   *(HORTENSIO stands, moves to PETRUCHIO Down Right.)*
33   HORTENSIO: How now! What's the matter? My old friend
34   Grumio!
35   And my good friend Petruchio! How do you all at Verona?

1	Tell me now, sweet friend, what happy gale
2	Blows you to Padua here from Old Verona?
3	PETRUCHIO: Such wind as scatters young men through the
4	world,
5	To seek their fortunes farther than at home,
6	Where small experience grows. But in a few,
7	Signior Hortensio, thus it stands with me:
8	Antonio, my father, is deceased,
9	And I have thrust myself into this maze,
10	Haply to wive and thrive as best I may.
11	Crowns in my purse I have, and goods at home,
12	And so am come abroad to see the world.
13	HORTENSIO: Petruchio, shall I then come roundly to thee,
14	And wish thee to a shrewd ill-favour'd wife?
15	Thou'st thank me but a little for my counsel;
16	And yet I'll promise thee she shall be rich,
17	And very rich. But thou'rt too much my friend,
18	And I'll not wish thee to her.
19	PETRUCHIO: Signior Hortensio, 'twixt such friends as we
20	Few words suffice; and therefore, if thou know
21	One rich enough to be Petruchio's wife,
22	Tell me of her, my good friend.
23	I come to wive it wealthily in Padua;
24	If wealthily, then happily in Padua.
25	HORTENSIO: Petruchio, since we are stepp'd thus far in,
26	I will continue that I broach'd in jest.
27	I can, Petruchio, help thee to a wife
28	With wealth enough, and young, and beauteous;
29	Brought up as best becomes a gentlewoman.
30	Her only fault (and that is faults enough)
31	Is that she is intolerably curst,
32	And shrewd and froward, so beyond all measure
33	That, were my state far worser than it is,
34	I would not wed her for a mine of gold.
35	PETRUCHIO: Hortensio, peace! Thou know'st not gold's effect!

1   Tell me her father's name, and 'tis enough;
2   For I will board her, though she chide as loud
3   As thunder when the clouds in autumn crack.
4   HORTENSIO: Her father is Baptista Minola,
5   An affable and courteous gentleman:
6   Her name is Katharina Minola,
7   Renown'd in Padua for her scolding tongue.
8   PETRUCHIO: I know her father, though I know not her,
9   And he knew my deceased father well.
10   I will not sleep, Hortensio, till I see her;
11   And therefore let me be thus bold with you,
12   To give you over at this first encounter,
13   Unless you will accompany me thither.
14   HORTENSIO: Tarry, Petruchio, I must go with thee,
15   For in Baptista's keep; my treasure is.
16   He hath the jewel of my life in hold,
17   His youngest daughter, beautiful Bianca,
18   And her withholds from me and other more,
19   Suitors to her, and rivals in my life,
20   Supposing it a thing impossible,
21   For those defects I have before rehearsed,
22   That ever Katharina will be woo'd.
23   Therefore this order hath Baptista ta'en,
24   That none shall have access unto Bianca,
25   Till Katharina the curst have got a husband.
26   *(HORTENSIO returns to his seat as BAPTISTA moves to sit on*
27   *the bench center; there he is joined by GREMIO and*
28   *PETRUCHIO.)*
29   GREMIO: Good-morrow, neighbour Baptista.
30   BAPTISTA: Good-morrow, neighbour Gremio. God save you,
31   gentlemen!
32   PETRUCHIO: And you, good sir! Pray, have you not a
33   daughter
34   Call'd Katharina, fair, and virtuous?
35   BAPTISTA: I have a daughter, sir, call'd Katharina.

1 GREMIO: You are too blunt: go to it orderly.
2 PETRUCHIO: You wrong me, Signior Gremio; give me leave.
3   I am a gentleman of Verona, sir,
4   That, hearing of her beauty, and her wit,
5   Her affability, and bashful modesty,
6   Her wondrous qualities and mild behaviour,
7   Am bold to show myself a forward guest
8   Within your house, to make mine eyes the witness
9   Of that report which I so oft have heard.
10 BAPTISTA: You're welcome, sir;
11   But for my daughter Katharina, this I know,
12   She is not for your turn; the more my grief.
13 PETRUCHIO: I see you do not mean to part with her,
14   Or else you like not of my company.
15 BAPTISTA: Mistake me not; I speak but as I find. *(Stand, move*
16   *to PETRUCHIO)*
17   Whence are you, sir? What may I call your name?
18 PETRUCHIO: Petruchio is my name, Antonio's son;
19   A man well known throughout all Italy.
20 BAPTISTA: I know him well; you are welcome for his sake.
21 PETRUCHIO: Signior Baptista, my business asketh haste,
22   And every day I cannot come to woo.
23   You knew my father well, and in him, me,
24   Left solely heir to all his lands and goods,
25   Which I have better'd rather than decreased.
26   Then tell me. If I get your daughter's love,
27   What dowry shall I have with her to wife?
28 BAPTISTA: After my death, the one half of my lands,
29   And, in possession, twenty thousand crowns.
30 PETRUCHIO: And, for that dowry, I'll assure her of
31   Her widowhood, be it that she survive me,
32   In all my lands and leases whatsoever.
33   Let specialties be therefore drawn between us,
34   That covenants may be kept on either hand.
35 BAPTISTA: Ay, when the special thing is well obtain'd,

1   **That is, her love; for that is all in all.**

2   **PETRUCHIO: Why, that is nothing; for I tell you, father,**

3   **I am as peremptory as she proud-minded;**

4   **And where two raging fires meet together,**

5   **They do consume the thing that feeds their fury.**

6   **Though little fire grows great with little wind,**

7   **Yet extreme gusts will blow out fire and all;**

8   **So I to her, and so she yields to me,**

9   **For I am rough, and woo not like a babe.**

10   **BAPTISTA: Well may'st thou woo, and happy be thy speed!**

11   **But be thou arm'd for some unhappy words.**

12   **PETRUCHIO: Ay, to the proof; as mountains are for winds,**

13   **That shake not, though they blow perpetually.**

14   **BAPTISTA: Well, go with me, and be not so discomfited.**

15   **Signior Petruchio, will you go with us,**

16   **Or shall I send my daughter Kate to you?**

17   **PETRUCHIO: I pray you do; I will attend her here.** *(All leave*

18   *but PETRUCHIO, taking Upstage seats.)*

19   *(To himself, sitting on bench center)*

20   **And woo her with some spirit when she comes.**

21   **Say that she rail; why, then I'll tell her plain,**

22   **She sings as sweetly as a nightingale.**

23   **Say that she frown; I'll say she looks as clear**

24   **As morning roses newly wash'd with dew.**

25   **Say she be mute, and will not speak a word;**

26   **Then I'll commend her volubility,**

27   **And say she uttereth piercing eloquence.**

28   **If she do bid me pack, I'll give her thanks,**

29   **As though she bid me stay by her a week.**

30   **If she deny to wed, I'll crave the day**

31   **When I shall ask the banns, and when be married.**

32   *(KATHARINA stalks Down Center.)*

33   **But here she comes;**

34   **And now, Petruchio, speak.**

35   *(Standing to address her. Decision must be made here as to*

1   *whether this scene is to be played with all of its physical violence*
2   *or not. If so, it must be memorized and done without scripts — and*
3   *played to the hilt!)*
4   **Good-morrow, Kate, for that's your name, I hear.**
5   **KATHARINA: Well have you heard, but something hard of**
6   **hearing.**
7   **They call me Katharine that do talk of me.**
8   **PETRUCHIO: You lie, in faith! For you are call'd plain Kate,**
9   **And bonny Kate, and sometimes Kate the curst;**
10   **But, Kate, the prettiest Kate in Christendom;**
11   **Kate of Kate-Hall, my super-dainty Kate,**
12   **For dainties are all Kates; and therefore, Kate,**
13   **Take this of me, Kate of my consolation;**
14   **Hearing thy mildness praised in every town,**
15   **Thy virtues spoke of, and thy beauty sounded,**
16   **Yet not so deeply as to thee belongs,**
17   **Myself am mov'd to woo thee for my wife.**
18   **KATHARINA: Mov'd! In good time! Let him that mov'd you**
19   **hither,**
20   **Remove you hence. I knew you at the first,**
21   **You were a moveable.**
22   **PETRUCHIO: Why, what's a moveable?**
23   **KATHARINA: A join'd stool.**
24   **PETRUCHIO: Thou hast hit it! Come, sit on me.**
25   **Alas, good Kate, I will not burden thee;**
26   **For, knowing thee to be but young and light, —**
27   **KATHARINA: Too light for such a swain as you to catch,**
28   **And yet as heavy as my weight should be.**
29   **PETRUCHIO: Should be? Should buzz!**
30   **KATHARINA: Well ta'en, and like a buzzard.**
31   **PETRUCHIO: O, slow-winged turtle! Shall a buzzard take**
32   **thee?**
33   **KATHARINA: Ay, for a turtle, as he takes a buzzard!**
34   **PETRUCHIO: Come, come, you wasp! I'faith, you are too**
35   **angry.**

1	KATHARINA:	If I be waspish, best beware my sting.
2	PETRUCHIO:	My remedy is then to pluck it out.
3	KATHARINA:	Ay, if the fool could find it where it lies.
4	PETRUCHIO:	Who knows not where a wasp doth wear his
5		sting?
6		In his tail.
7	KATHARINA:	In his tongue.
8	PETRUCHIO:	Whose tongue?
9	KATHARINA:	Yours, if you talk of tails; and so farewell.
10	PETRUCHIO:	What! With my tongue in your tail?
11		Nay, come again!
12		Good Kate, I am a gentleman.
13	KATHARINA:	That I'll try.
14		*(Striking him)*
15	PETRUCHIO:	I swear I'll cuff you, if you strike again.
16	KATHARINA:	So may you lose your arms.
17		If you strike me you are no gentleman,
18		And if no gentleman, why then no arms.
19	PETRUCHIO:	A herald, Kate? O, put me in thy books!
20	KATHARINA:	What is your crest? A coxcomb?
21	PETRUCHIO:	A combless cock, so Kate will be my hen.
22	KATHARINA:	No cock of mine; you crow too like a craven.
23	PETRUCHIO:	Nay, come, Kate, come! You must not look so
24		sour.
25	KATHARINA:	It is my fashion, when I see a crab.
26	PETRUCHIO:	Why, here's no crab, and therefore look not
27		sour.
28	KATHARINA:	There is, there is!
29	PETRUCHIO:	Then show it me.
30	KATHARINA:	Had I a glass, I would.
31	PETRUCHIO:	What, you mean my face?
32	KATHARINA:	Well aim'd of such a young one.
33	PETRUCHIO:	Now, by Saint George, I am too young for you.
34	KATHARINA:	Yet you are withered.
35	PETRUCHIO:	'Tis with cares.

1   KATHARINA: I care not.

2   PETRUCHIO: Nay, hear you, Kate. In sooth, you 'scape not so.

3   KATHARINA: I chafe you, if I tarry. Let me go.

4   PETRUCHIO: Did ever Dian so become a grove

5   As Kate this chamber with her princely gait?

6   O, be thou Dian, and let her be Kate;

7   And then let Kate be chaste, and Dian sportful!

8   KATHARINA: Where did you study all this goodly speech?

9   PETRUCHIO: It is extempore, from my mother-wit.

10   KATHARINA: A witty mother! Witless else her son.

11   PETRUCHIO: Am I not wise?

12   KATHARINA: Yes; keep you warm.

13   PETRUCHIO: Marry, so I mean, sweet Katharine, in thy bed.

14   And therefore, setting all this chat aside,

15   Thus in plain terms: your father hath consented

16   That you shall be my wife; your dowry 'greed on,

17   And will you, nill you, I will marry you.

18   Now, Kate, I am a husband for your turn;

19   For, by this light, whereby I see thy beauty,

20   Thy beauty, that doth make me like thee well,

21   Thou must be married to no man but me;

22   For I am he am born to tame you, Kate,

23   And bring you from a wild Kate to a Kate

24   Conformable as other household Kates.

25   *(Sees BAPTISTA coming; also GREMIO and TRANIO.)*

26   Here comes your father. Never make denial;

27   I must and will have Katharine to my wife.

28   BAPTISTA: Now, Signior Petruchio, how speed you with my

29   daughter?

30   PETRUCHIO: How but well, sir? How but well?

31   It were impossible I should speed amiss.

32   BAPTISTA: Why, how now, daughter Katharine! In your

33   dumps?

34   KATHARINA: Call you me daughter? Now, I promise you,

35   You have show'd a tender fatherly regard,

33

1	To wish me wed to one half lunatic,
2	A mad-cap ruffian and a swearing Jack,
3	That thinks with oaths to face the matter out.
4	PETRUCHIO: Father, 'tis thus: yourself and all the world,
5	That talk'd of her, have talk'd amiss of her.
6	If she be curst, it is for policy,
7	For she's not froward, but modest as the dove;
8	She is not hot, but temperate as the morn;
9	And to conclude, we have 'greed so well together,
10	That upon Sunday is the wedding-day.
11	KATHARINA: I'll see thee hang'd on Sunday first.
12	GREMIO: Hark, Petruchio; she says she'll see thee hang'd
13	first.
14	PETRUCHIO: Be patient, gentlemen: I choose her for myself.
15	If she said I be pleas'd, what's that to you?
16	'Tis bargain'd 'twixt us twain, being alone,
17	That she shall still be curst in company.
18	I tell you, 'tis incredible to believe
19	How much she loves me. O, the kindest Kate!
20	She hung about my neck, and kiss on kiss
21	She vied so fast, protesting oath on oath,
22	That in a twink she won me to her love.
23	O, you are novices! 'Tis a world to see,
24	How tame, when men and women are alone,
25	A meacock wretch can make the curstest shrew.
26	Give me thy hand, Kate; I will unto Venice,
27	To buy apparel 'gainst the wedding-day.
28	Provide the feast, father, and bid the guests,
29	I will be sure my Katharine shall be fine.
30	BAPTISTA: I know not what to say; but give me your hands;
31	God send you joy, Petruchio! 'Tis a match.
32	GREMIO and TRANIO: Amen, say we; we will be witness-
33	es.
34	PETRUCHIO: Father, and wife, and gentlemen, adieu.
35	I will to Venice; Sunday comes apace.

1   **We will have rings and things and fine array;**

2   **And, kiss me, Kate! We will be married o' Sunday.**

3   *(All move as KATHARINA screams, hits PETRUCHIO, etc.*

4   *PETRUCHIO laughs loudly, as he and GREMIO take their seats.*

5   *BAPTISTA, and TRANIO sit on the bench; KATHARINA*

6   *stands to the right and BIANCA to the left of the bench.)*

7   **BAPTISTA:** *(To TRANIO)* **This is the 'pointed day**

8   **That Katherina and Petruchio should be married,**

9   **And yet we hear not of our son-in-law.**

10   **What will be said? What mockery will it be**

11   **To want the bridegroom when the priest attends**

12   **To speak the ceremonial rites of marriage!**

13   **What says Lucentio to this shame of ours?**

14   **KATHARINA: No shame but mine! I must, forsooth, be**

15   **forc'd**

16   **To give my hand, oppos'd against my heart,**

17   **Unto a mad-brain rudesby, full of spleen;**

18   **Who woo'd in haste and means to wed at leisure.**

19   **I told you, I, he was a frantic fool,**

20   **Hiding his bitter jests in blunt behaviour;**

21   **And, to be noted for a merry man,**

22   **He'll woo a thousand, 'point the day of marriage,**

23   **Make feasts, invite friends, and proclaim the banns;**

24   **Yet never means to wed where he hath woo'd.**

25   **Now must the world point a poor Katharina,**

26   **And say, "Lo, there is mad Petruchio's wife,**

27   **If it would please him come and marry her!"**

28   **TRANIO: Patience, good Katharina, and Baptista too.**

29   **Upon my life, Petruchio means but well;**

30   **Whatever fortune stays him from his word,**

31   **Though he be blunt, I know him passing wise;**

32   **Though he be merry, yet withal he's honest.**

33   **KATHARINA: Would Katharina had never seen him though!**

34   *(Exit, weeping, followed by BIANCA and others, BAPTISTA*

35   *stands.)*

1	BAPTISTA: Go, girl; I cannot blame thee now to weep;
2	For such an injury would vex a very saint,
3	Much more a shrew of thy impatient humor.
4	*(BIONDELLO stands and rushes to BAPTISTA Down Left.)*
5	BIONDELLO: Master, master! News and such old news as
6	you never heard of!
7	BAPTISTA: Is it new and old too? How may that be?
8	BIONDELLO: Why, is it not news to hear of Petruchio's
9	coming?
10	BAPTISTA: Is he come?
11	BIONDELLO: Why, no, sir.
12	BAPTISTA: What then?
13	BIONDELLO: He is coming.
14	BAPTISTA: When will he be here?
15	BIONDELLO: When he stands where I am, and sees you there.
16	BAPTISTA: But say, what to thine old news?
17	BIONDELLO: Why, Petruchio is coming, in a new hat and
18	an old jerkin; a pair of old breeches thrice turn'd; a pair
19	of boots that have been candle-cases, one buckled,
20	another laced; an old rusty sword ta'en out of the town
21	armoury, with a broken hilt, and chapeless; with two
22	broken points: his horse hipped with an old mothy saddle,
23	and stirrups of no kindred!
24	BAPTISTA: *(Interrupting)* Who comes with him?
25	BIONDELLO: O, sir, his lackey, for all the world
26	caparisoned like the horse; with a linen stock on one leg
27	and a kersey boot-hose on the other, gartered with a red
28	and blue list; an old hat; and not like a Christian footboy,
29	or a gentleman's lackey.
30	TRANIO: 'Tis some odd humour pricks him to this fashion;
31	Yet oftentimes he goes but mean-apparell'd.
32	BAPTISTA: I am glad he is come, howsoe'er he comes.
33	*(PETRUCHIO and GRUMIO stand, move Down Center.)*
34	PETRUCHIO: Come, where be these gallants? Who's at home?
35	BAPTISTA: You are welcome, sir. *(Move to PETRUCHIO at center.)*

1   PETRUCHIO: And yet I come not well.

2   BAPTISTA: And yet you halt not.

3   TRANIO: Not so well apparell'd, as I wish you were. *(Move*
4   *into scene)*

5   PETRUCHIO: Were it better, I should rush in thus.
6   But where is Kate? Where is my lovely bride?
7   How does my father? Gentles, methinks you frown;
8   And wherefore gaze this goodly company,
9   As if they saw some wondrous monument,
10   Some comet or unusual prodigy?

11   BAPTISTA: Why, sir, you know this is your wedding-day;
12   First were we sad, fearing you would not come;
13   Now sadder, that you come so unprovided.
14   Fie, doff this habit, shame to your estate,
15   An eye-sore to our solemn festival!

16   TRANIO: And tell us, what occasion of import
17   Hath all so long detain'd you from your wife,
18   And sent you hither so unlike yourself?

19   PETRUCHIO: Tedious it were to tell, and harsh to hear.
20   Sufficeth, I am come to keep my word,
21   Though in some part enforced to digress;
22   Which, at more leisure, I will so excuse
23   As you shall well be satisfied withal.
24   But, where is Kate? I stay too long from her;
25   The morning wears, 'tis time we were at church.

26   TRANIO: See not your bride in these unreverent robes.
27   Go to my chamber; put on clothes of mine.

28   PETRUCHIO: Not I, believe me! Thus I'll visit her.

29   BAPTISTA: But thus, I trust, you will not marry her.

30   PETRUCHIO: Good sooth, even thus. Therefore ha' done
31   with words!
32   To me she's married, not unto my clothes.
33   Could I repair what she will wear in me
34   As I can change these poor accoutrements,
35   'Twere well for Kate, and better for myself.

1   But what a fool am I to chat with you
2   When I should bid good-morrow to my bride
3   And seal the title with a lovely kiss!
4   *(PETRUCHIO and GRUMIO move Up Right, and freeze with*
5   *their backs to the audience. GREMIO stands and moves*
6   *Downstage to TRANIO.)*
7   TRANIO: Signior Gremio, came you from the church?
8   GREMIO: As willingly as e'er I came from school.
9   TRANIO: And is the bride and bridegroom coming home?
10   GREMIO: A bridegroom, say you? 'Tis a groom indeed,
11   A grumbling groom, and that the girl shall find.
12   TRANIO: Curster than she? Why, 'tis impossible.
13   GREMIO: Why, he's a devil, the devil's dam. But hark! hark!
14   Here comes the wedding party.
15   *(PETRUCHIO, KATE, and all of the cast except PETRUCHIO's*
16   *servants move On-stage, with PETRUCHIO, KATE, and*
17   *BAPTISTA center; others, Down Right and Down Left.)*
18   PETRUCHIO: Gentlemen and friends, I thank you for your
19   pains.
20   I know you think to dine with me today,
21   And have prepared great store of wedding cheer;
22   But so it is, my haste doth call me hence,
23   And therefore here I mean to take my leave.
24   BAPTISTA: Is't possible you will away to-night?
25   PETRUCHIO: I must away to-day, before night come:
26   Make it no wonder. If you knew my business,
27   You would entreat me rather go than stay.
28   And, honest company, I thank you all
29   That have beheld me give away myself
30   To this most patient, sweet, and virtuous wife.
31   Dine with my father, drink a health to me,
32   For I must hence; and farewell to you all.
33   TRANIO: Let us entreat you stay till after dinner.
34   PETRUCHIO: It may not be.
35   GREMIO: Let me entreat you.

1	PETRUCHIO:	It cannot be.
2	KATHARINA:	Let me entreat you.
3	PETRUCHIO:	I am content.
4	KATHARINA:	Are you content to stay?
5	PETRUCHIO:	I am content you shall entreat me stay,
6		But yet not stay, entreat me how you can.
7	KATHARINA:	Now if you love me, stay!
8	PETRUCHIO:	Grumio, my horse!
9	GRUMIO:	Ay, sir, they be ready. The oats have eaten the
10		horses.
11	KATHARINA:	Nay, then,
12		Do what thou canst, I will not go to-day!
13		No, nor to-morrow! Not till I please myself.
14		The door is open, sir; there lies your way;
15		You may be jogging whiles your boots are green.
16		For me, I'll not be gone till I please myself.
17		'Tis like you'll prove a jolly surly groom
18		That take it on you at the first so roundly.
19		*(Crowd reactions throughout scene)*
20	PETRUCHIO:	O, Kate, content thee; prithee be not angry.
21	KATHARINA:	I will be angry. What hast thou to do?
22		Father, be quiet! He shall stay my leisure.
23	GREMIO:	Ay, marry, sir, now it begins to work.
24	KATHARINA:	Gentlemen, forward to the bridal dinner.
25		I see a woman may be made a fool,
26		If she had not a spirit to resist.
27	PETRUCHIO:	They shall go forward, Kate, at thy command.
28		Obey the bride, you that attend on her.
29		Go to the feast, revel and domineer,
30		Carouse full measure to her maidenhead,
31		Be mad and merry, or go hang yourselves!
32		But for my bonny Kate, she must with me.
33		Nay, look not big, nor stamp, nor stare, nor fret!
34		I will be master of what is mine own.
35		She is my goods, my chattels; she is my house,

39

1   **My household-stuff, my field, my barn,**

2   **My horse, my ox, my ass, my any thing!**

3   **And here she stands, touch her whoever dare.**

4   **I'll bring mine action on the proudest he**

5   **That stops my way in Padua. Grumio,**

6   **Draw forth thy weapon, we're beset with thieves!**

7   **Rescue thy mistress, if thou be a man.**

8   **Fear not, sweet wench! They shall not touch thee, Kate!**

9   **I'll buckler thee against a million.**

10   *(Scuffling, KATE screaming, crowd reactions, as PETRUCHIO*

11   *drags KATE out. All follow. PETRUCHIO and KATE may freeze*

12   *Up Right or Up Left, backs to audience. NATHANIEL, PHILIP,*

13   *JOSEPH, and NICHOLAS enter from Off-stage Right, and join*

14   *GRUMIO Down Right.)*

15   **NATHANIEL:**   **Welcome home, Grumio!**

16   **PHILIP:**   **How now, Grumio!**

17   **JOSEPH:**   **What, Grumio!**

18   **NICHOLAS:**   **Fellow Grumio!**

19   **NATHANIEL:**   **How now, old lad?**

20   **GRUMIO:**   **Welcome, you. How now, you? What you? Fellow,**

21   **you! — and thus much for greeting. Now, my spruce**

22   **companions, is all ready, and all things neat?**

23   **NATHANIEL:**   **All things are ready. How near is our master?**

24   **GRUMIO:**   **E'en at hand, alighted by this; and therefore be**

25   **not —**

26   **Cock's passion, silence! I hear my master.**

27   *(Storms into Down Right scene.)*

28   **PETRUCHIO:**   **Where be these knaves? What! No man at the**

29   **door**

30   **To hold my stirrup, nor to take my horse?**

31   **Where is Nathaniel, Gregory, Philip?**

32   **ALL SERVANTS:**   **Here! Here, sir! Here, sir!**

33   **PETRUCHIO:**   **Here, sir! Here, sir! Here, sir! Here, sir!**

34   **You logger-headed and unpolish'd grooms!**

35   **What, no attendance? No regard? No duty?**

1	Where is the foolish knave I sent before?
2	GRUMIO: Here, sir; as foolish as I was before.
3	PETRUCHIO: You peasant swain! You whoreson malt-horse
4	drudge!
5	Did I not bid thee meet me in the park,
6	And bring along these rascal knaves with thee?
7	GRUMIO: Nathaniel's coat, sir, was not fully made,
8	And Gabriel's pumps were all unpink'd i' the heel;
9	There was no link to colour Peter's hat,
10	And Walter's dagger was not come from sheathing.
11	There were none fine, but Adam, Ralph, and Gregory;
12	And the rest were ragged, old, and beggarly;
13	Yet, as they are, here are they come to meet you.
14	PETRUCHIO: Go, rascals, go, and fetch my supper in! *(Sit on*
15	*bench Down Right.)*
16	*(SERVANTS exit, talking among selves.)*
17	*(Sing)* **Where is the life that late I led?**
18	**Where are those** — *(Interrupt singing as KATE drags in,*
19	*beaten-looking.)* **Sit down, Kate, and welcome.**
20	**Soud, soud, soud, soud!** *(She sits beside him — as far away*
21	*as possible.)*
22	*(SERVANTS re-enter, pantomiming.)*
23	**Why, when, I say? — Nay, good sweet Kate, be merry.**
24	**Off with my boots, you rogues!** *(SERVANT tries.)* **You**
25	**villains, when?**
26	*(Sings.)* **It was the friar of orders grey,**
27	**As he forth walked on his way: —**
28	**Out, you rogue! You pluck my foot awry.**
29	**Take that, and mend the plucking off the other.** *(Shoves*
30	*SERVANT with his foot.)*
31	**Be merry, Kate. Some water, here; what, ho!**
32	**Where's my spaniel Troilus? Sirrah, get you hence,**
33	**And bid my cousin Ferdinand come hither: —**
34	*(SERVANT exits.)*
35	**One, Kate, that you must kiss, and be acquainted with.**

1	Where are my slippers? Shall I have some water?
2	Come, Kate, and wash, and welcome heartily.
3	*(SERVANT lets ewer fall, pantomime.)*
4	You whoreson villain! Will you let it fall? *(Strikes him.)*
5	KATHARINA: *(Getting up to walk away)* Patience, I pray you.
6	'Twas a fault unwilling.
7	PETRUCHIO: A whoreson, bettleheaded, flap-ear'd knave!
8	Come, Kate, sit down; I know you have a stomach. *(Pulls*
9	*her down.)*
10	Will you give thanks, sweet Kate, or else shall I?
11	What's this? Mutton?
12	SERVANT: Ay.
13	PETRUCHIO: Who brought it?
14	SERVANT: I, sir!
15	PETRUCHIO: 'Tis burnt; and so is all the meat.
16	What dogs are these! Where is the rascal cook?
17	How durst you, villains, bring it from the dresser,
18	And serve it thus to me that love it not?
19	There, take it to you, trenchers, cups, and all.
20	*(Pantomime: throws the meat.)*
21	You heedless joltheads, and unmanner'd slaves!
22	What! Do you grumble? I'll be with you straight.
23	KATHARINA: I pray you, husband, be not so disquiet;
24	The meat was well, if you were so contented.
25	PETRUCHIO: I tell thee, Kate, 'twas burnt and dried away;
26	Be patient; to-morrow't shall be mended,
27	And for this night we'll fast for company.
28	Come, I will bring thee to thy bridal chamber. *(Gets up*
29	*and drags her out, a noisy exit. But as PETRUCHIO sits, she*
30	*sneaks back Down Right to GRUMIO.)*
31	GRUMIO: No, no, forsooth! I dare not, for my life.
32	KATHARINA: The more my wrong, the more his spite
33	appears.
34	What, did he marry me to famish me?
35	Beggars, that come unto my father's door

1	Upon entreaty have a present alms;
2	If not, elsewhere they meet with charity;
3	But I, who never knew how to entreat,
4	Nor never needed that I should entreat,
5	Am starv'd for meat, giddy for lack of sleep,
6	With oaths kept waking, and with brawling fed.
7	And that which spites me more than all these wants,
8	He does it under name of perfect love;
9	As who should say, if I should sleep or eat,
10	'Twere deadly sickness or else present death.
11	I prithee go and get me some repast;
12	I care not what, so it be wholesome food. *(GRUMIO sees*
13	*PETRUCHIO approaching and makes a hasty exit. HORTEN-*
14	*SIO enters with PETRUCHIO.)*
15	PETRUCHIO: How fares my Kate? What, sweeting, all amort?
16	HORTENSIO: Mistress, what cheer?
17	KATHARINA: 'Faith, as cold as can be.
18	PETRUCHIO: Pluck up thy spirits; look cheerfully upon me.
19	And now, my honey love,
20	Will we return unto thy father's house,
21	And revel it as bravely as the best,
22	With silken coats and caps, and golden rings,
23	With ruffs and cuffs and farthingales and things;
24	With scarfs and fans and double change of bravery,
25	With amber bracelets, beads, and all this knavery.
26	No, our purses shall be proud, our garments poor;
27	For 'tis the mind that makes the body rich;
28	And as the sun breaks through the darkest clouds,
29	So honour peereth in the meanest habit.
30	What, is the jay more precious than the lark
31	Because his feathers are more beautiful?
32	Or is the adder better than the eel
33	Because his painted skin contents the eye?
34	O, no, good Kate! Neither art thou the worse
35	For this poor furniture and mean array.

1	If thou account'st it shame, lay it on me;
2	And therefore frolic! We will hence forthwith
3	To feast and sport us at thy father's house.
4	Go, call my men, and let us straight to him;
5	And bring our horses unto Long Lane end;
6	There will we mount, and thither walk on foot.
7	Let's see; I think 'tis now some seven o'clock,
8	And well we may come there by dinner-time.
9	KATHARINA: I dare assure you, sir, 'tis almost two,
10	And 'twill be supper time ere you come there.
11	PETRUCHIO: It shall be seven ere I go to horse.
12	Look, what I speak, or do, or think to do,
13	You are still crossing it. Sirs, let't alone.
14	I will not go to-day; and, ere I do,
15	It shall be what o'clock I say it is.
16	*(Transition as the three move to Down Center area.)*
17	PETRUCHIO: Come on, i' God's name! Once more toward
18	our father's.
19	Good Lord, how bright and goodly shines the moon.
20	KATHARINA: The moon? The sun. It is not moonlight now.
21	PETRUCHIO: I say it is the moon that shines so bright.
22	KATHARINA: I know it is the sun that shines so bright.
23	PETRUCHIO: Now, by my mother's son, and that's myself,
24	It shall be moon, or star, or what I list,
25	Or ere I journey to your father's house.
26	Go on, and fetch our horses back again.
27	Evermore cross'd, and cross'd; nothing but cross'd!
28	HORTENSIO: *(Sotto voce)* Say as he says, or we shall never go.
29	KATHARINA: Forward, I pray, since we have come so far,
30	And be it moon, or sun, or what you please;
31	And if you please to call it a rush candle,
32	Henceforth, I vow, it shall be so for me.
33	PETRUCHIO: I say it is the moon.
34	KATHARINA: I know it is the moon.
35	PETRUCHIO: Nay, then you lie! It is the blessed sun.

1　KATHARINA:　Then, God be blesse'd, it is the blessed sun!
2　　　　　But sun it is not when you say it is not,
3　　　　　And the moon changes even as your mind.
4　　　　　What you will have it named, even that it is;
5　　　　　And so it shall be so for Katharine.
6　HORTENSIO:　*(Sotto voce)* Petruchio, go thy ways; the field is
7　　　　　won.
8　PETRUCHIO:　Well, forward, forward! Thus the bowl should
9　　　　　run,
10　　　　And not unluckily against the bias.
11　　　*(Move to Down Left, then Up Left, at the same time entire cast,*
12　　　*except PETRUCHIO's servants, move Down Center, Down Right,*
13　　　*and Down Left. Leads take seats on the benches.)*
14　BAPTISTA:　Now, in good sadness, son Petruchio,
15　　　　I think thou hast the veriest shrew of all.
16　PETRUCHIO:　*(Sit next to BAPTISTA on bench center. GRUMIO*
17　　　　*stands behind and to the right of PETRUCHIO.)* Well, I say no;
18　　　　and therefore, for assurance,
19　　　　Let's each one send unto his wife,
20　　　　And he whose wife is most obedient,
21　　　　To come at first when he doth send for her,
22　　　　Shall win the wager which we will propose.
23　HORTENSIO:　*(On bench Down Right)* Content. What is the wager?
24　LUCENTIO:　*(On bench Down Left. BIONDELLO stands above the*
25　　　　*bench.)* Twenty crowns.
26　PETRUCHIO:　Twenty crowns!
27　　　　I'll venture so much on my hawk, or hound,
28　　　　But twenty times so much upon my wife.
29　LUCENTIO:　A hundred then.
30　HORTENSIO:　Content.
31　PETRUCHIO:　A match! 'Tis done.
32　HORTENSIO:　Who shall begin?
33　LUCENTIO:　That will I.
34　　　　Go, Biondello, bid your mistress come to me.
35　　　*(Freezes, back to audience, Up Left.)*

1	BIONDELLO: I go.
2	BAPTISTA: Son, I'll be your half, Bianca comes.
3	LUCENTIO: I'll have no halves. I'll bear it all myself.
4	How now! What news?
5	BIONDELLO: *(From Up Left)* Sir, my mistress sends you word
6	That she is busy, and she cannot come!
7	PETRUCHIO: How? She is busy, and she cannot come!
8	Is that an answer?
9	GREMIO: Ay, and a kind one too;
10	Pray God, sir, your wife send you not a worse.
11	PETRUCHIO: I hope, better.
12	HORTENSIO: *(Calling)* Sirrah Biondello, go and entreat my
13	wife
14	To come to me forthwith.
15	PETRUCHIO: O ho! Entreat her?
16	Nay, then she must needs come.
17	HORTENSIO: I am afraid sir,
18	Do what you can, yours will not be entreated.
19	Now, where's my wife?
20	BIONDELLO: *(Calling back from Up Left)* She says you have
21	some goodly jest in hand.
22	She will not come; she bids you come to her.
23	PETRUCHIO: Worse, and worse! She will not come! O vile!
24	Intolerable, not to be endur'd!
25	Sirrah, Grumio, go to your mistress; say,
26	I command her come to me. *(GRUMIO goes to KATHARINA*
27	*Upstage.)*
28	HORTENSIO: I know her answer.
29	PETRUCHIO: What?
30	HORTENSIO: She will not.
31	PETRUCHIO: The fouler fortune mine, and there an end.
32	BAPTISTA: Now, by my holidame, here comes Katharina!
33	*(KATHARINA comes down to right of PETRUCHIO.)*
34	KATHARINA: What is your will, sir, that you send for me?
35	PETRUCHIO: Where is your sister, and Hortensio's wife?

1 KATHARINA: They sit conferring by the parlour fire.

2 PETRUCHIO: Go, fetch them hither. If they deny to come

3   Swinge me them soundly forth unto their husbands.

4   Away, I say, and bring them hither straight.

5   *(Moves Upstage Center; freezes, back to audience.)*

6 **KATHARINA: Yes, my lord.**

7 LUCENTIO: Here is a wonder, if you talk of a wonder.

8 HORTENSIO: And so it is. I wonder what it bodes.

9 PETRUCHIO: Marry, peace it bodes, and love, and quiet life,

10   An awful rule, and right supremacy;

11   And, to be short, what not that's sweet and happy.

12 BAPTISTA: Now, fair befall thee, good Petruchio!

13   The wager thou hast won; and I will add

14   Unto their losses twenty thousand crowns;

15   Another dowry to another daughter,

16   For she is chang'd, as she had never been.

17 PETRUCHIO: Nay, I will win my wager better yet,

18   And show more sign of her obedience,

19   Her new-built virtue and obedience.

20   *(KATHARINA returns with BIANCA and the WIDOW.)*

21   See, where she comes, and brings your froward wives

22   As prisoners to her womanly persuasion.

23   Katharine, that cap of yours becomes you not.

24   Off with that bauble, throw it under-foot.

25 **KATHARINA: Yes, my lord.** *(Pantomimes doing so. Stands at left*

26   *end of bench center.)*

27 WIDOW: Lord, let me never have a cause to sigh,

28   Till I be brought to such a silly pass!

29 BIANCA: *(Joins LUCENTIO on bench Down Left.)* **Fie! What a**

30   **foolish duty call you this?**

31 LUCENTIO: I would your duty were as foolish too.

32   The wisdom of your duty, fair Bianca,

33   Hath cost me an hundred crowns since supper-time.

34 BIANCA: The more fool you, for laying on my duty!

35 PETRUCHIO: Katharine, I charge thee, tell these headstrong

47

1   women
2   What duty they do owe their lords and husbands.
3   WIDOW: Come, come, you're mocking! We will have no telling.
4   PETRUCHIO: Come on, I say; and first begin with her.
5   WIDOW: She shall not. *(Sits determinedly on bench to left of*
6   *PETRUCHIO.)*
7   PETRUCHIO: I say she shall. And first begin with her.
8   KATHARINA: *(Walk above and to left of WIDOW, thus talking*
9   *down to her.)* Fie, fie! Unknit that threatening unkind brow
10   And dart not scornful glances from those eyes,
11   To wound thy lord, thy king, thy governor!
12   It blots thy beauty as frosts do bite the meads,
13   Confounds thy fame, as whirlwinds shake fair buds,
14   And in no sense is meet or amiable.
15   Thy husband is thy lord, thy life, thy keeper,
16   Thy head, thy sovereign; one that cares for thee,
17   And for thy maintainance commits his body
18   To painful labour both by sea and land,
19   To watch the night in storms, the day in cold,
20   While thou liest warm at home, secure and safe;
21   And craves no other tribute at thy hands
22   But love, fair looks, and true obedience —
23   Too little payment for so great a debt!
24   PETRUCHIO: Why, there's a wench! *(Stands, goes to her.)* Come
25   on, and kiss me, Kate.
26   LUCENTIO: Well, go thy ways, old lad, for thou shalt ha't.
27   GREMIO: 'Tis a good hearing when children are toward.
28   LUCENTIO: But a harsh hearing when women are froward.
29   PETRUCHIO: Come, Kate, we'll to bed.
30   We three are married, but you two are sped.
31   *(To LUCENTIO)* 'Twas I won the wager, though you hit
32   the white;
33   And, being a winner, God give you good night!
34   *(PETRUCHIO may carry KATHARINA off as the curtain falls.)*
35

THE CROOKED TOWN*

by Gordon C. Bennett
From *Happy Tales, Fables, and Plays* by Gordon C. Bennett

CAST OF CHARACTERS

Five readers including one male to interpret the Peddler. If a larger cast is desired, townspeople as kazoo players, singers, and/or dancers may be added, including children.

NARRATOR: A good storyteller, man or woman.

VOICE 1, 2, 3: Contrasting vocal and physical types, men or women, who are storytellers, too.

PEDDLER: A portly fellow with a way of smiling all over his body.

This modern parable, originally intended for religious purposes, treating the nature of the church, has been adapted by Melvin R. White, Ph.D. with only slight changes for general use. A bit of imagination in directing and acting will produce a delightful "holding up of mirrors to nature." Mr. Bennett wrote, "Whatever supports the mood of celebration is good."

The Crooked Town may be performed simply with a few stools, chairs, or benches. One suggested arrangement:

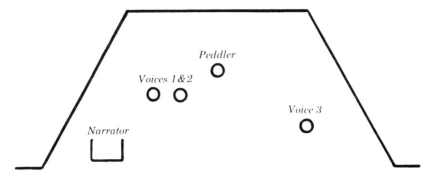

*From *Happy Tales, Fables, and Plays* by Gordon C. Bennett. Atlanta: John Knox Press, copyright © 1975. Adapted and reprinted by permission of the author and John Knox Press. This arrangement may be presented by bona fide educational groups without payment of a royalty fee.

1   *(As the reading starts, VOICES 1, 2, 3 enter, sit on their stools,*
2   *and freeze, facing front. PEDDLER enters with them, but freezes*
3   *on his stool with his back to the audience. Then NARRATOR*
4   *enters and takes his place behind the lectern, Down Right.)*
5   **NARRATOR:**   *(To the audience, direct and personal)* **You all know**
6   **the rhyme, I suspect, about the crooked man who lived**
7   **in a crooked house, but believe it or not there was once**
8   **a whole town that was crooked. It was called Bent Town,**
9   **and it was where all the Bent People lived. I don't know**
10   **if it is true or not, but they say it happened because an**
11   **evil witch once put a curse on the place. At any rate,**
12   **VOICE 2:**   *(VOICES 1, 2, and 3 are storytellers, too, except when*
13   *given dialog.)* **Bent Town was the oddest town you ever**
14   **saw. Everything was crooked,**
15   **VOICE 3:**   **From the judge's bench to the street corner**
16   **lamp posts,**
17   **VOICE 1:**   **From calisthenics to coffee pots,**
18   **VOICE 2:**   **From recipes to radio aerials.**
19   **VOICE 3:**   **The streets were crooked,**
20   **VOICE 1:**   **The calendar was crooked,**
21   **VOICE 2:**   **And the government was crooked.**
22   **VOICE 3:**   **This, of course, means that the people were**
23   **crooked. They looked very bony, for their arms and legs**
24   **stuck out at strange angles.** *(The cast may suit the action to*
25   *the word and become misshapen if desired.)*
26   **VOICE 1:   Their   backs   were   twisted   and   misshapen.**
27   *(Pantomime)*
28   **VOICE 2:**   **Their faces were bent into perpetual scowls.** *(All*
29   *scowl and may freeze in twisted and misshapen positions and*
30   *with scowls during the narration which follows.)*
31   **NARRATOR:**   **The people of Bent Town even walked funny,**
32   **zigzagging and bumping into each other. And their ways**
33   **were mean and devious. Any man or woman would,**
34   **without provocation, stomp, steal, slander and slobber,**
35   **or shun, shiver, and shame his wife or husband, neighbor,**

1   or fellow citizen. Conversation in Bent Town was devious
2   and indirect. If you said, "Good morning," the reply was
3   always something like,
4   **VOICE 2:**   *(On dialog, use On-stage focus, reacting to others in the*
5   *cast.)* **Is it?**
6   **VOICE 1:**   **Or ...**
7   **VOICE 2:**   **In a manner of speaking, perhaps ...**
8   **VOICE 1:**   **Or ...**
9   **VOICE 2:**   **You don't say.**
10   **NARRATOR:**   **And if you asked, "What time is it?" the answer**
11   **might be,**
12   **VOICE 3:**   **Time to look out for yourself, pal, heh-heh.**
13   **NARRATOR:**   **That was the best you could expect. The worst**
14   **would be some sort of insult like:**
15   **VOICE 3:**   **It's time to fix your face, ugly.**
16   **VOICE 1:**   **Or ...**
17   **VOICE 3:**   **It's way past your bedtime, dummy.**
18   **VOICE 1:**   **Or worse. Such was life in Bent Town — sinister,**
19   **sad, morose, and melancholy ... *until the Peddler came.***
20   **NARRATOR:**   **No one had ever seen the Peddler before, and**
21   **since the town seldom had visitors (for obvious reasons),**
22   **he was a curiosity.** *(PEDDLER turns around on his stool, and*
23   *as the narration provides motivation to do so, stands and comes*
24   *Down Center a bit.)* **The Peddler was a portly fellow with**
25   **a red flannel shirt and a way of smiling all over his body.**
26   **He walked beside a cart pulled by a donkey.** *(PEDDLER*
27   *comes Downstage toward the audience.)* **Suddenly one**
28   **morning, the donkey, the cart, and the Peddler appeared**
29   **in the twisted alleys of Bent Town and pulled to a stop**
30   **in the skewed square that passed for a marketplace.**
31   **PEDDLER:**   *(Calling out his wares, grinning from ear to ear)*
32   **Trinkets for sale! Ho-ho! Trinkets for sale! Ho-ho!**
33   **NARRATOR:**   **Nobody bought anything, for that was not the**
34   **way in Bent Town. Everyone simply grabbed what he**
35   **wanted, and soon the Peddler's cart was empty — that is,**

1   **except for a brown bag and a grey canvas that stretched**
2   **over the floor. The Peddler, still smiling in spite of the**
3   **way his trinkets had been taken, turned to the assembled**
4   **bent townspeople.**
5   **PEDDLER:** *(Talks to VOICES 1, 2, 3 and others, if others have*
6   *been added to the cast.)* **Friends, you have taken all that I**
7   **have. That is, all that I have except for these two items —**
8   *(A gesture to point out the imaginary items in the bottom of his*
9   *imaginary cart)* **two items which have been designed to —**
10   **uh — improve your — uh — dispositions!** *(PEDDLER*
11   *pantomimes the action that follows.)*
12   **NARRATOR:** **And he removed the canvas from the floor of**
13   **the cart, uncovering the first item and holding it up for**
14   **them to see.**
15   **VOICE 1: It's a full-length mirror!** *(Others ad-lib their*
16   *agreement, their interest, and their amazement.)*
17   **NARRATOR:** **Now the witch had broken all of their mirrors,**
18   **long ago, long before any of these people of Bent Town**
19   **were born. So, for the first time, everyone could see**
20   **himself and realize that he, as well as his neighbors, was**
21   **crooked. This was very upsetting indeed.**
22   **VOICE 2: Look at me! Help straighten me out!**
23   **VOICE 3: Yes — and then you help me!**
24   **VOICE 1: There, that's better. Now, your arm a little . . . and**
25   **the other leg. Now, look in the mirror!** *(During this, VOICES*
26   *1, 2, 3 work on each other, admire each other, and admire*
27   *themselves in the mirror, imaginary though it is.)*
28   **NARRATOR:** **So each person asked his fellow townsmen to**
29   **straighten him out, which they did. You never heard such**
30   **a rending,**
31   **VOICE 1: And cracking,**
32   **VOICE 2: And bending,**
33   **VOICE 3: And racking**
34   **NARRATOR:** *(Continuing)* **In all your life. And that's not all.**
35   **When they had finished with each other, they set about**

1　　　　transforming the town. Everything was straightened —
2　　　　from the judge's bench to the street corner lamp posts.
3　　　　Such a change!
4　　**VOICE 2:**　The people all walked straight and tall.
5　　**VOICE 3:**　Everyone spoke the truth.
6　　**NARRATOR:**　But they were still sad. Everyone felt guilty for
7　　　　the past.
8　　**PEDDLER:**　Friends, listen to me! It's all right! The past is
9　　　　preparation. Live and forget. Forget and live! *(Again,*
10　　　*pantomime, but use a real kazoo.)*
11　　**NARRATOR:**　And he took his brown bag out of his cart, and
12　　　　he put the funny little thing to his mouth. It was a kazoo.
13　　　*(PEDDLER plays a note on his kazoo.)* **He played a gay little**
14　　　**tune.** *(Does so.)* **The people were enchanted, for long ago,**
15　　　**the witch had destroyed all of their musical instruments.**
16　　**PEDDLER:**　In the bag — help yourselves. *(TOWNSPEOPLE*
17　　　*do so. PEDDLER plays a lively tune, perhaps "Lord of the Dance,"*
18　　　*and as each gets a kazoo from the imaginary bag, he joins in*
19　　　*and starts to play. If the cast has been enlarged, others may enter,*
20　　　*attracted by the music and laughter, dance — or join in the*
21　　　*singing. When the NARRATOR speaks, the music continues*
22　　　*softly in the background.)*
23　　**NARRATOR:**　The Peddler passed out kazoos all over town,
24　　　　and everyone made merry until two o'clock in the
25　　　　morning. The town rang with shrieks of laughter and the
26　　　　beat of dancing feet. The witches spell was broken, and
27　　　　no one was sad anymore. *(Music and dance up to climax and*
28　　　*conclusion. Cast freezes, perhaps making "living statues.")*
29　　**NARRATOR:**　The Peddler was gone the next day. No one is
30　　　　sure what happened to him. Rumor has it that he was
31　　　　drowned in a river by the angry witch whose spell he
32　　　　had broken. But no one wanted to believe that — and
33　　　　others claimed that he appeared in several other towns
34　　　　years later. One thing is certain. Bent Town was never
35　　　　the same again. Life there goes on very differently since

1   **the Peddler held up mirrors — and passed out kazoos!**

2   *(To the cast)* **Right?**

3   **ALL:**   *Right! (And if desired, all play a lively tune on their kazoos,*

4   *sing, and dance, to final curtain or tableau of smiling, happy*

5   *faces atop straight and tall bodies.)*

6

7

8

9

10

11

12

13

14

15

16

17

18

19

20

21

22

23

24

25

26

27

28

29

30

31

32

33

34

35

THE IMPORTANCE OF BEING EARNEST*

by Oscar Wilde
Adapted for Readers Theatre by Melvin R. White, Ph.D.

CAST OF CHARACTERS

ERNEST "JACK" WORTHING: Straight juvenile lead type, but temperamental. Voice suggestive of 29 years.

ALGERNON MONCRIEFF: A "smart-alec" juvenile, about the same age as Ernest Worthing. Voice may suggest aestheticism and tendency to think he is cute.

CECILY CARDEW: A saccharine-sweet ingenue of about 18 years.

GWENDOLYN FAIRFAX: A hard and brittle ingenue of character type. A little older than Cecily, and in direct contrast to the latter's excessive sweetness.

LADY BRACKNELL: A "gorgon" or domineering character of powerful voice and personality. Age, 50 to 60 years.

LANE and MERRIMAN: Typical middle-aged character butlers; may be played by the same man.

MISS PRISM: A fluttery middle-aged old maid.

MASTER OF CEREMONIES

In the production of this play, much consideration should be given to matters of tempo. The lines are clever, and must be read with meaning. Guard against unnecessary pauses between speeches or, as it is said, "Pick up your cues." The actor may pause within his own speeches for emotional and dramatic effects, but not between his speech and that of another.

The Importance of Being Earnest, a comedy of manners, is a play of lines and not a play of action. As a result, the tempo must be brisk. Oscar Wilde was having fun at the expense of the "manners" of his

---

*Adapted for Readers Theatre by Melvin R. White. Amateur performance rights of this adaptation are granted with the purchase of this book.

day. Keep this in mind as you develop your character, remembering to play it in a serious manner for the comedy that will result from this very seriousness. The characters are types, and may be overdrawn for comedy effect.

Although this play can be given with On-stage focus, movement for character relationships, and all, it works extremely well with eight lecterns, eight chairs or stools, and Off-stage focus. The notes in the script are for such an arrangement, with the cast standing and moving to stands to read when in a scene, and retiring to the seats to freeze when not on the stage.

Suggested Stage Arrangement for an Off-stage Focus Production

Lane	*Algy*	*Jack*	*Gwen*	*Cecily*	*Lady B.*	*Prism*	*M.C.*
☐	☐	☐	☐	☐	☐	☐	☐

1 (*As the reading starts, the MASTER OF CEREMONIES stands,*
2 *walks to the Downstage Left lectern and reads:*)
3 **M.C.:**   The first act of *The Importance of Being Earnest* takes
4 place in the morning room of Algernon Moncrieff's flat
5 in London. It is luxuriously and artistically furnished.
6 As the curtain rises, we hear the sound of a piano in an
7 adjoining room. Lane is arranging afternoon tea on the
8 table. (*LANE rises.*) After the music stops, Algernon enters.
9 (*ALGERNON rises.*)
10 **ALGY:**   Did you hear what I was playing, Lane?
11 **LANE:**   I didn't think it polite to listen, sir.
12 **ALGY:**   I'm sorry for that, for your sake. I don't play accurately
13 — anyone can play accurately — but I play with
14 wonderful expression.
15 **LANE:**   Yes, sir.
16 **ALGY:**   Have you got the cucumber sandwiches cut for Lady
17 Bracknell?
18 **LANE:**   Yes, sir.
19 **ALGY:**   Oh! . . . by the way, Lane, I see from your book that on
20 Thursday night, when Lord Shoreman and Mr. Worthing
21 were dining with me, eight bottles of champagne are
22 entered as having been consumed.
23 **LANE:**   Yes, sir; eight bottles and a pint.
24 **ALGY:**   Why is it that at a bachelor's establishment the
25 servants invariably drink the champagne? I ask merely
26 for information.
27 **LANE:**   I attribute it to the superior quality of the wine, sir. I
28 have often observed that in married households the
29 champagne is rarely of a first-rate brand.
30 **ALGY:**   Good heavens! Is marriage so demoralizing as that?
31 **LANE:**   I believe it is a very pleasant state, sir. I have had very
32 little experience of it myself up to the present. I have
33 only been married once. That was in consequence of a
34 misunderstanding between myself and a young woman.
35 **ALGY:**   (*Languidly*) I don't know that I am much interested in

57

1   your family life, Lane.

2 LANE: No, sir; it is not a very interesting subject. I never

3   think of it myself.

4 ALGY: Very natural, I am sure. That will do, Lane, thank you.

5 LANE: Thank you, sir. *(LANE sits.)*

6 ALGY: Lane's views on marriage seem somewhat lax. Really,

7   if the lower orders don't set us a good example, what on

8   earth is the use of them? They seem, as a class, to have

9   absolutely no sense of moral responsibility.

10 LANE: *(Stands.)* **Mr. Ernest Worthing.** *(JACK stands. LANE sits.)*

11 ALGY: How are you, my dear Ernest? What brings you up to

12   town?

13 JACK: Oh, pleasure, pleasure! What else should bring one

14   anywhere? Eating as usual, I see, Algy!

15 ALGY: *(Stiffly)* I believe it is customary in good society to

16   take some slight refreshment at five o'clock. Where have

17   you been since last Thursday?

18 JACK: In the country.

19 ALGY: What on earth do you do there?

20 JACK: When one is in town one amuses oneself. When one is

21   in the country one amuses other people. It is excessively

22   boring.

23 ALGY: And who are the people you amuse?

24 JACK: *(Airily)* Oh, neighbors, neighbors.

25 ALGY: Got nice neighbors in your part of Shropshire?

26 JACK: Perfectly horrid! Never speak to one of them.

27 ALGY: How immensely you must amuse them! By the way,

28   Shropshire is your county, is it not?

29 JACK: Eh? Shropshire? Yes, of course. Hallo! Why all these

30   cups? Why cucumber sandwiches? Why such reckless

31   extravagance in one so young? Who is coming to tea?

32 ALGY: Oh! Merely Aunt Augusta and Gwendolyn.

33 JACK: How perfectly delightful!

34 ALGY: Yes, that is all very well; but I am afraid Aunt Augusta

35   won't quite approve of your being here.

1	JACK:	May I ask why?
2	ALGY:	My dear fellow, the way you flirt with Gwendolyn is
3		perfectly disgraceful. It is almost as bad as the way
4		Gwendolyn flirts with you.
5	JACK:	I am in love with Gwendolyn. I have come up to town
6		expressly to propose to her.
7	ALGY:	I thought you had come up for pleasure? I call that
8		business.
9	JACK:	How utterly unromantic you are!
10	ALGY:	I really don't see anything romantic in proposing. It
11		is very romantic to be in love. But there is nothing
12		romantic about a definite proposal. Why, one may be
13		accepted. One usually is, I believe. Then the excitement
14		is over. The very essence of romance is uncertainty. If
15		ever I get married, I'll certainly try to forget the fact.
16	JACK:	I have no doubt about that, dear Algy. The Divorce
17		Court was specially invented for people whose memories
18		are so curiously constituted.
19	ALGY:	Oh! There is no use speculating on that subject.
20		Divorces are made in heaven. Please don't touch the
21		cucumber sandwiches. They are specially for Aunt
22		Augusta.
23	JACK:	Well, you have been eating them all the time.
24	ALGY:	That is quite a different matter. She is my aunt. Have
25		some bread and butter. The bread and butter is for
26		Gwendolyn. Gwendolyn is devoted to bread and butter.
27	JACK:	And very good bread and butter it is, too.
28	ALGY:	Well, my dear fellow, you need not eat as if you were
29		going to eat it all. You behave as if you were married to
30		her already. You are not married to her already, and I
31		don't think you ever will be.
32	JACK:	Why on earth do you say that?
33	ALGY:	Well, in the first place, girls never marry the men they
34		flirt with. Girls don't think it right.
35	JACK:	Oh, that is nonsense!

1	ALGY:	It isn't. It is a great truth. It accounts for the
2		extraordinary number of bachelors that one sees all over
3		the place. In the second place, I don't give my consent.
4	JACK:	Your consent?
5	ALGY:	My dear fellow, Gwendolyn is my first cousin. And
6		before I allow you to marry her, you will have to clear
7		up the whole question of Cecily.
8	JACK:	*(Lying)* Cecily! What on earth do you mean? What do
9		you mean, Algy, by Cecily? I don't know anyone of the
10		name of Cecily.
11	ALGY:	No? Do you remember this cigarette case you left the
12		last time you dined here?
13	JACK:	*(Indignantly)* Do you mean to say you have had my
14		cigarette case all this time?
15	ALGY:	Your cigarette case?
16	JACK:	Yes — mine.
17	ALGY:	Well, according to the inscription inside, this case is a
18		present from Cecily, and you said you didn't know anyone
19		of that name.
20	JACK:	*(Reluctantly)* Well, if you want to know, Cecily happens
21		to be my aunt.
22	ALGY:	Your aunt?
23	JACK:	Yes. Charming old lady she is, too. Lives at Tunbridge
24		Wells.
25	ALGY:	Oh! And why does your aunt call you her uncle? The
26		inscription says: "From little Cecily, with her fondest love
27		to her dear Uncle Jack." Besides, your name isn't Jack
28		at all; it's Ernest.
29	JACK:	It isn't Ernest; it's Jack.
30	ALGY:	You have always told me it was Ernest. I have
31		introduced you to everyone as Ernest. You answer to the
32		name of Ernest. You look as if your name was Ernest.
33		You are the most earnest-looking person I ever saw in
34		my life. Perfectly absurd saying your name isn't Ernest.
35		It's on your cards. I have one here. "Mr. Ernest Worthing;

1   Room 4, the Albany." I'll keep it as proof that your name
2   is Ernest, if ever you attempt to deny it to me, or to
3   Gwendolyn, or to anyone else.
4   JACK: *(Sighs.)* Well, my name is Ernest in town and Jack in
5   the country, and the cigarette case was given to me in
6   the country.
7   ALGY: Yes, but that doesn't account for the fact that your
8   small Aunt Cecily calls you her dear uncle. You know, I
9   suspect you of being a confirmed Bunburyist.
10 JACK: Bunburyist? What on earth do you mean by a
11   Bunburyist?
12 ALGY: I'll explain after you tell me why you are Ernest in
13   town and Jack in the country.
14 JACK: Very easy! Old Mr. Thomas Cardew, who adopted me
15   when I was a little boy, made me in his will guardian to
16   his granddaughter, Miss Cecily Cardew. Cecily, who
17   addresses me as her uncle from motives of respect, lives
18   at my place in the country under the charge of her
19   governess, Miss Prism.
20 ALGY: Now, go on. Why are you Ernest in town and Jack in
21   the country?
22 JACK: As Cecily's guardian, I have to adopt a high moral tone
23   on all subjects. In order to get up to town, I pretend to
24   have a younger brother named Ernest, who lives at The
25   Albany, and gets into the most dreadful scrapes. That,
26   my dear Algy, is the whole truth, pure and simple.
27 ALGY: The truth is rarely pure and never simple. However,
28   what you really are is a Bunburyist, Ernest, as I am. In
29   fact, you are a very advanced Bunburyist.
30 JACK: What on earth do you mean?
31 ALGY: You have invented a very useful younger brother
32   called Ernest, in order that you may be able to come up
33   to town as often as you like. I have invented an invaluable
34   permanent invalid called Bunbury, in order that I may
35   be able to escape Aunt Augusta and go down into the

1   country whenever I choose.

2 JACK: *(Indignantly)* I'm not a Bunburyist at all. If Gwendolyn

3   accepts me, I am going to kill my brother. Indeed, I think

4   I'll kill him in any case. Cecily is a little too much

5   interested in him. So I'm going to get rid of Ernest. I

6   strongly advise you to kill off Mr. — er — Bunbury.

7 ALGY: *(Firmly)* Never! Excuse me! There's Aunt Augusta and

8   Gwendolyn now. *(GWENDOLYN stands.)*

9 GWEN: Good afternoon, Algernon.

10 ALGY: Oh, hello, Gwendolyn! Where's Aunt Augusta?

11 GWEN: She's waiting at the foot of the stairs for you to help

12   her up.

13 ALGY: Oh, certainly! Mr. Worthing's here. I'll be back in no

14   time. *(ALGERNON sits.)*

15 JACK: Charming day it has been, Miss Fairfax.

16 GWEN: Pray don't talk to me about the weather, Mr. Worthing.

17   Whenever people talk to me about the weather, I always

18   feel they mean something else.

19 JACK: I do mean something else.

20 GWEN: I thought so.

21 JACK: Miss Fairfax, ever since I met you, I have admired you

22   more than any girl I have ever met.

23 GWEN: Yes, I am quite aware of that fact. For me you have

24   always had an irresistible fascination. Even before I met

25   you I was far from indifferent to you.

26 JACK: *(Pleased)* You mean you . . . ?

27 GWEN: My ideal has always been to love someone of the

28   name of Ernest. There is something in that name that

29   inspires absolute confidence.

30 JACK: You really love me, Gwendolyn?

31 GWEN: Passionately!

32 JACK: Darling! You don't know how happy you've made me.

33 GWEN: *(Fondly)* My own Ernest!

34 JACK: But you don't really mean to say that you couldn't love

35   me if my name wasn't Ernest?

1   GWEN: But your name is Ernest.
2   JACK: *(Quickly)* Yes, I know it is. But supposing it was
3   something else? Personally, darling, I don't much care
4   for the name of Ernest. I think Jack, for instance, a
5   charming name.
6   GWEN: *(Shocked)* Jack? Oh, no! Jack is a notorious domesticity
7   for John! I pity any woman who is married to a man
8   called John. The only really safe name is Ernest.
9   JACK: Gwendolyn, I must get christened at once — I mean
10   we must get married at once. There is no time to be lost.
11   GWEN: *(In surprise)* Married, Mr. Worthing?
12   JACK: Well — surely! You know that I love you, and you said that...
13   GWEN: I adore you. But you haven't proposed to me yet.
14   Nothing's been said at all about marriage. The subject
15   has not even been touched on.
16   JACK: Well — may I propose to you now?
17   GWEN: I think it would be an admirable opportunity. To
18   spare you any possible disappointment, I think it only
19   fair to tell you that I am determined to accept you.
20   JACK: Gwendolyn, will you marry me?
21   GWEN: Of course I will, darling. How long you have been
22   about it! I am afraid you have had very little experience
23   in how to propose.
24   JACK: My own one, I have never loved any one in the world
25   but you.
26   GWEN: Yes, but men often propose for practice. I know my
27   brother Gerald does. All my girlfriends tell me so. What
28   wonderfully blue eyes you have, Ernest! They are quite,
29   quite blue. I hope you will always look at me just like
30   that, especially when there are other people present.
31   *(LADY BRACKNELL stands.)*
32   LADY B.: Mr. Worthing! Rise, sir, from this semirecumbent
33   posture. It is most indecorous.
34   GWEN: Mamma! I must beg you to retire. This is no place for
35   you. Besides, Mr. Worthing has not quite finished yet.

1   LADY B.:   Finished what, may I ask?
2   GWEN: I am engaged to Mr. Worthing, Mamma.
3   LADY B.:   Pardon me, you are not engaged to anyone. When
4   you do become engaged to someone, I, or your father,
5   should his health permit him, will inform you of the fact.
6   An engagement should come on a young girl as a surprise,
7   pleasant or unpleasant, as the case may be. It is hardly
8   a matter that she could be allowed to arrange for herself.
9   ... And now I have a few questions to put to you, Mr.
10   Worthing. While I am making these inquiries, you,
11   Gwendolyn, will wait for me below in the carriage.
12   GWEN: *(Reproachfully)* **Mamma!**
13   LADY B.:   In the carriage, Gwendolyn! Gwendolyn, the
14   carriage!
15   GWEN: Yes, Mamma. *(GWENDOLYN sits.)*
16   LADY B.:   Mr. Worthing, I feel bound to tell you that you are
17   not down on my list of eligible young men, although I
18   have the same list as the dear Duchess of Bolton has. We
19   work together, in fact. However, I am quite ready to enter
20   your name, should your answers be what a really
21   affectionate mother requires. Do you smoke?
22   JACK: Well, yes, I must admit I smoke.
23   LADY B.:   I am glad to hear it. A man should always have an
24   occupation of some kind. There are far too many idle
25   men in London as it is. How old are you?
26   JACK: Twenty-nine.
27   LADY B.:   A very good age to be married at. I have always
28   been of the opinion that a man who desires to get married
29   should know either everything or nothing. Which do you
30   know?
31   JACK: *(After some hesitation)* I know nothing, Lady Bracknell.
32   LADY B.:   I am pleased to hear it. I do not approve of anything
33   that tampers with natural ignorance. Ignorance is like a
34   delicate exotic fruit; touch it and the bloom is gone. The
35   whole theory of modern education is radically unsound.

1   Fortunately in England, at any rate, education produces
2   no effect whatsoever. If it did, it would prove a serious
3   danger to the upper classes, and probably lead to acts of
4   violence in Grosvenor Square. What is your income?
5 JACK: Between seven and eight thousand a year.
6 LADY B.: In land, or in investments?
7 JACK: In investments, chiefly.
8 LADY B.: That is satisfactory. What between the duties
9   expected of one during one's lifetime, and the duties
10   exacted from one after one's death, land has ceased to
11   be either a profit or a pleasure. It gives one position, and
12   prevents one from keeping it up. That's all that can be
13   said about land.
14 JACK: I have a country house with some land, of course,
15   attached to it, about fifteen hundred acres, I believe.
16 LADY B.: A country house! How many bedrooms? Well, that
17   point can be cleared up afterwards. You have a town
18   house, I hope? A girl with a simple, unspoiled nature like
19   Gwendolyn, could hardly be expected to reside in the
20   country.
21 JACK: Well, I own a house in Belgrave Square, but it is let by
22   the year to Lady Bloxham. Of course, I can get it back
23   whenever I like, at six months' notice.
24 LADY B.: Lady Bloxham? I don't know her.
25 JACK: Oh, she goes about very little. She is a lady considerably
26   advanced in years.
27 LADY B.: Ah, nowadays that is no guarantee of respectability
28   of character. What number in Belgrave Square?
29 JACK: One forty-nine.
30 LADY B.: *(Shaking her head)* The unfashionable side. I thought
31   there was something. However, that could easily be
32   altered. .... Now to minor affairs. Are your parents living?
33 JACK: I have lost both my parents.
34 LADY B.: Both? That seems like carelessness. Who was your
35   father? He was evidently a man of some wealth. Was he

1   born in what the Radical papers call the purple of
2   commerce, or did he rise from the ranks of the
3   aristocracy?
4 JACK: I am afraid I really don't know. The fact is, Lady
5   Bracknell, I said I had lost my parents. It would be nearer
6   the truth to say that my parents seem to have lost me. I
7   don't actually know who I am by birth. I was . . . well, I
8   was found.
9 LADY B.: Found!
10 JACK: The late Mr. Thomas Cardew, an old gentleman of a
11   very charitable and kindly disposition, found me, and
12   gave me the name of Worthing, because he happened to
13   have a first-class ticket for Worthing in his pocket at the
14   time. Worthing is a place in Sussex. It is a seaside resort.
15 LADY B.: Where did the charitable gentleman who had a
16   first-class ticket for this seaside resort find you?
17 JACK: *(Gravely)* In a handbag.
18 LADY B.: A handbag?
19 JACK: *(Very seriously)* Yes, Lady Bracknell. I was in a
20   handbag — a somewhat large, black leather handbag,
21   with handles to it — an ordinary handbag in fact.
22 LADY B.: In what locality did this Mr. James, or Thomas,
23   Cardew come across this ordinary handbag?
24 JACK: In the cloakroom at Victoria Station. It was given to
25   him in mistake for his own.
26 LADY B.: The cloakroom at Victoria Station?
27 JACK: Yes. The Brighton line.
28 LADY B.: The line is immaterial. Mr. Worthing, I confess I feel
29   somewhat bewildered by what you have just told me. To
30   be born, or at any rate bred, in a handbag, whether it
31   had handles or not, seems to me to display a contempt
32   for the ordinary decencies of family life that remind one
33   of the worst excesses of the French Revolution. And I
34   presume you know what that unfortunate movement led
35   to? As for the particular locality in which the handbag

1   was found, a cloakroom at a railway station, might serve
2   to conceal a social indiscretion — has probably, indeed,
3   been used for that purpose before now — but it could
4   hardly be regarded as an assured basis for a recognized
5   position in good society.
6 **JACK:**   May I ask you then what you would advise me to do? I
7   need hardly say I would do anything in the world to
8   ensure Gwendolyn's happiness.
9 **LADY B.:**   I would strongly advise you, Mr. Worthing, to try
10   and acquire some relations as soon as possible, and to
11   make a definite effort to produce at any rate one parent,
12   of either sex, before the season is quite over.
13 **JACK:**   Well, I don't see how I could possibly manage to do
14   that. I can produce the handbag at any moment. It is in
15   my dressing room at home. I really think that should
16   satisfy you, Lady Bracknell.
17 **LADY B.:**   Me, sir! What has it to do with me? You can hardly
18   imagine that I and Lord Bracknell would dream of
19   allowing our only daughter — a girl brought up with the
20   utmost care — to marry into a cloakroom, and form an
21   alliance with a parcel? Good morning, Mr. Worthing!
22   *(LADY BRACKNELL sits in majestic indignation.)*
23 **JACK:**   Good morning! *(ALGERNON stands, whistling the*
24   *wedding march.)* **For goodness' sake, don't whistle that**
25   ghastly tune, Algy! How idiotic you are!
26 **ALGY:**   Didn't it go off all right, old boy? You don't mean to
27   say Gwendolyn refused you? I know it is a way she has.
28   She is always refusing people. I think it is most ill-natured
29   of her.
30 **JACK:**   Oh, Gwendolyn is as right as a trivet. As far as she is
31   concerned, we are engaged. Her mother is perfectly
32   unbearable. Never met such a Gorgon. . . . I don't really
33   know what a Gorgon is like, but I am quite sure that Lady
34   Bracknell is one. I beg your pardon, Algy, I suppose I
35   shouldn't talk about your own aunt in that way before you.

1   ALGY: My dear boy, I love hearing my relations abused. It is
2   the only thing that makes me put up with them at all.
3   Relations are simply a tedious pack of people who
4   haven't got the remotest knowledge of how to live, nor
5   the smallest instinct about when to die.
6   JACK: *(Pause)* You don't think there is any chance of
7   Gwendolyn becoming like her mother in about a hundred
8   and fifty years, do you, Algy?
9   ALGY: All women become like their mothers. That is their
10   tragedy. No man does. That's his. By the way, did you tell
11   Gwendolyn the truth about your being Ernest in town,
12   and Jack in the country?
13   JACK: *(In a very patronizing manner)* My dear fellow, the truth
14   isn't the sort of thing one tells to a nice, sweet, refined
15   girl. What extraordinary ideas you have about the way
16   to behave to a woman!
17   ALGY: The only way to behave to a woman is to make love to
18   her, if she is pretty, and to someone else if she is plain.
19   JACK: Oh, that is nonsense.
20   ALGY: What about your brother? What about the profligate
21   Ernest?
22   JACK: Oh, before the end of the week I shall have got rid of
23   him. I'll say he died in Paris of apoplexy. Lots of people
24   die of apoplexy, quite suddenly, don't they?
25   ALGY: Yes, but it's hereditary, my dear fellow. It's a sort of
26   thing that runs in families. You had much better say a
27   severe chill.
28   JACK: You are sure a severe chill isn't hereditary, or
29   anything of that kind?
30   ALGY: Of course it isn't!
31   JACK: Very well then. My poor brother Ernest is carried off
32   suddenly in Paris, by a severe chill. That gets rid of him.
33   ALGY: But I thought you said that Miss Cardew was a little
34   too much interested in your poor brother Ernest? Won't
35   she feel his loss a good deal?

1   **JACK:**   Oh, that is all right. Cecily is not a silly, romantic girl,
2   I am glad to say. She has got a capital appetite, goes for
3   long walks, and pays no attention at all to her lessons.
4   **ALGY:** I would rather like to see Cecily.
5   **JACK:**   Cecily and Gwendolyn are perfectly certain to be
6   extremely great friends. I'll bet you anything you like
7   that half an hour after they have met, they will be calling
8   each other sister.
9   **ALGY:** Women only do that when they have called each other
10   a lot of other things first. Now, my dear boy, if we want
11   to get a good table at Willis's, we really must go and dress.
12   Do you know it is nearly seven?
13   **JACK:**   *(Irritably)* Oh! It always is nearly seven.
14   **ALGY:** Well, I'm hungry.
15   **JACK:**   I never knew you when you weren't.
16   **ALGY:** What shall we do after dinner? Go to a theatre?
17   **JACK:**   Oh, no! I loathe listening.
18   **ALGY:** Well, let us go to the Club.
19   **JACK:**   Oh, no! I hate talking.
20   **ALGY:** Well, we might trot round to the Empire at ten?
21   **JACK:**   Oh, no! I can't bear looking at things. It is so silly.
22   **ALGY:** Well, what shall we do?
23   **JACK:**   Nothing!
24   **ALGY:** It is awfully hard work doing nothing. However, I
25   don't mind hard work where there is no definite object
26   of any kind. *(LANE stands.)*
27   **LANE:** Miss Fairfax. *(GWENDOLYN stands. LANE sits.)*
28   **ALGY:** Gwendolyn, upon my word.
29   **GWEN:** Algy, kindly turn your back. I have something very
30   particular to say to Mr. Worthing.
31   **ALGY:** Really, Gwendolyn, I don't think I can allow this at all.
32   **GWEN:** Algy, you aways adopt a strictly immoral attitude
33   towards life. You are not quite old enough to do that.
34   **JACK:**   My own darling!
35   **GWEN:** Ernest, we may never be married. From the

1   expression on Mamma's face I fear we never shall. Few
2   parents nowadays pay any regard to what their children
3   say to them. The old-fashioned respect for the young is
4   fast dying out. Whatever influence I ever had over
5   Mamma, I lost at the age of three. But although she may
6   prevent us from becoming man and wife, and I may marry
7   someone else, and marry often, nothing that she can
8   possibly do can alter my eternal devotion to you.
9   JACK: Dear Gwendolyn.
10   GWEN: The story of your romantic origin, as related to me by
11   Mamma, with unpleasing comments, has naturally
12   stirred the deeper fibers of my nature. Your Christian
13   name has an irresistible fascination. The simplicity of
14   your character makes you exquisitely incomprehensible
15   to me. Your town address at the Albany I have. What is
16   your address in the country?
17   JACK: The   Manor   House,   Woolton,   Hertfordshire.
18   *(ALGERNON, who has been carefully listening, smiles to*
19   *himself, and writes the address on his shirt cuff.)*
20   GWEN: There is a good postal service, I suppose? It may be
21   necessary to do something desperate. That, of course,
22   will require serious consideration. I will communicate
23   with you daily.
24   JACK: My own one.
25   GWEN: How long do you remain in town?
26   JACK: Till Monday.
27   GWEN: Good! Algy, you may turn round now.
28   ALGY: Thanks, I've turned round already.
29   GWEN: You may also ring the bell.
30   JACK: You will let me see you to your carriage, my own
31   darling?
32   GWEN: Certainly.
33   JACK: *(To LANE, who stands)* Lane, I will see Miss Fairfax
34   out.
35   LANE: Yes, sir. *(JACK and GWENDOLYN sit.)*

1	ALGY:	A glass of sherry, Lane.
2	LANE:	Yes, sir.
3	ALGY:	Tomorrow, Lane, I'm going Bunburying.
4	LANE:	Yes, sir.
5	ALGY:	I shall probably not be back till Monday. You can put
6		my dress clothes, my smoking jacket, and all the Bunbury
7		suits ...
8	LANE:	Yes, sir.
9	ALGY:	I hope tomorrow will be a fine day, Lane.
10	LANE:	Yes, sir.
11	ALGY:	Lane, you're a perfect pessimist.
12	LANE:	I do my best to give satisfaction, sir. *(JACK stands.*
13		*LANE sits.)*
14	JACK:	There's a sensible, intellectual girl! The only girl I
15		ever cared for in my life. *(ALGY is laughing immoderately.)*
16		What on earth are you so amused at?
17	ALGY:	Oh, I'm a little anxious about poor Bunbury, that's
18		all.
19	JACK:	If you don't take care, your friend Bunbury will get
20		you into a serious scrape some day.
21	ALGY:	I love scrapes. They are the only things that are never
22		serious.
23	JACK:	Oh, that's nonsense, Algy. You never talk anything but
24		nonsense.
25	ALGY:	Nobody ever does. *(JACK looks indignant and sits.*
26		*ALGERNON reads his shirt cuff, smiles, then laughs*
27		*uproariously as he sits.)*
28	M.C.:	Thus as Act I of *The Importance of Being Earnest* ends,
29		we know that Algernon has a plan — a plan to meet this
30		Cecily Cardew, Jack's ward. As the curtain rises on Act
31		II, we find ourselves in the garden of the Manor House,
32		Jack's home in the country. It's an old-fashioned garden,
33		full of roses. And there's a table covered with dull grey
34		and brown lugubrious-looking books. Miss Prism, the
35		governess, is seated at the table. Cecily is watering the

71

1   flowers. Miss Prism calls.

2   MISS P.: *(Calling)* Cecily, Cecily! Surely such a utilitarian

3   occupation as the watering of flowers is rather Moulton's

4   duty than yours? Especially at a moment when

5   intellectual pleasures await you. Your German grammar

6   is on the table. Pray open it at page fifteen. We will repeat

7   yesterday's lesson.

8   CECILY: *(Coming over very slowly)* But I don't like German. It

9   isn't at all a becoming language. I know perfectly well

10   that I look quite plain after my German lesson.

11   MISS P.: Child, you know how anxious your guardian is that

12   you should improve yourself in every way. He laid

13   particular stress on your German, as he was leaving for

14   town yesterday. Indeed, he always lays stress on your

15   German when he is leaving for town.

16   CECILY: Dear Uncle Jack is so very serious! Sometimes he

17   is so serious that I think he cannot be quite well.

18   MISS P.: *(Drawing herself up)* Your guardian enjoys the best

19   of health, and his gravity of demeanor is especially to be

20   commended in one so comparatively young as he is. I

21   know no one has a higher sense of duty and

22   responsibility.

23   CECILY: I suppose that is why he often looks a little bored

24   when we three are together.

25   MISS P.: Cecily! I am surprised at you. Mr. Worthing has

26   many troubles in his life. Idle merriment and triviality

27   would be out of place in his conversation. You must

28   remember his constant anxiety about that unfortunate

29   young man, his brother.

30   CECILY: I wish Uncle Jack would allow that unfortunate

31   young man, his brother, to come down here sometimes.

32   We might have a good influence over him, Miss Prism. I

33   am sure you certainly would. You know German, and

34   geology, and things of that kind influence a man very

35   much. *(CECILY begins to write in her diary.)*

1   **MISS P.:** *(Shaking her head)* **I do not think that even I could**
2   **produce any effect on a character that, according to his**
3   **own brother's admission, is irretrievably weak and**
4   **vacillating. Indeed, I am not sure that I would desire to**
5   **reclaim him. I am not in favor of this modern mania for**
6   **turning bad people into good people at a moment's notice.**
7   **As a man sows, so let him reap. You must put away your**
8   **diary, Cecily. I really don't see why you should keep a**
9   **diary at all.**
10 CECILY: I keep a diary in order to enter the wonderful
11 secrets of my life. If I didn't write them down, I should
12 probably forget all about them.
13 MISS P.: Memory, my dear Cecily, is the diary that we all
14 carry about with us.
15 CECILY: Yes, but it usually chronicles the things that have
16 never happened, and couldn't possibly have happened. I
17 believe that memory is responsible for nearly all the
18 three-volume novels that Mudie sends us.
19 MISS P.: Do not speak slightingly of the three-volume novel,
20 Cecily. I wrote one myself in earlier days.
21 CECILY: Did you really, Miss Prism? How wonderfully
22 clever you are! I hope it did not end happily. I don't like
23 novels that end happily. They depress me so much.
24 MISS P.: The good ended happily, and the bad unhappily.
25 That is what fiction means.
26 CECILY: I suppose so. But it seems very unfair. And was
27 your novel ever published?
28 MISS P.: Alas, no! The manuscript, unfortunately, was
29 abandoned. I use the word in the sense of lost or mislaid.
30 To your work, child, these speculations are profitless. I'll
31 leave you now to study your German, Cecily.
32 CECILY: *(Sighing)* Oh, very well, Miss Prism. *(MISS PRISM*
33 *sits.)* Horrid Political Economy! Horrid Geography!
34 Horrid, horrid German! *(MERRIMAN stands.)*
35 MERRIMAN: Mr. Ernest Worthing has just driven over

1   from the station. He has brought his luggage with him.

2   Here's his card.

3   CECILY: *(Takes the card and reads it.)* "**Mr. Ernest Worthing,**

4   **B4, the Albany, W.,**" Uncle Jack's brother! Did you tell

5   him Mr. Worthing was in town?

6   MERRIMAN: Yes, Miss. He seemed very much disappointed.

7   I mentioned that you and Miss Prism were in the garden.

8   He said he was anxious to speak to you privately for a

9   moment.

10   CECILY: Ask Mr. Ernest Worthing to come here. I suppose

11   you had better talk to the housekeeper about a room for

12   him.

13   MERRIMAN: Yes, Miss. *(MERRIMAN sits.)*

14   CECILY: I have never met any really wicked person before.

15   I feel rather frightened. I am so afraid he will look just

16   like everyone else. *(ALGERNON stands.)* **He does!**

17   ALGY: *(Raising his hat)* **You are my little cousin Cecily, I'm**

18   **sure.**

19   CECILY: You are under some strange mistake. I am not little.

20   In fact, I am more than usually tall for my age.

21   *(ALGERNON is rather taken aback.)* **But I am your cousin**

22   Cecily. You, I see from your card, are Uncle Jack's

23   brother, my cousin Ernest, my wicked cousin Ernest.

24   ALGY: Oh, I am not really wicked at all, cousin Cecily. You

25   mustn't think that I am wicked.

26   CECILY: If you are not, then you have certainly been

27   deceiving us all in a very inexcusable manner.

28   ALGY: *(Looks at her in amazement.)* **Oh, of course I have been**

29   rather reckless!

30   CECILY: I am glad to hear it.

31   ALGY: In fact, now you mention the subject, I have been very

32   bad in my own small way.

33   CECILY: I don't think you should be so proud of that, though

34   I am sure it must have been very pleasant.

35   ALGY: It is much pleasanter being here with you.

1 CECILY: I can't understand how you are here at all. Uncle
2   Jack won't be back until Monday afternoon.
3 ALGY: That is a great disappointment. I am obliged to go up
4   by the first train on Monday morning.
5 CECILY: I think you had better wait till Uncle Jack arrives.
6   I know he wants to speak to you about your emigrating.
7 ALGY: About my what?
8 CECILY: Your emigrating. He has gone up to buy your outfit.
9   Uncle Jack is sending you to Australia.
10 ALGY: Australia! I'd sooner die.
11 CECILY: Well, he said at dinner on Wednesday night that
12   you would have to choose between this world, the next
13   world and Australia.
14 ALGY: This world is good enough for me, cousin Cecily.
15 CECILY: Yes, but are you good enough for it?
16 ALGY: I'm afraid I'm not that. That is why I want you to
17   reform me. You might make that your mission, if you
18   don't mind, cousin Cecily.
19 CECILY: I'm afraid I've not time, this afternoon.
20 ALGY: Well, would you mind my reforming myself this
21   afternoon?
22 CECILY: That is rather quixotic of you. But I think you
23   should try.
24 ALGY: I will. I feel better already.
25 CECILY: You are looking a little worse.
26 ALGY: That is because I am hungry.
27 CECILY: How thoughtless of me. I should have remembered
28   that when one is going to lead an entirely new life, one
29   requires regular and wholesome meals. Won't you come
30   in?
31 ALGY: Thank you. *(They sit.)*
32 M.C.: And Cecily and Algernon leave to go into the house to
33   feed the ever-hungry Algy. After a few moments Miss
34   Prism returns, expecting to find Cecily hard at work. She
35   is somewhat taken aback to find the garden empty.

1   **MISS P.:** *(Humming)* **Oh, I wonder where Cecily is. Well, her**
2   **books are here — I'll just wait!** *(Humming)* **Oooh!**
3   *(Surprised)* **Mr. Worthing! This is indeed a surprise. We**
4   **did not look for you till Monday afternoon.**
5   **JACK:** *(Tragic)* **I have had to return sooner than I expected,**
6   **Miss Prism.**
7   **MISS P.:** **I trust your funereal garb does not betoken some**
8   **terrible calamity?**
9   **JACK:** **My brother!**
10   **MISS P.:** **More shameful debts and extravagance?**
11   **JACK:** **Dead!**
12   **MISS P.:** *(Surprised)* **Your brother Ernest dead?**
13   **JACK:** **Quite dead, Miss Prism.**
14   **MISS P.:** **What a lesson for him! I trust he will profit by it.**
15   **JACK:** **Poor Ernest! He had many faults, but it is a sad, sad**
16   **blow.**
17   **MISS P.:** **Very sad indeed. Were you with him at the end?**
18   **JACK:** **No. He died abroad — in Paris. I had a telegram last**
19   **night.**
20   **MISS P.:** **Will the interment take place here?**
21   **JACK:** **No. He seemed to have expressed a desire to be buried**
22   **in Paris.**
23   **MISS P.:** *(Shocked)* **In Paris! I fear that hardly points to any**
24   **very serious state of mind at the last. Shall I mention**
25   **your brother's demise to our minister, Dr. Chasuble, so**
26   **that he can make some slight allusion to this domestic**
27   **affliction next Sunday?**
28   **JACK:** **Do! Oh — and by the way — speaking of the minister,**
29   **I suppose Dr. Chasuble knows how to christen all right?**
30   **MISS P.:** **Certainly! Is there any particular infant in whom**
31   **you are interested, Mr. Worthing?**
32   **JACK:** **No! The fact is, I would like to be christened myself**
33   **this afternoon — say about five o'clock. Will you arrange**
34   **it for me, Miss Prism?**
35   **MISS P.:** **With pleasure, but . . .** *(CECILY stands.)*

1   JACK: Ah! Here is Cecily! My dear child, I . . .
2   CECILY: Uncle Jack! Oh, I am pleased to see you back. Why,
3   Uncle Jack — what's the matter? You look so sad!
4   JACK: Alas! — I —
5   CECILY: Cheer up! I've got such a surprise for you. Who do
6   you think is here? Your brother!
7   JACK: *(In amazement)* Who?
8   CECILY: Your brother Ernest. He arrived about half an hour
9   ago.
10 MISS P.:   These are very joyful tidings!
11 JACK: Nonsense! I haven't got a brother. I mean, he's dead!
12 CECILY: How absurd, Uncle Jack! Dead! *(ALGERNON*
13   *stands.)* Oh, Ernest!
14 JACK: Good Heavens!
15 ALGY: Brother John, I have come down from town to tell you
16   that I am very sorry for all the trouble I have given you,
17   and that I intend to lead a better life in the future. Won't
18   you shake hands?
19 JACK: No!
20 CECILY: Uncle Jack, do be nice. There is some good in
21   everyone. Ernest has just been telling me about his poor
22   invalid friend, Mr. Bunbury, whom he goes to visit so
23   often, and surely there must be much good in one who
24   is kind to an invalid, and leaves the pleasures of London
25   to sit by a bed of pain.
26 JACK: *(Indignantly)* Bunbury! I won't have him talk to you
27   about Bunbury! I won't have him talk to you about
28   Bunbury or about anything else. Come, Miss Prism! While
29   you are making arrangements with Dr. Chasuble about
30   the matter I mentioned — I'll order the dogcart for Mr.
31   Ernest.
32 CECILY: *(In surprise)* Dogcart, Uncle?
33 JACK: Yes! Mr. Ernest has been suddenly called back to
34   town. Come, Miss Prism! *(JACK sits.)*
35 MISS P.:   Yes, Mr. Worthing. *(MISS PRISM sits.)*

1   CECILY: Oh, dear, cousin Ernest, must we part?

2   ALGY: No indeed! I have no intention of going.

3   CECILY: But Uncle Jack . . .

4   ALGY: Oh, I don't care about Jack. I don't care for anybody

5   in the whole world but you. I love you, Cecily. You will

6   marry me, won't you?

7   CECILY: *(Happily)* You silly boy! Of course! I've loved you

8   ever since I knew Uncle Jack had a wicked brother.

9   ALGY: What a perfect angel you are, Cecily!

10   CECILY: You mustn't laugh at me, darling, but it has always

11   been a girlish dream of mine to love someone whose name

12   was Ernest.

13   ALGY: *(Startled)* But sweetheart, do you mean to say you

14   couldn't love me if I had some other name?

15   CECILY: What name?

16   ALGY: *(Anxiously)* Any name. Algernon — for instance.

17   Seriously, Cecily, if my name was Algy — couldn't you

18   love me?

19   CECILY: I might respect you, Ernest, I might admire your

20   character, but I fear that I should not be able to give you

21   my undivided attention.

22   ALGY: *(Gives an embarrassed cough.)* Ahem! Er — Cecily! Your

23   rector here is, I suppose, thoroughly experienced in the

24   practice of all the rites of the church?

25   CECILY: *(Surprised)* Oh, yes! Dr. Chasuble is a most learned

26   man. He has never written a single book, so you can

27   imagine how much he knows.

28   ALGY: I must see him at once on a most important

29   christening — er — I mean on most important business.

30   CECILY: *(Disappointed)* Oh!

31   ALGY: I shan't be away more than half an hour.

32   CECILY: Couldn't you make it twenty minutes?

33   ALGY: One kiss — and I'll be back in no time. Don't go away!

34   *(ALGY sits.)*

35   CECILY: *(Sighs deeply.)* What an impetuous boy he is! I like

1   his hair so much. I must enter his proposal in my diary.

2   *(MERRIMAN stands.)*

3   MERRIMAN: Excuse me, Miss?

4   CECILY: Well, Merriman?

5   MERRIMAN: A Miss Fairfax has just called to see Mr.

6   Worthing, on very important business, Miss Fairfax

7   states.

8   CECILY: *(Puzzled)* Miss Fairfax? I don't believe I —

9   MERRIMAN: Shall I show her in here, Miss?

10   CECILY: Yes!

11   MERRIMAN: Very good. *(Pause)* Miss Fairfax! *(Sits as GWEN*

12   *stands.)*

13   CECILY: How do you do, Miss Fairfax? Pray let me

14   introduce myself to you. My name is Cecily Cardew.

15   GWEN: Cecily Cardew? What a very sweet name! You are

16   here on a short visit, I suppose?

17   CECILY: Oh, no! I live here. I am Mr. Worthing's ward.

18   GWEN: *(In surprise)* Oh! Strange, Ernest never mentioned to

19   me that he had a ward.

20   CECILY: *(Startled)* I beg your pardon, did you say Ernest?

21   GWEN: Yes.

22   CECILY: *(Laughs.)* Oh, but Ernest Worthing isn't my

23   guardian — it is his older brother.

24   GWEN: Ernest never told me about a brother.

25   CECILY: I am sorry to say that they have not been on good

26   terms for a long time. *(In a very confidential tone)* Oh, Miss

27   Fairfax, perhaps I ought to tell you — Mr. Ernest

28   Worthing and I are engaged to be married.

29   GWEN: Married? Impossible! Mr. Worthing is engaged to me.

30   CECILY: You must be under some misconception, Miss

31   Fairfax. Ernest proposed to me — exactly five minutes

32   ago. See — I've entered it in my diary.

33   GWEN: Very curious! Ernest asked me to be his wife

34   yesterday afternoon at five-thirty. *(JACK stands.)*

35   CECILY: Oh, here's my guardian now!

1   JACK: Gwendolyn!

2   GWEN: *(Joyously)* **Ernest! My own Ernest!**

3   JACK: **Darling!**

4   GWEN: **One moment! May I ask if you are engaged to marry**

5   **this young lady?**

6   JACK: *(Horrified)* **Little Cecily? Of course not!**

7   GWEN: **There! You see, Miss Cardew.**

8   CECILY: **I knew there was a misunderstanding, Miss Fairfax.**

9   **The gentleman whose arm is at present around your**

10   **waist is my dear guardian, Mr. Jack Worthing.**

11   GWEN: **What?!**

12   CECILY: **This is Uncle Jack!**

13   GWEN: *(In horror)* **Jack! Oh!** *(ALGERNON stands.)*

14   CECILY: **Here comes Ernest now. Ernest!**

15   ALGY: **My love!**

16   CECILY: **One moment, Ernest! May I ask if you are engaged**

17   **to marry this young lady?**

18   ALGY: **What young lady? Good Heavens — Gwendolyn?!**

19   CECILY: **Yes — to "Good Heavens Gwendolyn"?**

20   ALGY: **Of course not!**

21   GWEN: **I knew there was some slight error, Miss Cardew.**

22   **The gentleman who is now embracing you is my cousin,**

23   **Mr. Algernon Moncrieff.**

24   CECILY: **Algernon Moncrieff! Are you called Algernon?**

25   ALGY: **I cannot deny it.**

26   GWEN: **Is your name really John?**

27   JACK: **I admit it! My name has been John for years.**

28   CECILY: **Miss Fairfax, a gross deception has been practiced**

29   **on both of us.**

30   GWEN: **My poor wounded Cecily!**

31   CECILY: **My sweet wronged Gwendolyn!**

32   JACK: **Gwendolyn — Cecily! It is very painful for me to be**

33   **forced to speak the truth — but I have no brother Ernest.**

34   **I have no brother at all.**

35   CECILY: **No brother at all?**

1   JACK: None!

2   GWEN: Had you never had a brother of any kind?

3   JACK: Never.

4   GWEN: Then, Cecily, I'm afraid it's quite clear that neither
5   of us is engaged to be married to anyone!

6   CECILY: It is not a very pleasant position for a young girl
7   suddenly to find herself in. Is it?

8   GWEN: Let us go into the house. They will hardly venture to
9   come after us there.

10 CECILY: No, men are so cowardly, aren't they? *(CECILY and*
11   *GWENDOLYN turn their backs or sit.)*

12 M.C.: Cecily and Gwendolyn retire into the house, casting
13   scornful looks back at Jack and Algernon. The third act
14   takes place in the morning room of the Manor House to
15   which the girls have retreated. The boys have finally
16   returned, and are being questioned by Cecily and
17   Gwendolyn. *(CECILY, GWENDOLYN and ALGERNON*
18   *return to scene.)*

19 CECILY: Mr. Moncrieff, why did you pretend to be my
20   guardian's brother?

21 ALGY: Why — so that I might have an opportunity of
22   meeting you, Cecily.

23 CECILY: *(Pleased)* Oh!

24 GWEN: Mr. Worthing, what explanation can you offer to me
25   for pretending to have a brother?

26 JACK: Why — so that I might have an opportunity of coming
27   up to town to see you, Gwendolyn.

28 GWEN: *(Pleased)* Oh!

29 CECILY: Gwendolyn, do you think we should forgive them?

30 GWEN: How can we, Cecily? Their Christian names are still
31   an insuperable barrier.

32 CECILY: Oh — yes! True.

33 JACK: My Christian name? But, Gwendolyn I've arranged
34   to be christened by Dr. Chasuble at five-thirty.

35 ALGY: You are? Why, that's funny! I've arranged to be

1   christened by Dr. Chasuble at five-thirty.

2 CECILY: You mean — you are both going to be christened

3   Ernest?

4 ALGY: Yes!

5 JACK: Yes!

6 GWEN: Darling! You're forgiven! You may kiss me.

7 CECILY: Darling! You may kiss me, too!

8 MERRIMAN: *(Stands.)* Ahem! Ahem!

9 JACK: Don't disturb us, Merriman.

10 MERRIMAN: Lady Bracknell!

11 JACK: Good Heavens!

12 LADY B.: *(Stands.)* Gwendolyn! What does this mean?

13 GWEN: Merely that I am engaged to be married to Mr.

14   Worthing, Mamma.

15 LADY B.: Algernon!

16 ALGY: Yes, Aunt Augusta?

17 LADY B.: Who is this young lady whose hand you are

18   holding?

19 JACK: That lady is Miss Cecily Cardew, my ward.

20 ALGY: I am engaged to be married to Cecily, Aunt Augusta.

21 LADY B.: I beg your pardon?

22 CECILY: Mr. Moncrieff and I are engaged to be married,

23   Lady Bracknell.

24 LADY B.: I do not know whether there is anything peculiarly

25   exciting in the air of this particular part of Hertfordshire,

26   but the number of engagements that go on seems to me

27   considerably above the proper average that statistics

28   have laid down for our guidance. I think some

29   preliminary inquiry on my part would not be out of place.

30   Mr. Worthing, is Miss Cardew at all connected with any

31   of the larger railway stations in London? I merely desire

32   information. Until yesterday I had no idea that there

33   were any families or persons whose origin was a

34   terminus. *(JACK looks perfectly furious, but restrains himself.)*

35 JACK: *(In clear, cold voice)* **Miss Cardew is the granddaughter**

1   of the late Mr. Thomas Cardew of 149 Belgrave Square,
2   S.W.; Gervase Park, Dorking Surrey; and the Sporran,
3   Fifeshire, N.B.
4   LADY B.:   That sounds not unsatisfactory. Three addresses
5   always inspire confidence, even in tradesmen. But what
6   proof have I of their authenticity?
7   JACK: Miss Cardew's family solicitors are Messrs. Markby,
8   Markby and Markby.
9   LADY B.:   Markby, Markby and Markby? A firm of the very
10   highest position in their profession. So far I am satisfied.
11   JACK: *(Very irritably)* How extremely kind of you, Lady
12   Bracknell! I have also in my possession, you will be
13   pleased to hear, certificates of Miss Cardew's birth,
14   baptism, whooping cough, registration, vaccination,
15   confirmation and the measles; both the German and the
16   English variety.
17   LADY B.:   Ah! A life crowded with incident, I see; though
18   perhaps somewhat too exciting for a young girl. I am not
19   myself in favor of premature experiences. Gwendolyn!
20   The time approaches for our departure. We have not a
21   moment to lose. As a matter of form, Mr. Worthing, I had
22   better ask you if Miss Cardew has any little fortune?
23   JACK: Oh, about a hundred and thirty thousand pounds in
24   the Funds. That is all. Goodbye, Lady Bracknell. So
25   pleased to have seen you.
26   LADY B.:   A moment, Mr. Worthing. A hundred and thirty
27   thousand pounds! And in the Funds! Miss Cardew seems
28   to me a most attractive young lady, now that I look at
29   her. Few girls of the present day have any really solid
30   qualities, any of the qualities that last, and improve with
31   time. We live, I regret to say, in an age of surfaces. *(To*
32   *CECILY)* Come over here, dear. Pretty child! Your dress
33   is sadly simple, and your hair seems almost as nature
34   might have left it. But we can soon alter all that. Kindly
35   turn round, sweet child. No, the side view is what I want.

1 Yes, quite as I expected. There are distinct social
2 possibilities in your profile. The two weak points in our
3 age are its want of principle and its want of profile. The
4 chin a little higher, dear. Style largely depends on the
5 way the chin is worn. They are worn very high, just at
6 present. Algernon!
7 ALGY: Yes, Aunt Augusta!
8 LADY B.: There are distinct social possibilities in Miss
9 Cardew's profile.
10 ALGY: Cecily is the sweetest, dearest, prettiest girl in the
11 whole world. And I don't care twopence about social
12 possibilities.
13 LADY B.: Never speak disrespectfully of society, Algernon.
14 Only people who can't get into it do that. *(To CECILY)*
15 Dear child, of course you know that Algernon has nothing
16 but his debts to depend upon. But I do approve of
17 mercenary marriages. When I married Lord Bracknell I
18 had no fortune of any kind. But I never dreamed for a
19 moment of allowing that to stand in my way. Well, I
20 suppose I must give my consent.
21 ALGY: Thank you, Aunt Augusta.
22 LADY B.: Cecily, you may kiss me!
23 CECILY: *(Kisses her.)* Thank you, Lady Bracknell.
24 LADY B.: You may also address me as Aunt Augusta for the
25 future.
26 CECILY: Thank you, Aunt Augusta.
27 LADY B.: The marriage, I think, had better take place quite
28 soon.
29 ALGY: Thank you, Aunt Augusta.
30 CECILY: Thank you, Aunt Augusta.
31 LADY B.: To speak frankly, I am not in favor of long
32 engagements. They give people the opportunity of
33 finding out each other's character before marriage,
34 which I think is never advisable.
35 JACK: I beg your pardon for interrupting you, Lady

1   Bracknell, but this engagement is quite out of the
2   question. I am Miss Cardew's guardian, and she cannot
3   marry without my consent until she comes of age. That
4   consent I absolutely decline to give.
5 LADY B.: Upon what grounds, may I ask? Algernon is an
6   extremely, I may almost say an ostentatiously, eligible
7   young man. He has nothing, but he looks everything.
8   What more can one desire?
9 JACK: It pains me very much to have to speak frankly to
10   you, Lady Bracknell, about your nephew, but the fact is
11   that I do not approve at all of his moral character. I
12   suspect him of being untruthful. *(ALGERNON and CECILY*
13   *look at him in indignant amazement.)*
14 LADY B.: Untruthful! My nephew Algernon? Impossible! He
15   is an Oxonian.
16 JACK: I fear there can be no possible doubt about the
17   matter. This afternoon, during my temporary absence in
18   London on an important question of romance, he
19   obtained admission to my house by means of the false
20   pretense of being my brother. He succeeded in the course
21   of the afternoon in alienating the affections of my only
22   ward. He subsequently stayed to tea, and devoured every
23   single muffin. And what makes his conduct all the more
24   heartless is that he was perfectly well aware from the
25   first that I have no brother, that I never had a brother,
26   and that I don't intend to have a brother, not even of any
27   kind. I distinctly told him so myself yesterday afternoon.
28 LADY B.: Ahem! Mr. Worthing, after careful consideration I
29   have decided entirely to overlook my nephew's conduct
30   to you.
31 JACK: That is very generous of you, Lady Bracknell. My own
32   decision, however, is unalterable. I decline to give my
33   consent.
34 LADY B.: *(To CECILY)* Come here, sweet child. How old are
35   you, dear?

1   CECILY: Well, I am really only eighteen, but I always admit
2   to twenty when I go to evening parties.
3   LADY B.: You are perfectly right in making some slight
4   alteration. Indeed, no woman should ever be quite
5   accurate about her age. It looks so calculating ... *(In*
6   *meditative manner)* Eighteen, but admitting to twenty at
7   evening parties. Well, it will not be very long before you
8   are of age and free from the restraints of tutelage. So I
9   don't think your guardian's consent is, after all, a matter
10   of any importance.
11   JACK: Pray excuse me, Lady Bracknell, for interrupting you
12   again, but it is only fair to tell you that according to the
13   terms of her grandfather's will, Miss Cardew does not
14   come legally of age till she is thirty-five.
15   LADY B.: That does not seem to me to be a grave objection.
16   Thirty-five is a very attractive age. London society is full
17   of women of the very highest birth who have, of their
18   own free choice, remained thirty-five for years.
19   CECILY: Algy, could you wait for me till I was thirty-five?
20   ALGY: Of course I could, Cecily. You know I could.
21   CECILY: Yes, I felt it instinctively, but I couldn't wait all
22   that time. I hate waiting even five minutes for anybody.
23   It always makes me rather cross. I am not punctual
24   myself, I know, but I do like punctuality in others, and
25   waiting, even to be married, is quite out of the question.
26   ALGY: Then what is to be done, Cecily?
27   CECILY: I don't know, Mr. Moncrieff.
28   LADY B.: My dear Mr. Worthing, as Miss Cardew states
29   positively that she cannot wait till she is thirty-five — a
30   remark which I am bound to say seems to me to show a
31   somewhat impatient nature — I would beg of you to
32   reconsider your decision.
33   JACK: But my dear Lady Bracknell, the matter is entirely in
34   your own hands. The moment you consent to my marriage
35   with Gwendolyn, I will most gladly allow your nephew

1   to form an alliance with my ward.
2 LADY B.:   *(Drawing herself up)* **You must be quite aware that**
3   **what you propose is out of the question.**
4 JACK: **Then a passionate celibacy is all that any of us can**
5   **look forward to.**
6 LADY B.:   **That is not the destiny I propose for Gwendolyn.**
7   **Algernon, of course, can choose for himself. Come, dear,**
8   **we have already missed five, if not six, trains. To miss**
9   **any more might expose us to comment on the platform.**
10   *(MISS PRISM stands.)*
11 JACK: **Oh, Miss Prism. Come here, would you?**
12 LADY B.:   *(Starting)* **Miss Prism! Did I hear you mention a Miss**
13   **Prism?**
14 JACK: **Yes, Lady Bracknell. Miss Prism has been for the last**
15   **three years Miss Cardew's esteemed governess and**
16   **valued companion.**
17 LADY B.:   *(In a severe, judicial voice)* **Prism!** *(MISS PRISM bows*
18   *her head in shame.)* **Come here, Prism! Where is that baby?**
19   *(General consternation)* **Twenty-eight years ago, Prism, you**
20   **left Lord Bracknell's house, Number 104, Upper**
21   **Grosvenor Street, in charge of a perambulator that**
22   **contained a baby, of the male sex. You never returned.**
23   **A few weeks later, through the elaborate investigations**
24   **of the Metropolitan police, the perambulator was**
25   **discovered at midnight, standing by itself in a remote**
26   **corner of Bayswater. It contained the manuscript of a**
27   **three-volume novel of more than usually revolting**
28   **sentimentality.** *(MISS PRISM starts in involuntary*
29   *indignation.)* **But the baby was not there!** *(Everyone looks at*
30   *MISS PRISM.)* **Prism, where is that baby?** *(A pause)*
31 MISS P.:   **Lady Bracknell, I admit with shame that I do not**
32   **know. I only wish I did. The plain facts of the case are**
33   **these. On the morning of the day you mention, a day that**
34   **is forever branded on my memory, I prepared as usual**
35   **to take the baby out in its perambulator. I had also with**

1   me a somewhat old but capacious handbag in which I
2   had intended to place the manuscript of a work of fiction
3   that I had written during my few unoccupied hours. In
4   a moment of mental abstraction, for which I can never
5   forgive myself, I deposited the manuscript in the
6   bassinette, and placed the baby in the handbag.
7   JACK: *(Who has been listening attentively)* **But where did you**
8   **deposit the handbag?**
9   MISS P.:   Do not ask me, Mr. Worthing.
10   JACK: Miss Prism, this is a matter of no small importance to
11   me. I insist on knowing where you deposited the handbag
12   that contained the infant.
13   MISS P.:   I left it in the cloakroom of one of the larger railway
14   stations in London.
15   JACK: What railway station?
16   MISS P.:   *(Quite crushed)* **Victoria. The Brighton line.**
17   JACK: I must retire to my room for a moment. Gwendolyn,
18   wait here for me.
19   GWEN: If you are not too long, I will wait here for you all my
20   life. *(JACK sits.)*
21   CECILY: What do you think this means, Lady Bracknell?
22   LADY B.:   I dare not even suspect, Cecily. I need hardly tell
23   you that in families of high position strange coincidences
24   are not supposed to occur. They are hardly considered
25   the thing.
26   CECILY: Oh, that noise! Uncle Jack seems strangely agitated.
27   LADY B.:   This noise is extremely unpleasant. It sounds as if
28   he was having an argument. I dislike arguments of any
29   kind. They are always vulgar, and often convincing.
30   *(Pause)* I wish he would arrive at some conclusion.
31   GWEN: This suspense is terrible. I hope it will last. *(JACK*
32   *stands.)*
33   JACK: Is this the handbag, Miss Prism? Examine it carefully
34   before you speak. The happiness of more than one life
35   depends on your answer.

1 MISS P.: *(Calmly)* It seems to be mine. Yes, here is the injury
2   it received through the upsetting of a Gower Street
3   omnibus in younger and happier days. Here is the stain
4   on the lining caused by the explosion of a temperance
5   beverage, an incident that occurred at Leamington. And
6   here, on the lock, are my initials. I had forgotten that in
7   an extravagant mood I had had them placed there. The
8   bag is undoubtedly mine. I am delighted to have it so
9   unexpectedly restored to me. It has been a great
10   inconvenience being without it all these years.
11 JACK: *(In a pathetic voice)* Miss Prism, more is restored to you
12   than this handbag. I was the baby you placed in it.
13 MISS P.: *(Amazed)* You?
14 JACK: Yes . . . mother!
15 MISS P.: *(Recoiling in indignant astonishment)* Mr. Worthing!
16   I am unmarried!
17 JACK: Unmarried! I do not deny that is a serious blow. But
18   after all, who has the right to cast a stone against one
19   who has suffered? Cannot repentance wipe out an act of
20   folly? Why should there be one law for men and another
21   for women? Mother, I forgive you.
22 MISS P.: Mr. Worthing, there is some error. Lady Bracknell
23   is the lady who can tell you who you really are.
24 JACK: *(After a pause)* Lady Bracknell, I hate to seem
25   inquisitive, but would you kindly inform me who I am?
26 LADY B.: I am afraid that the news I have to give you will not
27   altogether please you. You are the son of my poor sister,
28   Mrs. Moncrieff, and consequently Algernon's elder
29   brother.
30 JACK: Algy's elder brother! Then I have a brother after all. I
31   knew I had a brother! I always said I had a brother!
32   Cecily — how could you have ever doubted that I had a
33   brother?
34 GWEN: *(To JACK)* My own! But what own are you? What
35   is your Christian name, now that you have become

89

1   someone else?

2   JACK: Good Heavens! I had quite forgotten that point. Your

3   decision on the subject of my name is irrevocable, I

4   suppose?

5   GWEN: I never change, except in my affections.

6   CECILY: What a noble nature you have, Gwendolyn.

7   JACK: Then the question had better be cleared up at once.

8   Aunt Augusta, a moment. At the time when Miss Prism

9   left me in the handbag, had I been christened already?

10   LADY B.:   Every luxury that money could buy, including

11   christening, had been lavished on you by your fond and

12   doting parents.

13   JACK: Then I was christened! That is settled. Now, what

14   name was I given? Let me know the worst.

15   LADY B.:   Being the eldest son you were naturally christened

16   after your father — Lieut. Col. Ernest John Moncrieff.

17   JACK: Ernest. I always told you, Gwendolyn, my name was

18   Ernest, didn't I? Well, it is Ernest after all. I mean it

19   naturally is Ernest.

20   LADY B.:   Yes, the general was called Ernest. I knew I had

21   some particular reason for disliking the name.

22   GWEN: Ernest! My own Ernest! I felt from the first that you

23   could have no other name!

24   JACK: Gwendolyn, it is a terrible thing for a man to find out

25   suddenly that all his life he has been speaking nothing

26   but the truth. Can you forgive me?

27   GWEN: I can. For I feel that you are sure to change.

28   JACK: Gwendolyn, my own one!

29   ALGY: Cecily, my own one.

30   LADY B.:   My nephew, you seem to be displaying signs of

31   triviality.

32   JACK: On the contrary, Aunt Augusta, I've now realized for

33   the first time in my life the vital importance of being

34   *earnest*.

35

JOSEPH THE TAILOR

by Judy Wolfman

CAST OF CHARACTERS

NARRATOR: Storyteller leading into dialog.

JOSEPH: An enterprising tailor.

SARAH: A good, Jewish wife.

Jewish folktales are often told by one storyteller but they can be performed as a humorous dialog. Judy Wolfman has adapted this story into a simple drama that may be performed by two readers using pantomime to substitute for the various props such as the coat, the scissors, needle and thread for sewing and so on with all the items of the transformation for something out of nothing.

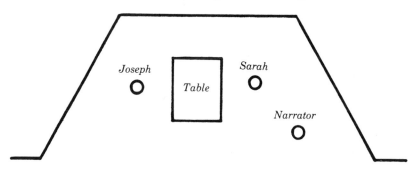

1   NARRATOR: Joseph was a very good tailor and, as a result,
2   was a very busy tailor. In fact, he was so busy that he
3   never had time to do his own clothes.
4   JOSEPH: I'm not complaining! I'm very pleased that people
5   like my work so much that they bring me their work. But
6   I wish I had some time to take care of my own needs.
7   Like this coat — it's my very favorite coat, but just look
8   at it — it's so worn. Oh well, perhaps some day . . .
9   NARRATOR: Yes, he loved his coat, and he wore it every day.
10   But his wife, Sarah, hated it.
11   SARAH: Joseph, dear Joseph. Just look at your coat. It's so
12   old — you wear it every day. Why don't you make yourself
13   a new one to wear?
14   JOSEPH: I'm much too busy, Sarah. But someday . . .
15   NARRATOR: Then, one day, Joseph took a good look at his
16   coat.
17   JOSEPH: Oh, no! Sarah! Sarah! Come here.
18   SARAH: What is it, Joseph? What's wrong?
19   JOSEPH: Just look at this coat — it's frayed all along the
20   edge. I can't wear a coat like this — my customers will
21   think I can't fix it.
22   SARAH: Ah, Joseph, my dear Joseph. Why don't you just
23   take your coat and throw it out?
24   JOSEPH: What? Why should I throw it out? I'm a tailor.
25   NARRATOR: So, Joseph cut and snipped and stitched and
26   sewed, and made a little jacket out of his coat.
27   JOSEPH: Look, Sarah — see the jacket I've made. I can wear
28   this on cool evenings.
29   SARAH: That's fine, Joseph. I am proud of you.
30   NARRATOR: Joseph loved his new jacket, and it became his
31   favorite thing to wear. He wore it every day until one
32   day he noticed a rip in the sleeve.
33   JOSEPH: Sarah, come here!
34   SARAH: What is it, Joseph?
35   JOSEPH: Just look at my favorite jacket! It has a rip in the

1   sleeve. I can't wear it with a rip in the sleeve.

2   SARAH: Ah, Joseph, then why don't you just take the jacket

3   and throw it out?

4   JOSEPH: What? Throw it out? Have you forgotten — I'm a

5   tailor.

6   NARRATOR: So, Joseph cut and snipped and stitched and

7   sewed, and made himself a fine vest.

8   JOSEPH: You see, Sarah — from the jacket I've made a

9   fine vest.

10   SARAH: Ah, dear Joseph. You are indeed a clever husband.

11   The vest is truly beautiful.

12   NARRATOR: Joseph became very attached to his new vest,

13   wearing it every day, since it was now his favorite piece

14   of clothing. Then one day . . .

15   JOSEPH: Sarah! Look! Look at my favorite vest! The pocket

16   is ripped. I surely can't wear it with a pocket ripped.

17   What'll my customers think of me?

18   SARAH: Joseph, dear Joseph. Why don't you just take your

19   vest and throw it out?

20   JOSEPH: Sarah — you know I can't throw it out. I am a

21   tailor!

22   NARRATOR: So, Joseph cut and snipped and stitched and

23   sewed, and from the vest, he made a beautiful, long scarf.

24   JOSEPH: Sarah, how do you like my scarf? Now I have a fine

25   scarf that I can wear to the synagogue on Friday nights.

26   SARAH: Your scarf is lovely, dear Joseph. I shall be proud

27   to be seen with you wearing your handsome scarf to the

28   synagogue.

29   NARRATOR: And wear it he did! Why, Joseph wore his

30   scarf every Friday night for several months, until one

31   day he noticed the scarf was very badly frayed.

32   JOSEPH: Oh, dear. My beautiful Sabbath scarf is so frayed,

33   I can no longer wear it to the synagogue.

34   SARAH: Then, Joseph, dear, why don't you just take your

35   scarf and throw it out?

1   JOSEPH: Sarah, you should know better than to tell me to
2   throw it out. After all — I'm a tailor!
3   NARRATOR: So, Joseph cut and snipped, and he stitched
4   and he sewed, and he made the scarf into a beautiful
5   necktie.
6   JOSEPH: You see, Sarah, from the scarf I've made a necktie,
7   and I'll wear this necktie when I get dressed up for special
8   events.
9   NARRATOR: And one day, Joseph had a chance to wear his
10   beautiful new tie.
11   SARAH: Joseph, we've been invited to attend a wedding.
12   Your new necktie would be the perfect thing to wear.
13   NARRATOR: But, at the wedding, Joseph was not very
14   careful about eating. In fact, it was well known that
15   Joseph was a rather sloppy eater. And so, by the end of
16   the meal, Joseph had food spots all over his lovely
17   necktie. When Joseph got home that evening, he removed
18   his tie and exclaimed:
19   JOSEPH: My goodness! Just look at this necktie! Why, it
20   looks terrible! Just look at all of these food spots. I
21   certainly can't wear this necktie again.
22   SARAH: You're quite right about that, Joseph. So, why don't
23   you just take the necktie and throw it out.
24   JOSEPH: Sarah, Sarah, as much as I know I can't wear the
25   necktie, I also know I can't throw it out. Have you
26   forgotten? I'm a tailor.
27   NARRATOR: So, once again, Joseph cut and snipped, and
28   stitched and sewed, and this time, he made a
29   handkerchief, which he wore around his neck. But, if you
30   remember, Joseph was a sloppy eater, and so when he
31   ate, the handkerchief got spotted until it became rather
32   disgusting. Even Joseph could see that!
33   JOSEPH: Ugh! I'm afraid my handkerchief is ruined. I
34   certainly can't wear anything that looks this disgusting!
35   SARAH: I'm glad you realize that, Joseph. So, why don't you

1   just take your handkerchief and throw it out?
2   JOSEPH: Sarah, how many times do I have to remind you? I
3   don't throw things out; I'm a tailor.
4   NARRATOR: So, Joseph cut and snipped, and he stitched
5   and he sewed, and made a button, which he wore on his
6   trousers to hold his suspenders up. But one day, as luck
7   would have it, he lost his button.
8   JOSEPH: Sarah, have you seen my button? It's come off my
9   pants, and I can't find it anywhere! I can't imagine where
10   my button might have gone!
11   SARAH: Ahhh, Joseph. Today I am a happy woman. You have
12   lost your button, so now you have nothing. And one thing
13   in this world that I'm sure of it this: You can't make
14   something out of nothing.
15   JOSEPH: What? What is it you say? You think I can't make
16   something out of nothing? Sarah, dear wife, not only am
17   I a tailor, but I am also a storyteller.
18   NARRATOR: With that, Joseph took out a pencil and wrote
19   down this story that we are telling you, which proves . . .
20   ALL: That you CAN make something out of nothing.
21
22
23
24
25
26
27
28
29
30
31
32
33
34
35

A HEN OR A HORSE

by Judy Wolfman

CAST OF CHARACTERS

NARRATOR: Storyteller leading into the dialog.

HUSBANDS AND WIVES: These may be the same for each visit or they may be different persons depending on available number of readers.

Once again this is a Jewish folktale adapted to a brief playlet. No props are required. Three imaginary houses are visited where the two men make their offer of a hen or a horse. They knock in pantomime and gesture to unseen horses.

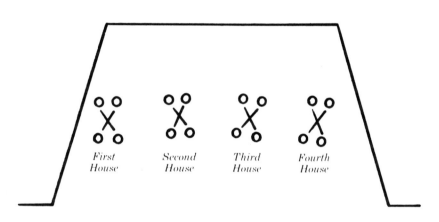

1	NARRATOR: Two men were having quite a dispute over who
2	is really the head of the house.
3	MAN 1: I believe that the husband is the head of the
4	house. After all, he's the one who works hard and sees
5	to it there's enough money to run the household.
6	MAN 2: True. But it's the woman who spends the money, and
7	she must make sure that she doesn't spend more than
8	her husband makes.
9	MAN 1: But who is stronger? The husband, of course. He is
10	strong like an ox.
11	MAN 2: Yes, he is strong like an ox, and also like an ox he can
12	be very stubborn.
13	NARRATOR: Each man advanced his opinion, and
14	supported his thinking with arguments that became
15	quite heated.
16	MAN 1: It appears to me that we're getting nowhere by
17	arguing. We'll have to prove ourselves, and see who's
18	right.
19	MAN 2: That's fine with me. We'll go from house to house,
20	and find out who runs the household — the husband or
21	the wife.
22	MAN 1: To every woman we find who is the head of the
23	household, I'll give a fine hen.
24	MAN 2: To every man we find who is the head of the house,
25	I'll give a horse.
26	NARRATOR: And so, the two men set out with two hens and
27	two horses. They went to the first house, where a slight
28	woman answered the door.
29	MAN 1: Good morning, Madam. I wonder if you would be
30	good enough to answer a question for us.
31	WOMAN: *(In a mild-mannered voice)* I'll try.
32	MAN 1: Would you please tell us — who is the head of this
33	house?
34	NARRATOR: Though the woman was little, and mild
35	mannered, she replied promptly, in a gentle but firm voice.

1   WOMAN: I am.

2   MAN 1:   Well, we have a hen here for you.

3   NARRATOR: They gave the woman the hen, and went to the

4   house next door. When they knocked, the door was

5   answered by a tall, thin, hard-faced woman.

6   MAN 2:   Madam, we'd like to know — who is the head of this

7   household?

8   NARRATOR: Without even hearing her words, the men

9   knew what her answer would be — and they were right.

10   WOMAN: Who do you think? I am, of course.

11   MAN 2:   Well, we have a hen for you. Thank you for your time.

12   NARRATOR: The men left, having given the woman her hen.

13   MAN 1:   Well, we have no more hens to give away. We'll have

14   to get some more.

15   NARRATOR: The men returned with another supply, and

16   went to a third home. This time a man answered the door.

17   MAN 1:   Sir, are you the head of this house?

18   NARRATOR: The man looked over his shoulder, and then

19   said in a voice hardly above a whisper . . .

20   MAN 3:   I am.

21   MAN 1:   Well, sir, we have a horse for you. We have two

22   horses here — one is a white horse, and the other is a

23   bay horse. You may take your choice.

24   MAN 3:   Well, I think I'll take the bay horse.

25   NARRATOR: Just then, a woman's voice called out:

26   WOMAN: No, John. You take the white horse.

27   MAN 3:   But, my dear, the bay horse is a much better animal.

28   WOMAN: Why, John, I'm surprised at you. Just look at the

29   white horse. It's so much prettier. Now, you just take the

30   white horse.

31   MAN 1:   Why don't you both talk it over, and we'll be back

32   presently to find out your decision.

33   NARRATOR: The two men left, and went to the next house,

34   where they lost another hen. Then they returned to get

35   the decision about the horse. When they reached the

1   door, they were met by both the man and the woman.

2   MAN 1:   Well, have you decided which horse you will take?

3   MAN 3:   Yes, we have. *We* have decided to take the white

4   horse.

5   MAN 1:   Oh, no, you don't. You won't get any horse. Instead,

6   you get a hen!

BEOWULF'S HANG-UP

by Charles R. Larson
Adapted for Readers Theatre by Melvin R. White, Ph.D.

CAST OF CHARACTERS

THE PROFESSOR: He teaches a seminar.

CLARA LEPAGE: A sophomore.

STUDENTS: Ten assorted, five above and five below the long table; they do not speak.

The setting is simple, a long table with 12 chairs:

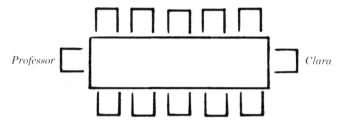

If desired, such items as a portable blackboard to suggest a classroom may be added, but this is not necessary.

Humor may be found as the heads of the ten non-talking students turn to focus on Clara and on the Professor as they speak (like watching a tennis match, perhaps).

Used by permission of Martin Levin. From Phoenix Nest, *Saturday Review*, Jan. 17, 1970, pages 8 and 10.

1   CLARA: Was Beowulf married?
2   PROFESSOR: What?
3   CLARA: Was Beowulf married?
4   PROFESSOR: *(Stands to move down to talk with the audience.)*
5   She — Miss LePage, a student in my survey of English
6   Literature seminar, repeated her question. I could tell it
7   was going to be another of those semesters. You see, the
8   year before, Miss LePage had been in both semesters of
9   my freshman English classes, and hardly a day had
10   passed when I didn't live in perpetual fear of her
11   unorthodox questions. Once she'd written a paper on
12   "Rip Van Winkle," claiming he was impotent — using as
13   her chief evidence the fact that Rip's gun didn't work.
14   Now it is another year, another semester, and Miss
15   LePage is a sophomore, sitting in that chair at the other
16   end of the table — back to haunt me for another year.
17   After fighting all summer to get to teach this section of
18   English Literature survey by discussion instead of
19   lecture, who shows up but Clara LePage? And here it is,
20   only the second class. I mean, it's pretty difficult to
21   teach the English Lit survey without beginning with
22   *Beowulf.*
23 CLARA: Was he?
24 PROFESSOR: *(Returning to his seat)* I don't think so. It's
25   difficult to tell. No, I guess not. The textual evidence . . .
26 CLARA: *(Interrupting)* That's what I thought.
27 PROFESSOR: Does it matter?
28 CLARA: Haven't you ever thought about it before?
29 PROFESSOR: *(Giving up)* OK. What's the reason Beowulf
30   never married?
31 CLARA: *(Very serious)* Well, I don't know if this is the only
32   reason, but it's fairly obvious after reading the poem that
33   he's a homosexual.
34 PROFESSOR: *(Voice shows he is losing his "cool.")* How can you
35   tell? How do you know?

101

1   CLARA: Well, certainly if from nothing else, just about by
2   everything he does. I mean, haven't you ever paid any
3   attention to the little things he's always doing throughout
4   the whole story?
5   PROFESSOR: I guess I haven't, Miss LePage. Like what?
6   CLARA: Oh, you know, like always going around hugging
7   everyone — I mean all the other males in the story.
8   PROFESSOR: *(Explodes a bit.)* You're being absurd!
9   CLARA: I'm serious. You're just not very observant. Didn't
10   you ever notice that when Beowulf kills someone, he does
11   it by hugging him to death? That he's always got to have
12   his arms around some other male? *(Perhaps one or more of*
13   *the other students nods head in agreement.)* And can you
14   imagine anything so stupid as getting undressed when
15   he knows he's going to have to fight Grendel? I mean,
16   after all, Heorot Hall isn't exactly the safest place to spend
17   a night — and yet the first thing Beowulf does when he
18   goes there is take his clothes off. The text says, if I may
19   read it for you . . . *(PROFESSOR nods assent. Reading:)*
20   "He stripped off his shirt, his helmet, his sword/
21   Hammered from the hardest iron, and handed/
22   All his weapons and armor to a servant."
23   Don't you think that's fairly clear?
24 PROFESSOR: *(Vehemently)* But he knew his strength! He was
25   going to crush Grendel to death!
26 CLARA: *(Quite controlled)* Then why doesn't he do the same
27   thing with Grendel's mother? When he goes off to kill
28   her, he's decked out in all the armor he can find. He
29   doesn't fight her all stripped down like that — he's afraid
30   to touch a female.
31 PROFESSOR: But . . .
32 CLARA: *(Keeps right on talking.)* He's simply got a thing for
33   males. He's always swimming naked with other young men —
34   like Breca, for instance. And a passion for hugging them.
35   If you remember, that's the way he kills the dragon, too.

102

1   PROFESSOR: *(Trying to be funny, perhaps)* **Was it a male**
2   **dragon?** *(One of the students snickers.)* **So what's your point?**
3   CLARA: Well, I think it's pretty clear. Beowulf was homo-
4   sexual — and if you look at the poem that way the whole
5   meaning's changed. He's not the one you're supposed to
6   sympathize with.
7   PROFESSOR: *(Intrigued in spite of himself)* **Who then, Grendel?**
8   CLARA: Grendel's mother. Who else? That's the one we're
9   supposed to feel sorry for. Grendel was an only child. His
10   poor mother. What really bothers Beowulf — and the
11   reason he puts on all that stuff before he goes to fight
12   her — is that a female has come to revenge Grendel's
13   death. It's too humiliating. If it had been Grendel's father
14   instead . . .
15   PROFESSOR: *(Impatiently)* **Grendel doesn't have a father!**
16   CLARA: How do you know?
17   PROFESSOR: There's no textual evidence.
18   CLARA: There isn't any textual evidence that he doesn't
19   either.
20   PROFESSOR: Anything else you've got on your mind now
21   that you've ruined the poem?
22   CLARA: Just one thing.
23   PROFESSOR: What?!
24   CLARA: I think it's fairly clear from the end of the tale —
25   Beowulf's lack of masculinity.
26   PROFESSOR: How?!
27   CLARA: Well, usually when a hero in an epic does some sort
28   of great, heroic deed, he's given a boon, isn't he?
29   PROFESSOR: *He is* — all that treasure — or did you forget?
30   CLARA: That's exactly my point. It should have been a
31   woman. Why didn't Hrothgar give Beowulf a wife for
32   killing Grendel, if he was such a brave young man? He
33   knew he was gay.
34   PROFESSOR: *(Sneering)* **So instead he lives happily ever**
35   **after — childless.**

1   **CLARA:** *(Very sure of herself)* **Hrothgar knows what's going on.**
2   **That's why he sends him away. You think he wants**
3   **someone around his court who's a fetishist?**
4   **PROFESSOR:** *(Completely perplexed)* **A fetishist? Whatever**
5   **are you referring to?**
6   **CLARA:** **The arm. Grendel's arm — didn't you see how**
7   **Beowulf tried to keep it?** *(PROFESSOR gives up. If he has*
8   *books or notes on the table, may grab them, and then stalk out.*
9   *CLARA stands, grins for the first time, clasps her hands above*
10   *her head in triumph as the other ten students applaud her, and*
11   *the curtain falls.)*
12
13
14
15
16
17
18
19
20
21
22
23
24
25
26
27
28
29
30
31
32
33
34
35

THE ENDLESS AUTUMN

by Arthur Hoppe
Adapted for Performance by Melvin R. White, Ph.D.

CAST OF CHARACTERS

NARRATOR

IRMA: A friend of Sophie; wife of Fred, a fan of football.

SOPHIE: A friend of Irma

FRED: Who likes to watch football on TV; he does not speak.

This skit is based on an Arthur Hoppe column which first appeared in the San Francisco Chronicle on March 24, 1987. It calls for three ordinary chairs, and a small table — perhaps a card table. The tea which is served may be real or it may be imaginary, pantomimed.

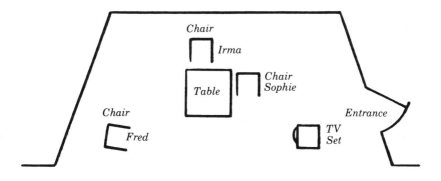

1   **NARRATOR:** The National Football League signed new
2   television contracts that will enable viewers to watch
3   eleven straight hours of football on Sundays this fall.
4   **IRMA:** Come right in, Sophie, and make yourself
5   comfortable. *(As SOPHIE does so, IRMA motions her to a seat*
6   *at the table.)* **How about a nice cup of tea?**
7   **SOPHIE:** Thank you, Irma, don't mind if I do. *(Throughout the*
8   *skit, the ladies enjoy their tea.)* **How's Fred?** *(Glancing over at*
9   *him. FRED is sitting staring at a TV set, imaginary, a "little*
10   *smile" on his face.)*
11   **IRMA:** *(Glance at FRED.)* **The same, as you can see. He just**
12   **sits there with that little smile on his face.**
13   **SOPHIE:** *(Look at TV.)* **What's the score?**
14   **IRMA:** It's 12,042 to 12,040. The Cowhawks are still ahead.
15   **SOPHIE:** They've been ahead since the kick-off a year ago
16   last May, haven't they?
17   **IRMA:** Yes, that's why Fred's still smiling. *(Pantomime business*
18   *with sugar; might take some herself and stir it.)* **Sugar, Sophie?**
19   **SOPHIE:** No, thank you, Irma. *(Look at FRED.)* **But he looks**
20   **different, somehow.**
21   **IRMA:** It's his new sweater. When I painted the room, I
22   decided to re-cover him and the love seat. *(Business)*
23   **Cream?**
24   **SOPHIE:** A drop. *(Business)* **Between you and me, Irma, I**
25   **think this idea of having a perpetual football game going**
26   **around the clock, month in and month out, is really dumb.**
27   **IRMA:** Well, once people got to watching all day Saturday,
28   all day and all evening on Sundays, plus Monday and
29   Thursday nights, it was just a matter of filling in the gaps,
30   and the beer industry is certainly happy. Imagine, 342
31   commercials a day!
32   **SOPHIE:** Maybe so, but look what it's done to Fred there.
33   *(Glance at him.)*
34   **IRMA:** Oh, he's not much trouble, Sophie. I dust him once a
35   week, and you'd be amazed at how long a man can survive

1   on a diet of Bud Light and corn chips.

2   SOPHIE: Does he ever sleep?

3   IRMA: Oh, he gets at least eight hours. He catnaps during
4   commercials.

5   SOPHIE: Really, Irma, you're a saint. *(May reach across to touch*
6   *her.)* He can't be much company. He never says a word.

7   IRMA: That's not so, Sophie. Every once in a while he'll say
8   something like, *(Yell it out)* "It's fourth and one, you idiot!
9   Go for it!" And I like to think he recognizes me.

10   SOPHIE: What about the children?

11   IRMA: Little Billie enjoys him. Just last week he used him for
12   the left wall of his fort. But Millicent's older, and she
13   wants me to move him up to the attic. She says that when
14   she has her friends over, he's kind of a party pooper. But
15   I said, "Millicent, he's your father. He stays in the living
16   room, and that's that." You know, Sophie, it isn't easy
17   keeping a family together.

18   SOPHIE: Really, Irma, you're a saint. But he's such a burden
19   to you. Look, I don't know how to say this, but what you
20   ought to do is pull the plug.

21   IRMA: Sophie, I couldn't do that! Father O'Hanrahan says it
22   would be a sin!

23   SOPHIE: Father O'Hanrahan's just saying that because he's
24   a Cowhawks fan, too.

25   IRMA: That's not true, Sophie. The Father says Fred's happy
26   that the Cowhawks are winning, and as long as he's
27   happy, I've got no right to pull the plug! *(FRED stirs, leans*
28   *forward a bit in his chair, and stops smiling. SOPHIE sees this.)*

29   SOPHIE: Irma, I do believe Fred's stirring! What's happened
30   on the TV? *(They both look.)*

31   IRMA: I think the Seagulls are going to attempt a field goal.
32   Yes, look at that! *(Getting up excitedly)* It's up and it's . . . it's
33   good! My heavens, that puts the Seagulls ahead for the
34   first time!

35   SOPHIE: *(Getting up, moving toward IRMA)* Pull the plug, Irma,

1 **pull the plug!** *(IRMA moves rapidly to the wall behind the TV*
2 *set, imaginary or real, and pulls the plug! The two women may*
3 *hug as FRED collapses back into his chair in total dismay.)*
4
5
6
7
8
9
10
11
12
13
14
15
16
17
18
19
20
21
22
23
24
25
26
27
28
29
30
31
32
33
34
35

THE SANDWICH LINE

by John M. Kaman
Adapted to Readers Theatre by Melvin R. White, Ph.D.

CAST OF CHARACTERS

SHE: Waitress

SIR: Customer

EXTRAS: As needed

This column by John M. Kaman, a San Francisco attorney and short-story writer, appeared in the San Francisco Chronicle's "Sunday Punch," page 2, on January 21, 1988. It calls for a cast of two: a waitress or order-taker, and a "sir," trying to order a sandwich. The setting is anything which suggests a luncheon counter, a fast-food place, or even a deli. Others may be in line behind him.

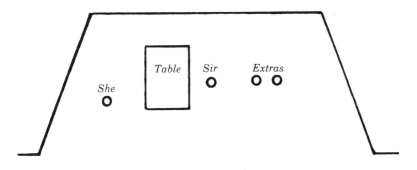

The Sandwich Line is reprinted by permission of the author. Copyright © 1988 Chronicle Publishing Co. John M. Kaman is a published poet and short-story writer. He also practices law in San Francisco, CA.

1   SHE: Can I help you, sir?

2   SIR: Pastrami with jack cheese on dark rye to go. Everything

3   — mustard, mayonnaise, lettuce, tomato and onions.

4   SHE: That's a pastrami?

5   SIR: Yes, with jack cheese.

6   SHE: Want any cheese on that, sir?

7   SIR: Jack cheese.

8   SHE: What kind of bread?

9   SIR: Dark rye.

10   SHE: Mustard or mayonnaise?

11   SIR: Both.

12   SHE: You want both, it's a nickel extra. You want both?

13   SIR: Yeah, I want both.

14   SHE: Lettuce, tomato, onions?

15   SIR: Yes, everything.

16   SHE: Pickles, too?

17   SIR: No, hold the pickles.

18   SHE: Sweet or dill, sir?

19   SIR: No pickles.

20   SHE: No pickles?

21   SIR: No pickles.

22   SHE: For here or to go, sir?

23   SIR: To go. I said, "To go."

24   SHE: Four-ninety-five plus the mayo is five dollars.

25   SIR: *(Holding out a twenty dollar bill)* Here you go.

26   SHE: Sorry, sir. We don't break twenties.

27   SIR: You don't break twenties?

28   SHE: No, sir. No large bills.

29   SIR: I don't have anything else.

30   SHE: You can get some change across the street at the bank.

31   I'll hold the sandwich for you.

32   SIR: Hey, I'm good for it. I come in here every day. Catch you

33   tomorrow.

34   SHE: Sorry, sir, no credit. Next in line. Your order, please.

35   SIR: Just a minute. Every day I come in here we go through

1   **the same routine. I tell you what I want, same thing every**

2   **day, you make me repeat the whole damn order.** *(Increases*

3   *volume as anger increases.)* **I waste ten minutes here every**

4   **day repeating myself, and you can't trust me until**

5   **tomorrow?**

6   SHE: *(Unperturbed)* **Move along, sir, please. You're holding up**

7   **the line. Next, please.** *(If others are in line, move them up.)*

8   **Can I help you, Ma'am?** *(Or sir)*

9

10

11

12

13

14

15

16

17

18

19

20

21

22

23

24

25

26

27

28

29

30

31

32

33

34

35

SORRY ABOUT THAT, LORD

by Al Martinez
Adapted for Readers Theatre by Melvin R. White, Ph.D.

CAST OF CHARACTERS

HUSBAND: Enthusiastic man, any age. Must be an effective story-teller, as he also serves as the narrator.

WIFE: Housewife; about the same age as the husband.

BUILDING INSPECTOR: Man or woman, tough.

COAST GUARD: Man or woman, tough.

S.P.C.A.: Man or woman, tough.

VOICE OF GOD: Deep and resonant male voice; unearthly quality.

A newspaper column by Al Martinez, "Sorry About That, Lord," comments humorously on what would happen today if anyone tried to build an ark as Noah once did.

With one person per role a cast of six is required. The only prop needed is one ordinary chair for the wife placed far to one side and facing Upstage, away from the audience. No special costuming is necessary.

As the skit opens, the Husband as Narrator enters the empty stage, crosses Down Center to talk with the audience. As he does so, the Wife unobtrusively seats herself on the single chair, facing Upstage, away from the audience.

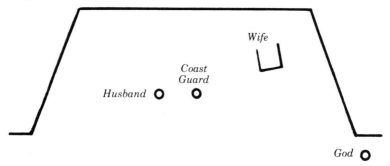

112

1   HUSBAND: *(Narrating)* **It was in the winter of 19____. Rain**
2   **had fallen for thirty days and thirty nights. I was in the**
3   **kitchen cooking some fondue when suddenly a voice from**
4   **above said:**

5   WIFE: *(From her seat, sounding like God)* **You'd better build an**
6   **ark.**

7   HUSBAND: *(Startled)* **Huh?** *(Looking up)*

8   WIFE: *(Herself, vocally)* **I said you'd better build an ark. Either**
9   **that, or fix the holes in the roof.**

10   HUSBAND: *(Calling back, liking the idea)* **You know what? I**
11   **think I *will* build an ark! Yes, I'm going to!**

12   WIFE: *(Calling back, patiently)* **That's fine, dear. Are you stirring**
13   **the fondue?**

14   HUSBAND: *(To audience)* **The next day I went downtown and**
15   **got me some lumber and a groovy little hammer and went**
16   **to work, whack, whack, whack. What a beautiful little**
17   **craft it would be, forty cubits by . . .**

18   INSPECTOR: *(Coming over to HUSBAND and interrupting)* **You**
19   **got a permit for that, buddy?**

20   HUSBAND: **This, sir,** *(or lady)* **is an ark. I had a sign from the**
21   **Lord to build it.**

22   INSPECTOR: **You got it in writing?**

23   HUSBAND: **Well, no . . . but . . .**

24   INSPECTOR: **Then you need a building permit.**

25   HUSBAND: **You don't understand, sir** *(Or lady)* **. . .**

26   INSPECTOR: **I understand, buddy. That thing don't meet the**
27   **requirements of a multiple-dwelling unit as contained in**
28   **Section 21, Paragraph 5, of the Building Code. You got to**
29   **have studs on sixteen-inch centers, two electrical outlets**
30   **in each compartment, half-inch sheetrock on the inside,**
31   **and waterproofing all over.** *(Returns to his seat.)*

32   HUSBAND: *(To audience)* **I had to dismantle the ark, draw up**
33   **plans, submit them to the county building department**
34   **and get a permit. Then I began, whack, whack, whack.**
35   *(COAST GUARD stands, comes down to HUSBAND.)*

1   **COAST GUARD:**   *(Loud and gruff)* **You plan to put that tub in**
2   **the water, Mac?**
3   **HUSBAND:**   **I do.**
4   **COAST GUARD:**   **You know anything about boats? Navigation?**
5   **Rules of safety and courtesy afloat? License requirements**
6   **for passenger craft? One life jacket for each living**
7   **creature aboard?**
8   **HUSBAND:**   **Man, this is an ark, not a luxury liner.**
9   **COAST GUARD:**   **No difference, Mac. Gotta have a license . . .**
10   **put that tub in the water the way it is, we'll sink it as a**
11   **navigation hazard.** *(Returns to seat.)*
12   **HUSBAND:**   **So I hired a crew and I bought life jackets and a**
13   **two-way radio and radar and lifeboats and went back to**
14   **work, whack, whack, whack. I paid a guy to help me and**
15   **we finished the job on the thirty-ninth day of rain.**
16   *(S.P.C.A. walks down to HUSBAND.)*
17   **S.P.C.A.:**   *(Loud and mean)* **Hey, you got permission to keep**
18   **them elephants here, fella? And them kangaroos? How**
19   **about them timber wolves, they had their rabies shots?**
20   **We gotta report from your neighbors that your pythons**
21   **are all over the place.** *(Returns to seat.)*
22   **HUSBAND:**   **I gave up the project, but fortunately, it stopped**
23   **raining after thirty-nine and a half days. It's a good thing,**
24   **too. I got word the Carpenters' Union was ready to lean**
25   **on me for scabbing an ark job.**
26   **VOICE OF GOD:**   *(Deep, resonant, unearthly)* **You'd better build**
27   **an ark.**
28   **HUSBAND:**   *(Looking up)* **Huh?**
29   **VOICE OF GOD:**   **You'd better build an ark.**
30   **HUSBAND:**   **Oh, Lord!**
31   **WIFE:**   *(Comes Down Center to him.)* **Wake up, for heaven's sake.**
32   **What're you dreaming about — threshing around. And**
33   **will you get out in the kitchen and empty those pans**
34   **where the roof leaks. I** *told* **you to fix the roof or build**
35   **an ark!**

1   **HUSBAND:**   *(Bluffing a bit)* **Don't be silly. Who needs an ark**
2   **these days, anyway?**
3   **WIFE:**   *(Taking him by the arm, yanking him Off-stage)* **Stop**
4   **stalling. You've had your nap. Now get to work on those**
5   **leaks!**
6
7
8
9
10
11
12
13
14
15
16
17
18
19
20
21
22
23
24
25
26
27
28
29
30
31
32
33
34
35

Mystery/Suspense

SIRE DE MALETROIT'S DOOR*

by Robert Louis Stevenson
Adapted for Readers Theatre by Melvin R. White, Ph.D.

CAST OF CHARACTERS

DENIS DE BEAULIEU: The leading man, traditionally tall, dark and handsome.

SIRE DE MALETROIT: An old man, polite, sly, cruel, crafty and domineering.

BLANCHE DE MALETROIT: The ingenue, leading lady type; of course, beautiful.

MEN: Some three male voices may be used, mature and masculine, heard from Off-stage — but they are not necessary.

Robert Louis Stevenson is considered one of Scotland's greatest writers — poet, novelist, short story writer. One of the best known and most enjoyed of his short stories is "Sire de Maletroit's Door."

This adaptation may be performed as a group story telling performance without any special dramatic enhancement — that is, no costuming, no setting, no special lighting, and so on. Or it may be offered as a period piece with the addition of costumes, make-up, and special lighting. In either case, no setting, no props and furniture are required. In short, the *story,* and the actors and actress are the important ingredients.

---

*Adapted for Readers Theatre by Melvin R. White. Amateur performance rights of this adaptation are granted with the purchase of this book.

1   **DENIS DE BEAULIEU:** *(Hereafter DENIS. Enters and crosses*
2   *Down Center to talk with the audience. If done as a play rather*
3   *than a telling of the story, he may be spotlighted.)* **You may**
4   **smile when I tell you my story. You may smile and say it**
5   **is only a story, that such things don't ever really happen.**
6   **But I tell you this story of the Sire de Maletroit's door** *is*
7   **the truth. What happened to me that stormy night in**
8   **Paris in the year 1429 changed the entire course of my**
9   **life. When the Sire de Maletroit's door closed behind me**
10   **that evening, it locked out one life and ushered in**
11   **another.**

12   **You see, I'd been calling on a friend that evening,**
13   **and was on my way back home. It was past midnight,**
14   **and it was storming. The wind pulled at my coat collar**
15   **as I hurried along the dark, narrow street.** *(Here, if the*
16   *Off-stage voices of three men wish to be inserted, we hear them*
17   *laughing, singing an old French song, talking.)* **As I turned a**
18   **corner, I saw three French soldiers coming towards me,**
19   **staggering along, laughing and talking. It was evident**
20   **they had been drinking heavily, and in their condition I**
21   **knew they would just as soon kill me as to pass me by.**
22   **So I turned and hurried back the way I had come, hoping**
23   **they would not see me.**

24   **MEN:**   *(If used)* **(One) Who goes there? (Two) Stop where you**
25   **are! (Three) After him, men!**

26   **DENIS:**   **It was too late. They had already seen me. I turned**
27   **back around the corner and ran. Suddenly I noticed a**
28   **large mansion with a dark entryway, and thought I might**
29   **hide there in the shadows until the soldiers passed. I**
30   **hurried up the steps, and onto the porch. I held myself**
31   **close against the door,** *(Re-living it all)* **hoping I would be**
32   **unobserved. To my surprise, the door sprang open behind**
33   **me, and I stumbled into the house. The door swung shut**
34   **and locked itself behind me. For a moment, I just stood**
35   **there, trying to catch my breath, realizing that at least I**

1   was safe from the drunken soldiers. Then I looked
2   around, peering into the gloom of this dark, old mansion.
3   I listened, but there was not a sound. Minutes passed,
4   and I decided it was safe to leave. But when I tried the
5   door, I found to my dismay that it was locked. Suddenly
6   a hall door opened, and I saw a determined-looking old
7   man standing with his hand on the doorknob.

8   **SIRE DE MALETROIT:** *(Hereafter SIRE)* **Come in. I've been**
9   **expecting you.**

10   **DENIS:** *(Startled)* **Uh? Expecting me?**

11   **SIRE:** **Yes, of course.** *(Moves toward DENIS.)*

12   **DENIS:** *(Cross toward SIRE)* **But — there must be some mistake.**
13   **You couldn't have been expecting** *me.* **It was quite by**
14   **accident I happened to open your door and step in.**

15   **SIRE:** *(Chuckling to himself)* **Yes, yes! But no matter. The main**
16   **thing is that you are here. Just sit down and make**
17   **yourself comfortable. We shall arrange our little affair**
18   **presently.** *(Starts to walk away.)*

19   **DENIS:** *(Follows him, trying to explain.)* **But sir, I'm sure there's**
20   **some kind of a mistake. You see, I had no intention of**
21   **entering your house. If your door —**

22   **SIRE:** *(Stopping to interrupt)* **Oh yes, my door. It did its part,**
23   **too. I left it unlocked just for you.**

24   **DENIS:** **But it couldn't be for me. I'm a stranger in your**
25   **country. My name is Denis de Beaulieu. I'm here only**
26   **because of circumstances. I'm —**

27   **SIRE:** *(Back to DENIS. Interrupting)* **My young friend, you'll**
28   **permit me to have my own ideas on that subject. They**
29   **may differ from yours, probably do, but time will show**
30   **us which is right. But excuse me for a moment, please.**
31   **Someone else is here waiting to see you.** *(Calling)* **Blanche!**
32   **Blanche! Someone is here to see you. Come! Let him see**
33   **you in your beautiful wedding gown!** *(BLANCHE enters,*
34   *sees DENIS, and is horrified.)*

35   **BLANCHE DE MALETROIT:** *(Hereafter BLANCHE. Startled)*

121

1   Uncle! This is not the man!

2   SIRE: *(Chuckling and agreeing insincerely)* **Of course not,**

3   **Blanche. Of course he isn't the man.**

4   BLANCHE: *(Pleading)* **But it's true, Uncle. I've never seen this**

5   **man before in my life!**

6   SIRE: **Maybe so, maybe so. And I suppose the name Denis**

7   **de Beaulieu means nothing to you either.**

8   BLANCHE: **No, Uncle, it does not!**

9   SIRE: **Ah yes, innocent, so innocent.**

10   BLANCHE: *(Crossing toward DENIS)* **Monsieur de Beaulieu,**

11   **tell me, have I ever seen you, or have you ever seen me**

12   **before?**

13   DENIS: **I've never had that pleasure, Ma'amselle.** *(To SIRE)*

14   **This is the first time I've ever met your niece, Monsieur.**

15   SIRE: **Too bad. Too bad, indeed. But then** *(Shrugging his*

16   *shoulders)* **it's never too late to begin. I married my wife**

17   **after only a week's acquaintance, which proves these**

18   **impromptu marriages are often the best type after all,**

19   **as we were very happy together.**

20   DENIS: *(Astonished)* **Marriage? You mean that I —**

21   BLANCHE: *(Interrupting to run to her uncle)* **Oh, Uncle, you**

22   **can't realize what you are doing? Punish me if you must,**

23   **but please don't involve this young man — this stranger**

24   **who knows nothing about it. Please, won't you believe**

25   **me when I tell you that this is *not* the man you think he is?**

26   SIRE: *(Suddenly loses his slyness, becomes hard and cruel.)* **I no**

27   **longer believe anything you tell me, Blanche de Maletroit!**

28   DENIS: **Blanche de Maletroit? You are a member of that**

29   **distinguished family, Ma'amselle?**

30   SIRE: **She is. And *I* am the head of that family. *I* am Sire de**

31   **Maletroit.**

32   BLANCHE: *(Bitterly)* **Yes — and it has become an obsession**

33   **with him!**

34   SIRE: *(Cross to her as he flares up)* **Silence!** *(Then more quietly*

35   *after a pause)* **Blanche, when you decided to dishonor**

1   your family, one of the foremost families in all France,
2   you lost the right to question my plans for you. You must
3   do as I say and no questions asked!
4 BLANCHE: *(Pleading)* But Uncle —
5 SIRE: *(Interrupting)* Now, I've found a man for you — you may
6   take him or not. I don't care. But think it over carefully,
7   because if you turn this one down, the next one may not
8   be so handsome and refined.
9 BLANCHE: *(Sobbing)* Oh, how can you be so cruel?
10 SIRE: *(His old sly self again)* You two will want to be together
11   now for a while, so I'll go to the library and leave you
12   alone. As you can see, Monsieur Beaulieu, my niece has
13   on her wedding gown. It's now three o'clock. Monsieur,
14   you have two hours to make up for lost time. I shall have
15   a priest here by five o'clock to perform the ceremony.
16 DENIS: But Monsieur, surely you don't intend to carry out
17   this plan?
18 SIRE: *(Hard voice)* I most certainly do, Monsieur. And if you
19   have any ideas about escaping, forget them. I have the
20   house surrounded with guards. *(Starts to leave.)* Now I'll
21   leave you — until five o'clock. *(Exits.)*
22 BLANCHE: *(Sobbing, crosses to DENIS.)* Oh, Monsieur, this is
23   awful — awful! It's just like a bad dream!
24 DENIS: *(Confused)* I wish you'd tell me what this is all about!
25   I only know that I accidentally stumbled into your house
26   tonight, and now I must marry you.
27 BLANCHE: *(Sobbing)* I'll tell you. It's only right that you
28   should know. *(Gains control during the following.)* You see,
29   my Uncle, Sire de Maletroit, is my guardian, and he's
30   always made me promise to uphold the honor of the
31   Maletroits. He's been very strict with me — allowed me
32   to have no friends of my own. Well, three months ago a
33   young captain began to stand near me every day in
34   church. He never spoke, only smiled at me. I guess he
35   could tell my uncle wouldn't like to him to speak. One

123

1   day he passed a note to me, and since then I have received

2   many from him. Then last week he asked me to leave the

3   door open here some evening so that he might come and

4   speak to me on the stairs. He came twice.

5 DENIS: But how did your uncle come to suspect you were

6   seeing this young captain, Ma'amselle?

7 BLANCHE: *(Again sobbing a bit)* I don't know. I only know

8   that this morning in church Uncle forced my hand open,

9   took the note, and read it. When he finished, he handed

10   it back very politely, and without a word.

11 DENIS: What did the note say?

12 BLANCHE: It was another request to have the door open this

13   evening so we could talk on the stairs again. *(Increase*

14   *sobbing)* But it has become the ruin of us all!

15 DENIS: Evidently he laid the trap for the young captain, and

16   caught me instead.

17 BLANCHE: It's so unfair to you, Monsieur de Beaulieu!

18   You've had no part in this. It's bad enough for my uncle

19   to punish me, but not *you*.

20 DENIS: Do you love this captain?

21 BLANCHE: No, we're only friends. But my uncle wouldn't

22   believe that. He brought me home after church, and

23   locked me in my room. Then this evening he made me

24   put on this wedding dress.

25 DENIS: And in two hours we're to be married.

26 BLANCHE: *(Again sobbing)* Yes, Monsieur!

27 DENIS: *(Suddenly growing angry)* This is ridiculous! There's

28   no reason why two perfect strangers should be married

29   just to satisfy the foolish whims of a selfish old man!

30   Come, Ma'amselle, we'll talk with your uncle, reason with

31   him. *(Calling)* Sire de Maletroit! Sire de Maletroit!

32   Monsieur, may we speak with you? Monsieur!

33 SIRE: *(Enters.)* Well, here are the bride and groom.

34 DENIS: *(Cross to him)* Monsieur de Maletroit, this whole thing

35   has gone far enough. I'll be no part of it — the crime of

1   **forcing this young lady to be my wife. Under more**
2   **favorable circumstances I'd be very happy to have such**
3   **a beautiful woman for my bride. But as things are now,**
4   **I'll have no part of it.**
5   **SIRE:** *(Slyly, quietly)* **Monsieur de Beaulieu, I'm afraid you**
6   **don't quite understand the choice I have offered you.**
7   *(Crosses Downstage to Down Center to an imaginary window in*
8   *the fourth wall of the stage.)* **Here, come over to the window.**
9   *(DENIS does so.)* **Now, do you see the iron ring attached**
10   **to the window ledge?**
11   **DENIS:**   **Yes, Monsieur.**
12   **SIRE:**   **Through the ring you'll see a strong rope, a good rope,**
13   **such as a hangman uses.**
14   **BLANCHE:**   *(Coming down, horrified)* **Oh no, Uncle!**
15   **SIRE:**   *(Shoving BLANCHE aside; coldly but forcefully)* **Monsieur,**
16   **unless you decide to marry my niece I shall have you**
17   **hanged out of this window. I assure you the idea of having**
18   **your heels kicking against the side of my house is just**
19   **as unpleasant to me as it is to you. I have but one desire,**
20   **and that is to keep the honor of my family!**
21   **DENIS:**   **Then you offer me marriage or death?**
22   **SIRE:**   **There's nothing else I can do, Monsieur.**
23   **BLANCHE:**   *(Moving rapidly away)* **Oh, Uncle, you've gone mad!**
24   *(Sobbing)*
25   **SIRE:**   *(Follows her.)* **Is a person mad because he wishes to**
26   **keep the honor of his family pure?** *(Pause, and then)* **Is it**
27   **to be marriage or death? I'll return shortly to hear your**
28   **decision.** *(Exits.)*
29   **BLANCHE:**   *(Cross to DENIS)* **Oh, Monsieur, there's only one**
30   **choice to make. You must marry me.**
31   **DENIS:**   **Ma'amselle, I'm not afraid to die.**
32   **BLANCHE:**   **But it isn't that! It's for my sake that you mustn't**
33   **let yourself be killed. I couldn't bear to have you hanged**
34   **just because of me.**
35   **DENIS:**   **You're very kind, but I couldn't marry you, knowing**

1   that you had consented to be my wife just to save me
2   from death.
3   BLANCHE: But surely there must be something I can do,
4   some way to show my appreciation. And I can think of
5   worse things than being your wife.
6   DENIS: Thank you, Ma'amselle, but you can't make me forget
7   it was in pity and not in love.
8   BLANCHE: But Monsieur, I didn't ask you to marry me just
9   out of pity. It was because I respected and admired you,
10   and loved you from the moment you took my part against
11   my uncle!
12   DENIS: But Ma'amselle ...
13   BLANCHE: It's true, Monsieur. When I saw you stand up so
14   nobly against my uncle, I knew that I loved you — even
15   though you must despise me.
16   DENIS: But I don't despise you. I love you better than the
17   whole world. But I must be sure that —
18   BLANCHE: *(Interrupting excitedly)* Then if you love me and I
19   love you — what else matters? Oh Monsieur, what will
20   you tell my uncle when he returns? *(SIRE enters, comes*
21   *Down Center to stand between the two.)* Oh, here he is ...
22   SIRE: Well, Blanche — Monsieur — what have you decided?
23   Have I gained a new nephew? Or is there to be a corpse
24   hanging from my window this morning?
25   BLANCHE: *(Joyfully)* You've gained a nephew, Uncle.
26   DENIS: Yes, Monsieur, I've decided to marry your niece. But
27   not to save my neck. It is only because Blanche and I love
28   each other. There is no other reason.
29   SIRE: *(Chuckling)* Ahhh, yes, yes. Fine, fine. The family honor
30   has been restored! Blanche ... Denis de Beaulieu ... I
31   wish you long life and happiness. *(May bow a courtly bow*
32   *to each, and then exit, chuckling, as DENIS and BLANCHE*
33   *reach out to each other and hold hands — as the curtain falls.)*
34
35

THE GUNMAN

by John Keefauver
Adapted for Performance by Melvin R. White, Ph. D.

CAST OF CHARACTERS

NARRATOR: An effective storyteller, man or woman.

COUNTER WOMAN: An elderly, plumpish woman with gray hair, some of it straggling.

KLUTCH: The young man with a gun.

This dramatization of the short story, *The Gunman,* provides three challenging roles: an all-important Narrator to set the mood and sustain it; the Counter Woman who says, "When you get old, there's not much to be afraid of," and the Gunman, the young man with the gun in his pocket.

The scene is an ordinary diner; the portion we see is a counter with two or three stools. Downstage Right is a lectern, a tall stool behind it for the Narrator who observes everything that takes place.

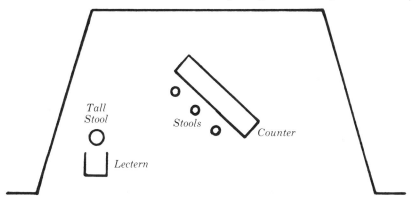

No special costumes are necessary, but if desired, the Counter Woman may wear a rather dirty apron; Klutch, a jacket such as a well-worn Navy pea coat, and a cap, an open shirt — all clothes to suggest that he is "down on his luck."

It is recommended that the Counter Woman and Klutch memorize their lines. However, the Narrator may either read the story, using the lectern and stool Downstage Right, or tell it if it is memorized. When action or business is described in the narration, the actors perform it, timing it with the narration.

As the play opens, the Counter Woman is found behind the counter, Center Stage, as the young man is entering. The Narrator is Downstage Right.

"The Gunman" adapted from a story by John Keefauver, copyright © 1958 by John Keefauver. First published in *Our Family* magazine. Used by permission.

1   NARRATOR: The young man with the gun in his pocket left
2   the dry shadow of the doorway and slushed through the
3   rain into the diner as the two predawn customers —
4   men — left the diner. He quickly sat down on a stool at
5   the counter. *(KLUTCH sits on one of the Upstage stools.)* **Rain**
6   **dripped from the soggy rim of his hat. It seeped into his**
7   **worn coat and streaked his face. An elderly, plumpish**
8   **woman was behind the counter. The gunman watched**
9   **her come toward him, smiling.** *(She does so.)*
10 COUNTER WOMAN: May I help you, sir?
11 KLUTCH: Uh . . . just coffee.
12 COUNTER WOMAN: Sugar? Cream?
13 KLUTCH: No thank you. Black.
14 NARRATOR: Sipping his coffee, the young man watched the
15   woman behind the counter. His eyes followed the elderly
16   woman, darting away when she suddenly turned toward
17   him. He squirmed on his stool, and when a downpour of
18   rain hit the window, he jumped. *(He does so, knocking over*
19   *his coffee cup, imaginary or real as desired.)* **His arm swung**
20   **around and knocked over his coffee cup, and the spoon**
21   **clattered to the floor. The Counter Woman came over to**
22   **the gunman.** *(She does so.)*
23 COUNTER WOMAN: Scare you?
24 KLUTCH: *(Chokes out the word.)* **No.**
25 COUNTER WOMAN: Here, let me clean this up. *(She sponges*
26   *up the spilled coffee, smiling.)* **Lot of wind tonight. Another**
27   **cup?**
28 KLUTCH: No.
29 COUNTER WOMAN: It's on the house.
30 KLUTCH: No. No thanks.
31 COUNTER WOMAN: *(Gives it to him.)* **Here it is anyway. You**
32   **need it; you're soaked through. Be good for you.** *(She walks*
33   *away, and stands back to the audience.)*
34 NARRATOR: The diner was empty. Coffee spilled over the
35   edge of the cup as the gunman raised it to his lips.

1　　　　Trembling, he lowered the cup to the counter and got up
2　　　　from the stool. *(Throughout, he suits the action to the*
3　　　　*narration.)* The diner was empty. His breathing was
4　　　　shallow and quick, his face colorless. His right hand was
5　　　　deep inside his gun pocket. *(COUNTER WOMAN puts*
6　　　　*change on the counter.)*
7　COUNTER WOMAN:　Don't forget your change. *(He scoops it up*
8　　　　*with his left hand.)* You're awfully nervous — like last
9　　　　night, running your hand in and out of your pocket. *(She*
10　　　　*reaches under the counter, brings out a newspaper clipping.)* I
11　　　　found this under your stool last night, after you'd left. It
12　　　　must have fallen out of your pocket, nervous like you
13　　　　were, running your hand in and out.
14　KLUTCH:　Not mine.
15　COUNTER WOMAN:　*(With a penetrating look)* Must be.
16　KLUTCH:　*(Lowering his eyes)* No.
17　COUNTER WOMAN:　It's all about a holdup. In a diner. *(He*
18　　　　*grunts nervously.)* They tell just how it happened. How this
19　　　　man came into this diner over on Fifth Street and sat
20　　　　around until nobody was left in the place. Then he held
21　　　　up the girl that was behind the counter. She yelled, and
22　　　　he shot her. *(She shakes her head sorrowfully, slowly.)* It's not
23　　　　right, telling how it happened. Makes it easier to see how
24　　　　to rob a place.
25　KLUTCH:　Uh-huh.
26　COUNTER WOMAN:　Not right at all.
27　KLUTCH:　I guess most diners keep a gun behind the counter.
28　　　　Ought to, seems to me.
29　COUNTER WOMAN:　I don't.
30　KLUTCH:　Seems to me you'd be afraid.
31　COUNTER WOMAN:　I used to be afraid when I was younger.
32　　　　*(Casually shoves the clipping toward him.)* But I'm old now.
33　　　　When you're old, there's not much to be afraid of. *(She*
34　　　　*walks away to get some coins.)* You're wet. Why don't you go
35　　　　home and go to bed? *(Returning)* Here's the change you

1   **forgot last night. And here's your clipping.** *(Pushes the*
2   *items across the counter.)*
3   **KLUTCH:** *(Backing away)* **It's not mine.**
4   **COUNTER WOMAN:** *(In a mother-quiet voice)* **Yes it is.**
5   **KLUTCH:** *(Turning away from the counter)* **No.**
6   **COUNTER WOMAN:** *(She may come out from behind the counter*
7   *here if desired.)* **I want you to read it. About the girl who**
8   **was shot.**
9   **KLUTCH:** *(Mumbling)* **Nothing to me.**
10   **COUNTER WOMAN: The girl died. She had two kids.**
11   **KLUTCH: I don't know nothing about it!**
12   **COUNTER WOMAN: I know you don't, even though the**
13   **description sounds like you.**
14   **KLUTCH: I just come in this town a few days ago. I'm broke.**
15   *(His voice begins to quiver.)* **I just want a job. That's all I want.**
16   **COUNTER WOMAN: Go on home and go to bed, son. Take this**
17   **clipping home and read it.** *(Getting closer to him)*
18   **KLUTCH: I just want a job. That's all. Honest.** *(Turns toward*
19   *her.)*
20   **COUNTER WOMAN: I'll help you get a job. Go on home and**
21   **go to bed.**
22   **KLUTCH:** *(Speaking directly to her, straight into her eyes)* **I've**
23   **never robbed nothing. I didn't have nothing to do with**
24   **no holdup.**
25   **COUNTER WOMAN:** *(Perhaps a hand on his shoulder)* **Come**
26   **back tomorrow. Eleven o'clock. I'll help you get a job.**
27   **I've been in this town a long time.** *(Smiles wanly.)* **I'm old.**
28   **You're young.**
29   **KLUTCH:** *(Mumbling, disbelieving)* **How you gonna help me**
30   **get a job?**
31   **COUNTER WOMAN:** *(She glances at the side of his coat.)* **Give me**
32   **that gun you got in your pocket, Vic.**
33   **KLUTCH:** *(Draws away from her.)* **I don't have no gun.**
34   **COUNTER WOMAN: Yes you do.**
35   **KLUTCH: I don't.** *(She smiles faintly.)* **And my name is not Vic,**

1   it's Klutch.

2 COUNTER WOMAN: *(Quietly)* **I know. Vic was my boy's name.**

3 *(A dampness begins to melt through her eyes.)* **You look a lot**

4   **like him. Young. He was a good boy . . . until he . . . until**

5   **something happened to him . . . inside.** *(Looks at the gun*

6   *pocket.)* **Please.**

7 KLUTCH: *(His head jumps.)* **No!**

8 COUNTER WOMAN: **Vic wouldn't give me his gun, either. He**

9   **got all twisted. About diners especially. He didn't like**

10   **diners, because I owned one. He said a diner was like a**

11   **jail, chaining me in.** *(Reaches toward him, asking for the gun.)*

12 KLUTCH: **I'll get rid of it.**

13 COUNTER WOMAN: **That's what Vic used to tell me. But he**

14   **never got rid of his gun . . . until the police got him. He**

15   **was holding up a diner.** *(Indicates the clipping.)* **That diner.**

16   *(Eyes become memory-soft.)* **Been almost a year now. He shot**

17   **the girl behind the counter. Killed her. Police killed him.**

18 KLUTCH: **I'm not going to shoot nobody.**

19 COUNTER WOMAN: *(She seems not to hear him.)* **I saved the**

20   **clipping. Kept it right under the counter. Don't know**

21   **why. Brought back so many bad memories. Unless I saved**

22   **it to show somebody like you.**

23 KLUTCH: **I told you it didn't belong to me.**

24 COUNTER WOMAN: *(Nodding)* **I made up that story about**

25   **you and the clipping. I noticed when you came in here**

26   **last night that you had that look in your eyes — like Vic**

27   **used to get. I knew what you were up to. I'm old. I knew.**

28   *(She stares at him. He almost puts his hand in the gun pocket,*

29   *but can't decide to actually do so.)* **Vic used to help me here.**

30   **I've never wanted anybody since. But maybe you'd like**

31   **to help me. I'm old. You're young . . . like Vic.**

32 KLUTCH: **I need a job.**

33 COUNTER WOMAN: **Give me the gun . . . Klutch.** *(He does so.*

34   *Add some sort of business as works with the particular cast —*

35   *shake hands, or she may squeeze his arm and head back behind*

the counter, or she may even hug him [but that is doubtful] as
the curtain falls.)

THE TELL-TALE HEART*

by Edgar Allan Poe
Adapted for Readers Theatre by Melvin R. White, Ph.D.

CAST OF CHARACTERS

JASPER QUINT: Old character, a very nasty person with an unpleasantly whining voice and a thin nonhumorous laugh; eighty-nine years of age.

HENRY FLACK: Young man, attractive, but very high-strung and emotional.

SERGEANT GRIMM: Policeman, middle-aged character type, mature and solid.

HODGES: Policeman, also a mature and solid middle-aged character type.

MESSENGER: A boy or a man, possibly played by Grimm or Hodges.

The stage is divided into several playing areas: Down Center is a combined living and dining room, set simply with a table and three chairs; Down Right, Jasper Quint's room which has a long bench to be used as a bed (or if a more real setting is desired, a cot); Up Right is the kitchen; Down Left, Henry Flack's bedroom; and Up Center, an imaginary (or real) outside door.

If special area lighting is used, the four playing areas may be lighted or dimmed as the action moves from one part of the house to another.

Sound effects add greatly to this play, but they are not necessary; they may be "heard" by the actors and thus by the audience. They can be real sounds of wind, of knocking, of a cat meowing. If the cat meow is employed, it must be produced vocally, the cries varying as indicated in the script.

Period costumes, policeman's attire, and the like will enhance the atmosphere, but these are not necessary.

NOTE: This version of Poe's "The Tell-Tale Heart" has also been produced simply with five tall stools, five lecterns, using Off-stage focus (the readers seeing the other characters in the realm of the audience). In this more theatrical version, many groups have found

---

*Adapted for Readers Theatre by Melvin R. White. Amateur performance rights of this adaptation are granted with the purchase of this book.

it necessary to memorize all of the dialog and dispense with their scripts, as the amount of movement and action and the final scene made handling scripts very difficult.

STAGING DIAGRAM

1 — Long bench to suggest a bed.

2-6 — Ordinary kitchen or dining room chairs; if the Messenger is not played by Grimm or Hodges, one more chair is needed Up Center.

7 — A table.

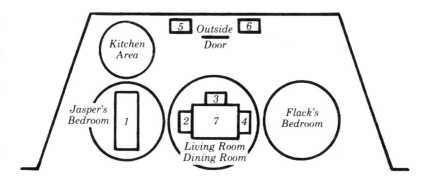

1   ***SETTING:***   As the curtain opens, FLACK is seated to the right of
2   the table Down Center in chair #2, with QUINT above the table
3   in chair #3. The two POLICEMEN are seated in chairs #5 and
4   #6, their backs to the audience, frozen. If special lighting is being
5   used, the lights concentrate on the living room/dining room
6   Down Center, a gloomy, shadowed room. If sound is being used,
7   the wind is a wailing, eerie one.

8   **QUINT:**   *(With distaste)* **Liver again, eh?**

9   **FLACK:**   **What's the matter with the liver?**

10   **QUINT:**   **You know I don't like it.**

11   **FLACK:**   **Well, uncle, I think I am entitled once in a while to**
12   **cook what I like. Toby likes it, too.** *(Reaching down to pat*
13   *an imaginary cat)* **Don't you, Toby?** *(Meow of cat)*

14   **QUINT:**   **That's all liver is fit for, cats!** *(Wind up)*

15   **FLACK:**   **What a horrible night! Listen to that wind!**

16   **QUINT:**   **It's strong enough to tear off the shutters. Why don't**
17   **you fix them, nephew?**

18   **FLACK:**   **I haven't had the time.**

19   **QUINT:**   *(Mimicking him)* **Haven't had the time. There are**
20   **twenty-four hours in every day. What do you do with**
21   **your time?**

22   **FLACK:**   *(Losing his too-short temper)* **You know what I do with**
23   **it! Wait on you — make your bed — clean your clothes —**
24   **cook your meals —**

25   **QUINT:**   *(Interrupting)* **Cook me liver!**

26   **FLACK:**   **Oh, stop harping on the liver! . . . And when I'm not**
27   **waiting on you, I'm tutoring a bunch of stupid,**
28   **uninteresting children . . .**

29   **QUINT:**   **Noisy brats! I wish you'd get some other place to**
30   **hold your classes.**

31   **FLACK:**   **You can't be left alone! That's why I have my pupils**
32   **come here to the house.** *(Voice rising)* **But they may not**
33   **come much longer — the few that are left.**

34   **QUINT:**   **Why not?**

35   **FLACK:**   **Because of you . . . you!** *(Angrily)* **Uncle, I've told you**

1	over and over to keep out of sight during school hours —
2	while my pupils are here. But today . . .
3	QUINT: I only opened the door a little bit and looked in.
4	FLACK: Yes. And that was enough. Afterward, some of my
5	pupils went home.
6	QUINT: What do you mean, went home?
7	FLACK: The sight of you frightens them — until they are
8	sick!
9	QUINT: Why should I frighten them?
10	FLACK: Why?! Don't you ever look in a mirror?
11	QUINT: *(Smirking bit of a laugh)* If you look as good at eighty-
12	nine as I do, nephew, you'll be lucky!
13	FLACK: I hope I'm dead before eighty-nine.
14	QUINT: *(Cackling)* Dead, eh?
15	FLACK: I don't want to live to be senile — disgusting —
16	loathsome . . .
17	QUINT: *(Cackling)* Heh-heh-heh . . .
18	FLACK: Pass me the butter. *(Pantomime business. If sound is*
19	*used, dish breaks.)* Good lord!
20	QUINT: There you go — another dish broken!
21	FLACK: *(Shakily)* I didn't do it. You dropped it! You're old —
22	your hands are shaky.
23	QUINT: *(Holding one out to show him)* Steadier than yours,
24	nephew, steadier than yours. You're getting jumpier
25	every day.
26	FLACK: *(Exploding again)* You're enough to shatter anybody's
27	nerves!
28	QUINT: *(Needling him)* You'll have to buy another butter dish
29	tomorrow.
30	FLACK: I will? Why not you? This is your house.
31	QUINT: I can't spare the money.
32	FLACK: Can't spare the money?! Ridiculous! You've plenty
33	put away. I know.
34	QUINT: *(Warily)* Now, nephew, you're wrong. I . . .
35	FLACK: *(Blasting out)* Don't lie to me! I tell you I know!

1	**QUINT:** *(Cackling)* **Heh-heh! You do, eh? And since you're the**
2	**only kin I've got, I suppose you think . . .**
3	**FLACK:** *(Emphatically)* **I don't want your money! I wouldn't**
4	**touch it!**
5	**QUINT:** **You wouldn't, eh?**
6	**FLACK:** **No. I only want the chance to earn my own living.**
7	**QUINT:** *(Sardonically)* **How noble that sounds, nephew!**
8	*(Cackling)* **Then why is it you creep into my room at night**
9	**and peer down at me? To see if I'm dead?**
10	**FLACK:** *(Taken aback)* **No, to — uh — to see if you're sleeping**
11	**comfortably.**
12	**QUINT:** **No! To see if I'm breathing . . . or if —**
13	**FLACK:** *(Interrupting)* **You're talking crazy! Maybe you are**
14	**crazy! But I warn you, Jasper Quint, if you make me lose**
15	**any more pupils — make me lose my means of living . . .**
16	**QUINT:** **Look at me, nephew. You don't really think that I**
17	**frighten your pupils?**
18	**FLACK:** **What else? You're enough to!**
19	**QUINT:** **Look at me, I say . . .**
20	**FLACK:** *(Shouting suddenly)* **I won't look at you! I hate the**
21	**sight of you!**
22	**QUINT:** *(Cackling)* **Heh-heh . . .**
23	**FLACK:** **That hideous eye . . .**
24	**QUINT:** **You don't like my eye?**
25	**FLACK:** **I loathe it!** *(Stands to cross Down Left away from the*
26	*table.)* **Go away! Leave me alone!**
27	**QUINT:** **All right. I'll go to my room — and to bed.** *(Cackling)*
28	**For I must take care of my health. I want to live to be at**
29	**least one hundred.** *(Cackling at the thought)*
30	**FLACK:** *(Yelling in frustration)* **Stop that cackling, and get out!**
31	*(QUINT turns to go out right to his room, but is interrupted by*
32	*a knock on the Up Center door. FLACK goes Up Center to open*
33	*the door. MESSENGER stands up from his chair.)*
34	**MESSENGER:** **Mr. Henry Flack?**
35	**FLACK:** **Yes, I'm Henry Flack. What is it?**

1   **MESSENGER:**   **A letter for you, sir.** *(Pantomiming holding it out*
2   *to FLACK)*
3   **FLACK:**   **Now what** ... *(Taking the imaginary letter, ripping it*
4   *open as he pantomimes closing the door. Opens it, and reads it*
5   *to himself.)*
6   **QUINT:**   **Nephew** ...
7   **FLACK:**   **I thought you'd gone to bed.**
8   **QUINT:**   **What's in the note?**
9   **FLACK:**   *(Irritably)* **How do I know? Can't you see I'm trying**
10   **to read it?!**
11   **QUINT:**   **Well?**
12   **FLACK:**   *(Tense, seething within)* **You've done it! You've done it**
13   **now!**
14   **QUINT:**   **Done what?**
15   **FLACK:**   **The thing I said you would, you fiend! Frightened**
16   **my pupils so they won't come back!**
17   **QUINT:**   *(Suggestion of cackling)* **Is that what the note says?**
18   **FLACK:**   **The parents of those students who went home today**
19   **have held a meeting and decided to withdraw their**
20   **children from my classes!**
21   **QUINT:**   **They probably found a better teacher.**
22   **FLACK:**   **No! It's you who frightened them away — you,**
23   **leering at them through cracks in the door, fixing them**
24   **with that hideous eye** ...
25   **QUINT:**   **Never mind my eye** ...
26   **FLACK:**   **You devil! As if I haven't endured enough from you**
27   **without this!**
28   **QUINT:**   **Do you think I've liked living with you? You're** ...
29   *(Sound of cat screaming as if stepped on)* **Confound that cat!**
30   **It nearly tripped me!**
31   **FLACK:**   *(Confronting QUINT face to face Down Center)* **I've**
32   **waited on you, stood for your eternal gibes and cackling**
33   **laughter. I've taken your insults, overlooked your**
34   **meanness** ...
35   **QUINT:**   *(Also angry)* **You can't talk to me like that! I** ...

1   **FLACK:**   And now — you're driving my pupils from me!

2   **QUINT:**   Me? It's you — your nasty disposition — that's

3   driving the brats away. If you . . . *(Cat screams again.)* **That**

4   **cat again, right at my feet. Get out!** *(Kicking the imaginary*

5   *cat; cat screams in fright and pain.)*

6   **FLACK:**   **You kicked Toby — curse you!**

7   **QUINT:**   **Yes, I kicked your cat — and if it doesn't stay out**

8   **from under my feet, I'll do it again!**

9   **FLACK:**   *(Trying to coax Toby from under the table)* **Kitty . . . Kitty**

10   **. . . Come, Toby . . .**

11   **QUINT:**   **I'd like to poison it!**

12   **FLACK:**   *(Standing, heads for QUINT.)* **Get out! Get out of**

13   **here!**

14   **QUINT:**   **Now, nephew, calm down . . .**

15   **FLACK:**   **Get out!**

16   **QUINT:**   **All right, I'll go — stop yelling.** *(Cross to Down Right*

17   *area, and stretch out on the bench; then freeze.)*

18   **FLACK:**   *(After QUINT exits, FLACK picks up the imaginary cat,*

19   *holds it in his lap, pets it, and talks to it tenderly.)* **Toby . . . poor**

20   **old Toby. He hurt you.** *(Cat meows.)* **Yes, he's a demon.**

21   **Evil. Cruel. He drives me past endurance.** *(Wind increases*

22   *in intensity.)* **He kicked you, Toby; he'll pay for that. I**

23   **wonder if he's asleep.** *(Putting the cat down. Then picks up*

24   *an imaginary knife from the table.)* **If he's awake, I'll frighten**

25   **him with this knife. No, Toby, stay here.** *(Moving Down*

26   *Right. If special lighting is used, black out center area as very*

27   *dim lights come up Down Right. As FLACK steathily approaches*

28   *the bed, he stumbles on something, mutters under his breath.)*

29   **QUINT:**   *(Jerks up in bed.)* **Who's there? What . . . uh . . . just**

30   **dreaming, I guess.** *(Lies down again.)* **No. There's**

31   **something . . .** *(Up again peering into the darkness)* **Nephew,**

32   **is that . . .** *(Shrieks as FLACK plunges his knife into him several*

33   *times.)*

34   **FLACK:**   **Done! At last I'm rid of him. Now I'll bury him**

35   **under those loose boards in the other room, and no one**

1   **will ever know.**

2   *(All lights black out to designate time passing. After a short*

3   *blackout, a clock strikes four deep, hollow notes, and lights come*

4   *up slightly Up Center to reveal the two POLICEMEN at the*

5   *door — imaginary or real. FLACK has crossed Down Left during*

6   *the blackout, and is standing frozen, his back to the audience.*

7   *QUINT has slipped Off-stage, out of sight.)*

8   **SERGEANT:**   **Sure this is the place, Hodges?**

9   **HODGES:**   **Sure, Sergeant. This is Henry Flack's house. But**

10   **everything looks quiet and peaceable.**

11   **SERGEANT:**   **Well, looks sometimes lie. Knock on the door.**

12   *(HODGES does so.)*

13   **HODGES:**   **I don't hear anybody.**

14   **SERGEANT:**   **Knock again, Hodges.** *(HODGES does so.)*

15   **Someone in this house is awake.**

16   **HODGES:**   **How do you know?**

17   **SERGEANT:**   **I saw a light flick off a moment ago, just as we**

18   **turned the corner.**

19   **HODGES:**   **You did, huh?**

20   **SERGEANT:**   **Shush . . . I hear someone. Yeah, someone's**

21   **coming to the door.**

22   **FLACK:**   *(Sleepily, opening the door)* **Good evening. Uh — who's**

23   **there? Oh, the police! I beg your pardon. I'm half-asleep,**

24   **didn't hear you knock. Did I keep you waiting long?**

25   **SERGEANT:**   **Is your name Henry Flack?**

26   **FLACK:**   *(Courteously)* **It is . . . and at your service.**

27   **SERGEANT:**   *(Gruff and abrupt)* **I'm Sergeant Grimm . . . and**

28   **this is Officer Hodges.**

29   **FLACK:**   *(Cordially)* **Come in, come in, gentlemen. Come in out**

30   **of this cold wind.**

31   **SERGEANT:**   *(With gruff sarcasm)* **Thanks for — inviting us!**

32   *(They move Down Center into the living room/dining room area,*

33   *FLACK leading.)*

34   **FLACK:**   **Here we are! This is much better than standing in**

35   **the door in the cold. Now . . . what can I do for you? Oh . . .**

1   **but have a seat.** *(SERGEANT sits at the right of the table,*
2   *chair #2; HODGES, chair #4.)*
3   **SERGEANT:** We're deputized to search your house, Mr.
4   **Flack.**
5   **FLACK:** *(Startled)* **To search my house? Good heavens!**
6   **Whatever for, Sergeant?**
7   **SERGEANT:** One of your neighbors heard a shriek tonight
8   **which seemed to come from your house. The information**
9   **was reported to police headquarters.**
10   **HODGES:** Yes. They seemed to suspect foul play.
11   **FLACK:** Foul play? Here in my house? *(Laughing)* That's good!
12   **That is good!**
13   **SERGEANT:** Glad it amuses you. Then we'll go ahead with
14   **our search.**
15   **FLACK:** Certainly. Go ahead. *(Laughing even more heartily)* **But**
16   **that shriek!** *(Breaks off in peals of laughter.)*
17   **HODGES:** You mean you heard it, too, Mr. Flack?
18   **FLACK:** Did I hear it, Officer Hodges! *(Laughs.)* Well, of course.
19   **SERGEANT:** You heard it, Flack?
20   **FLACK:** Yes, Sergeant. It was one of the most fiendish,
21   **bloodcurdling shrieks that ever came from a human**
22   **throat! It woke me up from a sound sleep.**
23   **HODGES:** The complaint said it came from this house, Mr.
24   **Flack.**
25   **FLACK:** *(Trying not to laugh)* **That's right, Officer. It did.**
26   *(Laughs.)* **It did come from this house. It came from my**
27   **bedroom. It came from me!**
28   **SERGEANT:** You mean to say . . .
29   **FLACK:** Yes. I had the most devilish nightmare! It made my
30   **blood run cold. I dreamed a huge black vulture grabbed**
31   **me in his claws and started to eat me — his naked head,**
32   **his pale blue filmy eyes, his hideous beak tearing at me.**
33   **I shrieked . . .**
34   **HODGES:** Ugh! That was a dream to make any man shriek!
35   **FLACK:** Yes . . . and the sound of my own cry woke me up.

1   That's all there was to it, Sergeant.
2   SERGEANT: Well . . . but we'd better search the house since
3   there was a formal complaint.
4   FLACK: *(Amiably)* **Of course, of course. I'll take you over it**
5   myself. The downstairs first?
6   SERGEANT: What's upstairs?
7   FLACK: Nothing but empty rooms. My uncle and I — uh, you
8   know my uncle lives here too?
9   SERGEANT: The old man, Jasper Quint. Yes, I know.
10   FLACK: We only use the lower floor.
11   SERGEANT: Go search the upstairs, Hodges.
12   HODGES: Sure, Sergeant. *(Crosses Up Left and freezes, his back*
13   *to the audience.)*
14   SERGEANT: Now, Mr. Flack, how many rooms on this lower
15   floor?
16   FLACK: Four. This one is a combination living and dining
17   room.
18   SERGEANT: *(Looking around)* **Mm-hm. And where's the**
19   kitchen?
20   FLACK: *(Crossing Up Right, the SERGEANT following)* **Here.**
21   SERGEANT: *(Looking around)* **I see. Well, there's nothing here**
22   that seems out of order.
23   FLACK: *(Returning Down Center and crossing Down Left, the*
24   *SERGEANT following)* **Two bedrooms open off the living**
25   room. Come this way, Sergeant.
26   SERGEANT: Hmm. This is your bedroom, I take it?
27   FLACK: Yes, this is where the fiendish nightmare had me in
28   its grip. *(Laughing, pointing to an imaginary bed)* **You can**
29   see how I pulled the bedclothes off in my struggle with
30   the vulture.
31   SERGEANT: This room seems all right. What about the other
32   room?
33   FLACK: Only my uncle's room. *(Leading to the Down Right*
34   *area)* **Come, I'll show you.**
35   SERGEANT: Too bad to wake the old man up if he's asleep.

1   **Why, he's not here! The bed's not been slept in!**

2   **FLACK: Oh, didn't I tell you? Uncle Jasper's gone to visit**

3   **friends in the country. Up around Overmere by the**

4   **Dilston River.**

5   **SERGEANT: So? A sudden departure?**

6   **FLACK: No. He'd been planning it for quite some time. I miss**

7   **him, too. I'm very fond of Uncle Jasper.**

8   **SERGEANT:** *(Leading the way back to the living room)* **Well, we**

9   **seem to have got you out of bed for nothing, Mr. Flack.**

10   *(Calling)* **Hodges!**

11   **HODGES:** *(Unfreezing, crossing Down Center)* **Here, Sergeant.**

12   **SERGEANT: Find anything out of the way upstairs?**

13   **HODGES: Nothing but empty rooms and cobwebs.**

14   **SERGEANT: Well — we'll have to go back to the station and**

15   **report a false alarm. With apologies to you, Mr. Flack,**

16   **for disturbing you.**

17   **FLACK: Oh, that's all right. But just a minute, gentlemen.**

18   *(Starts to cross up behind the table.)*

19   **SERGEANT: You've something else to show us?**

20   **FLACK: No . . . no. You've seen the whole of my house. No, I**

21   **was going to offer you a bit of refreshment before you**

22   **start out into that cold wind again.**

23   **HODGES: I call that nice of you, Mr. Flack.**

24   **FLACK: I have a bottle of old Burgundy . . .**

25   **HODGES:** *(Heartily)* **Ah, Sergeant, we can't pass that up, now**

26   **can we?**

27   **SERGEANT:** *(Hesitating)* **Uh . . . no, Hodges. I think . . . we'll**

28   **. . . stay.**

29   **FLACK: Good! Have a seat by the table. Sit down,**

30   **gentlemen, sit down.** *(They do so in chairs #2 and #4.)* **I'll**

31   **be back in a moment with the wine.** *(Crossing Up Right to*

32   *the kitchen area and freezing)*

33   **HODGES: Well, Sergeant, he's all right, I guess.**

34   **SERGEANT: I don't know. There's something about him — I**

35   **can't make him out.**

1 HODGES: You suspect him of hiding something?
2 SERGEANT: I don't know. There's not a sign of anything
3   suspicious. His manner — open . . . aboveboard . . .
4 HODGES: Sure it is. He's friendly, courteous, hospitable.
5   Yes, and he seemed perfectly willing, too, to show us the
6   house — let us search.
7 SERGEANT: I know, Hodges. And yet . . . I seem to feel . . .uh
8   . . . there's something here that bothers me.
9 HODGES: What? Where?
10 SERGEANT: In the air. I . . . I feel it in my bones. I don't know . . .
11 HODGES: You're getting creepy, Sergeant. That's not like
12   you. *(FLACK has started back, goes above the table, and*
13   *pantomimes with the two others the business of serving glasses*
14   *of wine.)* Ah, here's Mr. Flack now — and the Burgundy!
15   *(Lowly)* The wine'll fix you up.
16 FLACK: Now this is what I call cozy! A warm room, a bottle
17   of wine, and friends to share it with. A glass for each of
18   us. *(Pouring, and handing them each a glass)* Gentlemen!
19   *(Raising his glass to each; they respond in kind.)*
20 SERGEANT: Ah — very good wine, Mr. Flack.
21 FLACK: Thank you, Sergeant.
22 HODGES: Certainly feels good in your stomach on a cold
23   night like this!
24 FLACK: You mean morning, Officer. The clock just struck
25   four-thirty.
26 SERGEANT: What clock? I heard no clock strike.
27 FLACK: The town clock in the Hall tower.
28 SERGEANT: Flack, you couldn't hear the town clock from
29   this distance!
30 FLACK: You mean you couldn't, Sergeant. It chances that I
31   have a very acute sense of hearing.
32 HODGES: You've had it always?
33 FLACK: No. It developed from a sickness. Instead of dulling
34   my sense of hearing, the disease intensified it.
35 SERGEANT: I never heard of such a thing. You must

1   imagine it.

2   **HODGES:** But it is half-past four by my watch, Sergeant.

3   **SERGEANT:** Then he knew it by the clock out in the kitchen.

4   You noted the time when you went for the wine.

5   **FLACK:** *(Laughing, and sitting in chair #3 above the table)* **You're**

6   **a skeptical fellow, Sergeant, aren't you? Suppose I tell**

7   **you that right now I can hear the milk cart rattling up**

8   **the street several blocks away?**

9   **SERGEANT:** I'd still think you were imagining things. I don't

10   hear a sound. Do you, Hodges?

11   **HODGES:** No, I don't, Sergeant.

12   **FLACK:** *(Laughing)* **It's quite a trial to my pupils, I assure you,**

13   **to have my ears so quick. I catch them in the slightest**

14   **rustle of mischief, and they can never put their sly tricks**

15   **over. Listen. Now — do you hear?** *(Sound of horses' hoofs*

16   *and rattle of a cart in the distance)*

17   **HODGES:** It is the milk cart! I hear the horses' hoofs. And

18   the rattle of the cart, and even the clinking of the milk

19   cans!

20   **FLACK:** Now what do you say, Sergeant?

21   **SERGEANT:** *(Skeptical to the last)* **The milkman is as regular**

22   **as the clock. You knew he'd be coming past at this time.**

23   **FLACK:** *(Laughing)* **I see you're a hard man to convince,**

24   **Sergeant. But no matter. Have some more wine.**

25   **SERGEANT:** No more, thanks. *(Quickly, as FLACK starts to*

26   *pour more for HODGES)* **And no more for you, Hodges.**

27   **HODGES:** *(Reproachfully)* **Aw, Chief . . .**

28   **SERGEANT:** No, we've had enough. But before we go, there

29   is one thing I'd like to ask you.

30   **FLACK:** Yes. What is it?

31   **SERGEANT:** When did old Jasper Quint leave for the

32   country?

33   **FLACK:** Yesterday.

34   **SERGEANT:** Mmmm. Is he to visit long?

35   **FLACK:** He did not say — did not know how long he'd stay.

1	SERGEANT: You're very fond of him, you say?
2	FLACK: Very. We're more like father and son than uncle and
3	nephew.
4	SERGEANT: He's quite well-off, I've heard.
5	FLACK: He had a tidy little sum.
6	SERGEANT: Well, watch out that someone doesn't murder
7	him for it. There are many who'd stoop to that, you know.
8	FLACK: No one would murder Uncle Jasper, Sergeant. He's
9	too well-loved.
10	SERGEANT: What do you mean, well-loved? Why no one even
11	knows him! Nobody comes here, your neighbors say. And
12	he never even steps out of the house, I hear.
13	HODGES: I saw him once, Sergeant, hobbling about the
14	yard with a cane.
15	FLACK: Yes, unfortunately Uncle Jasper has grown quite
16	feeble these past few years.
17	HODGES: He has a glass eye, hasn't he, Mr. Flack?
18	FLACK: *(Off guard, getting up)* So you noticed it, too!
19	HODGES: *(Puzzled)* Noticed what?
20	FLACK: The eye. His hideous eye that stared at you!
21	HODGES: But a glass eye would stare, wouldn't it?
22	FLACK: *(Catching himself)* Yes . . . yes. Of course it would.
23	*(Anxiously)* Tell me, Sergeant, do you hear anything?
24	Anything — unusual?
25	SERGEANT: No. Not a thing. Uh, tell me about this glass eye
26	of Jasper Quint's.
27	FLACK: *(As if driven)* It wasn't a — I mean, it isn't a glass eye.
28	It's his own. I can see it now . . . now, staring at me!
29	*(Fearful)* Don't you hear anything yet?
30	SERGEANT: No. Nothing. So the eye stared at you, eh? Like
31	the eye of the vulture in your nightmare.
32	FLACK: *(From now on FLACK becomes more and more emotional,*
33	*more and more erratic, more insane. Breathlessly:)* Yes! . . . No!
34	What nonsense are we talking? That silly dream!
35	*(Laughing shakily)* You got me to thinking of it again.

147

1   ... Listen!

2   SERGEANT: Hodges, do you hear anything?

3   HODGES: Not a sound, Sergeant. Uh ... what's the matter

4   with him?

5   SERGEANT: I don't know. Flack, what does it sound like,

6   this thing you hear?

7   FLACK: *(Breath catching)* What? ... Oh, nothing, Sergeant.

8   Not a thing, really. *(Talking faster and louder)* I say, have

9   you gentlemen ever been to Overmere on the Dilston

10   River?

11   SERGEANT: You mean where your uncle's gone?

12   FLACK: Yes ... yes. They say the fishing's fine up there in

13   October — or maybe it was March. Better go up

14   sometime ...

15   SERGEANT: All right. We will.

16   FLACK: Be sure to take along plenty of blood — I mean

17   worms. You can't beat the Dilston River for cackling

18   and ...

19   SERGEANT: Look here, Flack, what's the matter with you?

20   HODGES: Maybe too much wine, Sergeant.

21   SERGEANT: No, he only had one glass. I watched. Flack,

22   are you talking to try to cover up something?

23   FLACK: *(Moving around more and more as he gets more excited.*

24   *Voice rising)* And the ducks! You ought to see how great

25   the hunting is in the marshes above Overmere. Plenty of

26   ducks to catch and fish to hunt. But the ducks have eyes —

27   pale, filmy eyes that stare at you! *(Covering ears with hands)*

28   There it is again!

29   SERGEANT: *(Getting up, going above the table to FLACK)* Get

30   hold of yourself, Flack. Buck up. You're talking crazy.

31   And I want to know, what is it you think you hear? What

32   can't you drown out?

33   FLACK: You know. You hear it, too!

34   SERGEANT: No, I ... *(Taking FLACK by the arm. HODGES*

35   *rises to be of help.)*

1 FLACK: *(Struggling to get away from the SERGEANT)* **You're**
2 **lying. I see it in your eyes. You hear it too! Low, dull,**
3 **quick, but getting louder! You hear it! You're only making**
4 **a mockery of my horror!**
5 SERGEANT: **Help me hold him, Hodges. He's raving.**
6 *(HODGES quickly takes the other arm.)*
7 HODGES: **What's he talking about, Sergeant?**
8 SERGEANT: **I don't know, but ...**
9 FLACK: *(Almost screaming in terror)* **There it goes again!**
10 **... I can't stand it any longer. ... But you know, anyway.**
11 **... You've caught me! ... It's getting louder ... louder ...**
12 **Oh, I confess! ... I did it! I — I killed him ...**
13 HODGES: **Great Scott!**
14 FLACK: *(Suddenly spent ... quietly)* **I murdered Uncle Jasper.**
15 HODGES: **Well, I'll be ...**
16 SERGEANT: **Sit down, Mr. Flack.** *(Helping him to chair #3, and*
17 *motioning HODGES to sit again in chair #4, eventually sitting*
18 *in chair #2 himself)* **Now, tell me, when did you kill the old**
19 **man, Flack?**
20 FLACK: *(Jumping from his chair to be followed at once by both of*
21 *the POLICEMEN in order to grab him once again)* **Tonight.**
22 **Not three hours ago ... in that room.** *(Pointing to the right)*
23 HODGES: **He's mad, Sergeant. He couldn't have killed him**
24 **here. There's not a sign. And he'd have to get rid of the**
25 **body, remember.**
26 SERGEANT: *(Sharply)* **Shut up, Hodges. Tell us about it,**
27 **Flack.**
28 FLACK: **Yes — yes, I'll tell you. I'll tell you everything — but**
29 **sit down — stop hanging on to me!**
30 SERGEANT: *(Motioning HODGES back to his seat, and returning*
31 *to his)* **All right. Now — begin. You murdered him for his**
32 **money.**
33 FLACK: **No. Though I needed it and hoped he'd die so I could**
34 **have it! But I wouldn't kill him for his money.**
35 SERGEANT: **What, then?**

1   FLACK: His eye ... his eye that looked like the eye of a
2   vulture! It got so on my nerves. I couldn't stand it staring
3   me in the face day after day. I had to put it out!
4   SERGEANT: And you chose tonight to do it?
5   FLACK: I tried other times. I'd creep into his room, clutching
6   my knife, after listening at his door until his breath was
7   heavy and regular and I'd think he was asleep. And
8   then ...
9   SERGEANT: Go on ...
10   FLACK: I told you! I'd open his door a crack. The room was
11   always black — he kept his shutters closed for fear of
12   burglars.
13   SERGEANT: You had no light at all?
14   FLACK: I carried a little lantern and blocked the light with a
15   shield. Then when I'd made a crack in the door, I'd open
16   a tiny slit in the lantern until a single dim ray of light
17   would shoot through the slit right into his face! Right
18   into his eye! But I couldn't kill him when it was staring
19   at me!
20   SERGEANT: And then tonight, Flack?
21   FLACK: We quarreled. Over little things at first. Then in
22   earnest. The parents of the children whom I tutor have
23   been withdrawing them from my classes. *(More upset)* I
24   lost four today!
25   SERGEANT: But what did that have to do with your uncle?
26   FLACK: *(Exploding a bit again)* It was his eye that did it! I told
27   him to stay in his room, to stay away from my classroom.
28   But he'd sneak around and peer at them through the
29   classroom door. Some children ran home, hysterical from
30   fear of him — him and that eye!
31   SERGEANT: Mmmm. You saw your living slipping away
32   from you ...
33   FLACK: That was it, Sergeant. And then tonight he kicked my
34   cat! Toby, the only living thing that cares for me and
35   treats me with affection — that loves me. I swore that

1   nothing in heaven or hell — eye or no eye — open or
2   shut — would stop me from killing him!

3 HODGES: Sergeant, do you suppose? . . .

4 SERGEANT: Keep quiet, Hodges.

5 FLACK: Luck was with me, I thought. For when I listened at
6   his door, I heard his heavy breathing. So I opened his
7   door. He heard me, but I had the shutter closed on my
8   lantern, and I heard him mutter that he was dreaming.
9   I waited and waited. Finally, I thought he was asleep, so
10   I opened the shutter just a small crack. He was awake,
11   and my light hit him right in his eye. He knew it was me,
12   so . . . I stabbed him, again and again — and he shrieked
13   as I did it.

14 SERGEANT: And that's how you killed him.

15 FLACK: Yes, that's how I killed him, Sergeant. You'll think
16   me mad, but for many minutes after I stabbed him his
17   heart beat on and on with a muffled sound. But finally,
18   it ceased.

19 SERGEANT: What did you do with the body, Mr. Flack?

20 FLACK: I used every precaution for concealment. I removed
21   three planks, loose ones, from the flooring of this room —
22   right underneath the spot your chair stands on, Sergeant.

23   *(SERGEANT gets up quickly and backs away from the area.)*

24 HODGES: *(Jumping up, too)* **Great Scott, Sergeant!**

25 FLACK: I put the body underneath the floor and then
26   replaced the planking. I did it all so carefully that even
27   you could not find anything amiss.

28 HODGES: That's the truth.

29 FLACK: There was no stain. No blood spot. I took care of that.

30 SERGEANT: What time did you finish?

31 FLACK: It was almost four o'clock. I had just put out the
32   light and was going to my room to go to bed when you
33   two knocked at my door.

34 HODGES: It's strange that you weren't afraid to let us in,
35   Flack.

1   **FLACK:**   But I'd left no trace! I'd been so clever — I thought I
2   was safe. And I would have been except for the awful
3   **beating** ... *(Breaks off, covers ears with hands, voice rises in*
4   *fear.)* **There it is again! Listen ... don't you hear it now?**
5   **It's tearing me to pieces! I can't stand it — I can't stand it!**
6   **HODGES:**   *(Moving to FLACK and grabbing his arm again)* **He's**
7   **off his head again, Sergeant.**
8   **SERGEANT:**   I wonder if his story can be true?
9   **FLACK:**   I've told you the truth. I swear it! *(Almost screaming,*
10   *hands to his ears)* **But the beating ... the beating ...**
11   **SERGEANT:**   *(Taking FLACK's other arm)* **Now tell me, Flack,**
12   **what is this sound you hear that terrified you into a**
13   **confession?**
14   **FLACK:**   Don't mock me any more! You hear it, too. A dull,
15   quick sound — such as a watch makes when wrapped up
16   in cotton. *(Wildly)* **There it is! It's his heart beating!** *(If*
17   *desired, the sound of a beating heart, getting louder and louder,*
18   *may be started here and increased to a climax as the play ends.)*
19   **HODGES:**   Shall I tear up the planking?
20   **SERGEANT:**   No, we'll do that after we take him to the station.
21   I fear he gave it to us straight — that he's telling the
22   truth. We'll send after the body.
23   **FLACK:**   What does the body matter? It won't haunt me. But
24   **his heart ... louder ... louder ...** *(The two POLICEMEN*
25   *are taking him Upstage to the door and out)* **'til I die — I'll**
26   **hear the awful beating of his hideous heart.** *(Builds to*
27   *emotional and vocally hysterical end, sobbing and screaming as*
28   *he is led away.)*
29
30
31
32
33
34
35

Christmas Specials

A CHRISTMAS CAROL*

by Melvin R. White, Ph.D.
Adapted from Charles Dickens

Charles Dickens, 1812-1870, was among the most popular of English novelists, and possibly the best known and loved of his novels was his Christmas story, *A Christmas Carol,* with its hopes for peace and good will. Its characters — Ebenezer Scrooge, Bob Cratchit, Tiny Tim and others — are so effectively drawn that they have come to be thought of as real people. Millions have read this story over and over again. It is performed each year on television and radio as well as in high school, college, community, and professional theatres, but *A Christmas Carol* remains as fresh and beloved as the spirit of Christmas itself.

The Physical Arrangement of the Scene

One reason why *A Christmas Carol* is not performed as a play more often is because of the many different settings in which it takes place. This version uses the *Our Town* idea of a simple setting, employing the mind, the imagination, rather than elaborate staging. Thus it is possible to stage this Christmas story very simply, arranging some 10 or 12 chairs, stools, or boxes toward the back of the stage, along with four benches Downstage Left and Right with a chair between them and slightly Upstage, and a lectern (if the Narrator is given one) Downstage Right. Suggestions are made throughout the script on when to move chairs and benches about a bit to change scenes and to which playing area: Down Right, Down Left, Down Center, Upstage Center, Upstage Right, and Upstage Left. (See Platform Arrangement for *A Christmas Carol.*)

The Narrator may carry a book, *A Christmas Carol,* and refer to it at times to emphasize that he is sharing with the audience the Dickens' story. In fact, in the first production of this adaptation, the cast approached the play in Readers Theatre style, carrying their scripts with them and at times referring to them. However, they were completely familiar with their lines, and could have dispensed with the books if they wished.

No sets, lights, or costumes are necessary, but since it is a period story, costumes — or some suggestion of costumes — would be helpful. Too, if desired, since many of the scenes are set in particular parts of the stage, selective lighting could be employed to enhance the production.

*Adapted for Readers Theatre by Melvin R. White. Amateur performance rights of this adaptation are granted with the purchase of this book.

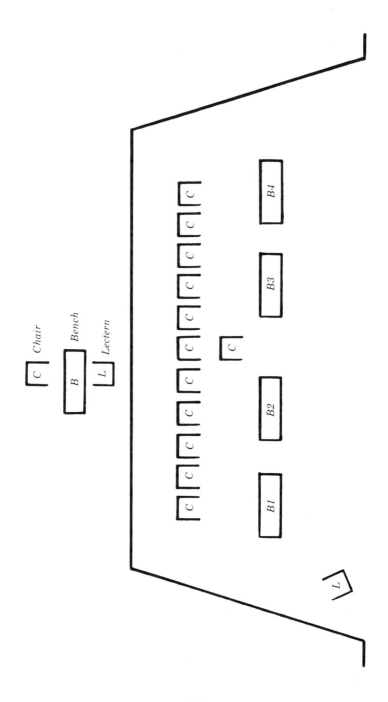

CAST OF CHARACTERS

The number of actors for Dickens' *A Christmas Carol* can be quite small or very large. If a separate actor is assigned to each role, the total would be 31. But many characters have only two or three speeches, so it is possible to assign some of these short roles to versatile actors who are capable of portraying many different characters, thus keeping the cast to 10 or 12. However, certain roles should be enacted by one person who interprets only the one part: The Narrator, Ebenezer Scrooge, Bob Cratchit and the other members of his family, and probably Fred, too.

NARRATOR: Effective storyteller, warm, friendly, and intimate with the audience.

MAN ONE: Mature in voice and physique.

MAN TWO: Mature in voice and physique; portly.

WOMAN: Mature in voice and physique.

CHILD ONE: May portray several small girls.

CHILD TWO: May portray several small boys.

FRED: Cheerful young man, leading man type.

EBENEZER SCROOGE: "A squeezing, wrenching, grasping, scraping, clutching, covetous old sinner."

BOB CRATCHIT: A young, middle-aged man of 35-40, ideally rather thin and "beaten-looking," but pleasant in voice and manner.

JACOB MARLEY: Old character, capable of projecting an unearthly, hollow, sepulchral voice; possibly MAN ONE or MAN TWO.

**GHOST OF CHRISTMAS
PAST:** Dickens described this man as ". . . a strange figure — like a child; yet not so like a child as like an old man . . . Its hair was white as if with age; and yet the face had not a wrinkle in it, and the tenderest bloom was on the skin."

FAN: A child, Scrooge's sister; possibly CHILD ONE.

FEZZIWIG: A fat and jovial character with a "comfortable, oily, rich, fat, jovial voice."

BELLE: A fair young girl, ingenue type; must be able to play herself at age 40-45 also.

BELLE'S DAUGHTER: A fair young girl, ingenue type; if possible, the twin of BELLE when she was young.

BELLE'S HUSBAND: A middle-aged father.

GHOST OF CHRISTMAS PRESENT: Young man, smiling and cheerful, full of good will.

MRS. CRATCHIT: A pleasant, motherly type, perhaps 35 years of age, a typical "home-body," outgoing and friendly; "plain;" not well-educated.

PETER CRATCHIT: The older of the two young Cratchit boys; later appears again as a mature young man.

SECOND YOUNG CRATCHIT: The younger of the two Cratchit boys; later appears again as a mature young man.

MARTHA CRATCHIT: A wholesome ingenue, 15-18 years of age, but "plain" like her mother; later is a woman of 25-30.

TINY TIM: A very small boy, ill and weak; may have a crutch.

FRED'S WIFE: A charming woman, leading lady type.

FAT MAN: Contrasting middle-aged or old-aged character
SECOND MAN: types; may be played by MAN ONE, MAN TWO,
THIRD MAN: and other actors.

GHOST OF CHRISTMAS FUTURE: A silent spirit who has no dialog, only pantomime. Dickens wrote that this phantom is silent and grave, "seemed to scatter gloom and mystery." A solemn phantom.

CHARWOMAN:
OLD JOE: Contrasting character types, middle-aged
LAUNDRESS: or old-aged.
UNDERTAKER'S MAN:

BOY: A young boy, 10-12 years of age; can be played by CHILD TWO.

This arrangement/adaptation of Dickens *A Christmas Carol* is intended for Readers Theatre purposes. However, it has been presented successfully as a play per se. For example, the community theatre in Fresno, California, Christopher Brown, director, staged it very effectively. Their set design provided a diagonal street running from Upstage Right to Downstage Left. Area One, Down Right, was occupied by a turntable, divided into three parts, each of which accommodated a simple set and a few props for small scenes such as Scrooge's countinghouse, Ebenezer's childhood room, the episodes with young Ebenezer and Belle and Belle and her husband, Fred and his family, and old Joe's shop. Area Two was a permanent platform Up Left, across the street and Upstage from the turntable, reached by several steps, replete with windows, doors, a four-poster bed, and capable of selective lighting, as was Area One. Downstage Left, an open area in which all large scenes were placed — Fezziwig's warehouse, the Cratchit house, and the cemetery. Carolers, townspeople, and cast members, all costumed in period attire, provided atmosphere and transitions as they strolled up and down the diagonal street. In the Fresno production, the Narrator, a costumed Charles Dickens, entered through a large copy of the book, *A Christmas Carol,* and then read from a small copy of the book to start the play. Then he moved to a period chair Down Left from which he was spotlighted to read narration as the performance progressed, and the story moved without pause to various areas of the wide stage.

1 *(As the play starts, if the cast is to appear and remain on stage,*
2 *with the suggested Upstage chairs, the actors enter from both*
3 *sides of the stage and take their seats, freezing. The exception is*
4 *the NARRATOR who, as the rest sit, either comes Down Center*
5 *to tell his story to the audience, or crosses to the lectern Down*
6 *Right, opening and placing his book on it. The various voices*
7 *who give the bits of dialog during the opening narration do not*
8 *unfreeze or come on stage; the first actors to enter — or leave their*
9 *Upstage seats are EBENEZER SCROOGE and his nephew*
10 *FRED, as indicated below. Or SCROOGE may take his position*
11 *in the Down Center chair on his first entrance, if preferred.)*
12 **NARRATOR: Marley was dead, to begin with. There is no**
13 **doubt whatever about that. The register of his burial was**
14 **signed by the clergyman, the clerk, the undertaker, and**
15 **the chief mourner, Scrooge. Old Marley was as dead as**
16 **a doornail. Scrooge knew he was dead? Of course he did.**
17 **How could it be otherwise? Scrooge and he were**
18 **partners — and Scrooge was his sole executor, his sole**
19 **administrator, his sole residuary legatee, his sole friend,**
20 **his sole mourner. Yes, Scrooge knew he was dead, but he**
21 **never painted out old Marley's name. There it stood, years**
22 **afterward, above the door — SCROOGE AND MARLEY.**
23 **It was all the same to him.** *(If SCROOGE has not gone directly*
24 *to the Down Center chair, moves there now.)* **Oh, but he was**
25 **a tightfisted hand at the grindstone, was Scrooge! A**
26 **squeezing, wrenching, grasping, scraping, clutching,**
27 **covetous old sinner! Nobody ever stopped him in the**
28 **street to say:**
29 **VOICE (MAN): My dear Scrooge, how are you? When will you**
30 **come to see me?**
31 **NARRATOR: No beggars implored him:**
32 **VOICE (WOMAN): Please, a farthing — or a crust of bread!**
33 **NARRATOR: No children asked him:**
34 **VOICE (CHILD): Do you have the time? Please, sir, what**
35 **time is it?**

1   NARRATOR: No one ever once in all his life inquired:

2   VOICE (MAN):   Can you tell me the way to the Exchange?

3   NARRATOR: But what did Scrooge care? It was the very

4   thing he liked — to edge his way along the crowded paths

5   of life, keeping all human sympathy at a distance. *(Change*

6   *of pace in the narration to mark a transition)* Once upon a

7   time — of all the good days in the year, upon a Christmas

8   Eve — old Scrooge sat busy in his countinghouse. It was

9   cold, bleak, biting, foggy weather, and the city clocks had

10   only just gone three, although it was quite dark already.

11   The door of Scrooge's countinghouse was open so he

12   could keep his eye on his clerk, Bob Cratchit, who, in a

13   dismal little cell beyond, was copying letters. Suddenly

14   the silence was broken by a cheerful voice, the voice of

15   Scrooge's nephew, Fred.

16   FRED: *(Stands and comes Down Center to right of SCROOGE, who*

17   *is seated Down Center.)* A merry Christmas, Uncle! God save

18   you!

19   SCROOGE: Bah! Humbug!

20   FRED: Christmas a humbug, Uncle? You don't mean that, I'm

21   sure!

22   SCROOGE: I do. Out upon merry Christmas! What's

23   Christmas time to you but a time for paying bills without

24   money, a time for finding yourself a year older and not

25   an hour richer. What right have you to be merry? What

26   reason have you to be merry? You're poor enough.

27   FRED: *(Determined to be cheerful)* Well then, what right have

28   you to be dismal? You're rich enough. Don't be cross,

29   Uncle.

30   SCROOGE: What else can I be when I live in such a world of

31   fools as this? Merry Christmas! If I could work my will,

32   every idiot who goes about with "Merry Christmas" on

33   his lips should be boiled with his own pudding!

34   FRED: *(Pleading)* Uncle!

35   SCROOGE: *(Standing)* Nephew, keep Christmas in your own

1   way, and let me keep it in mine.

2   FRED: Keep it! But you don't keep it!

3   SCROOGE: Let me leave it alone then! Much good may it do

4   you! Much good it has ever done you!

5   FRED: *(Placatingly)* Don't be angry, Uncle. Come! Dine with us

6   tomorrow!

7   SCROOGE: Good afternoon.

8   FRED: Uncle, I want nothing from you. I ask nothing of you.

9   Why can't we be friends?

10   SCROOGE: Good afternoon.

11   FRED: I'm sorry to find you so determined. We've never had

12   any quarrel to which I've been a party. I made this trial

13   in homage to Christmas, and I'll keep my Christmas

14   humor to the last. So — a merry Christmas, Uncle!

15   SCROOGE: Good afternoon!

16   FRED: And a happy New Year! *(Return to seat Up Center and*

17   *freeze.)*

18   SCROOGE: Good afternoon!

19   NARRATOR: Fred, the nephew, gave up, and left the room

20   without an angry word. *(Two men stand and come Down Left*

21   *of SCROOGE, who is still standing.)* The clerk, in letting

22   Scrooge's nephew out, had let two other people in. They

23   were pleasant, portly gentlemen, and now stood, hats off,

24   in Scrooge's office. They had books and papers in their

25   hands, and bowed to him.

26   MAN ONE: Scrooge and Marley's, I believe. Have I the

27   pleasure of addressing Mr. Scrooge or Mr. Marley?

28   SCROOGE: Scrooge. Marley's been dead these seven years.

29   He died seven years ago this very night.

30   MAN TWO: We have no doubt his liberality is well represented

31   by his surviving partner. At this festive season of the year,

32   Mr. Scrooge, it is more than usually desirable that we should

33   make some slight provision for the poor and the destitute.

34   Many thousands are in want of the common necessities;

35   hundreds of thousands are in want of common comforts.

1   SCROOGE: Are there no prisons? And the workhouses? Are
2   they not still in operation?
3   MAN ONE: *(Somewhat taken aback)* **Under the impression that**
4   **they scarcely furnish Christmas cheer of mind or body,**
5   **a few of us are endeavoring to raise a fund to buy the**
6   **poor some meat and drink, and means of warmth. What**
7   **shall I put you down for?**
8   SCROOGE: Nothing.
9   MAN ONE: *(Not understanding)* **You wish to be anonymous?**
10   SCROOGE: *(A bit vehemently)* **I wish to be left alone! I don't**
11   make merry myself at Christmas, and I can't afford to
12   make idle people merry. I help to support the
13   establishments I have mentioned — they cost enough;
14   and those who are badly off must go there.
15   MAN TWO: Many can't go there — and many would rather die.
16   SCROOGE: If they would rather die, they'd better do it and
17   decrease the surplus population. Besides, it's not my
18   business. It's enough for a man to understand his own
19   business, and not to interfere with other people's. Mine
20   occupies me constantly. Good afternoon, gentlemen! *(The*
21   *two men retreat to their seats and freeze; SCROOGE may pace*
22   *Down Right and back to meet BOB CRATCHIT Down Center.)*
23   NARRATOR: At length the hour of shutting up the counting-
24   house arrived. With an ill will Scrooge admitted the fact
25   to the expectant clerk in the tank, who instantly snuffed
26   out his candle and put on his hat. *(CRATCHIT moves Down*
27   *Center during this narration.)*
28   SCROOGE: You want all day tomorrow, I suppose?
29   CRATCHIT: If quite convenient, sir.
30   SCROOGE: It's not convenient, Cratchit, and it's not fair. If I
31   were to stop half a crown for it, you'd think yourself
32   mightly ill-used, I'll be bound?
33   CRATCHIT: Yes, sir.
34   SCROOGE: And yet you don't think *me* ill-used, when I pay
35   a day's wages for no work.

1   CRATCHIT: It's only once a year, sir.
2   SCROOGE: A poor excuse for picking a man's pocket every
3   twenty-fifth of December! But I suppose you must have
4   the whole day. Be here all the earlier the *next* morning.
5   CRATCHIT: Yes, sir. I promise. *(CRATCHIT and SCROOGE*
6   *return to their respective chairs, and freeze.)*
7   NARRATOR: Scrooge took his melancholy dinner in his
8   usual melancholy tavern, and having read all the
9   newspapers, went home to bed. He lived in chambers
10   which had once belonged to Old Marley. They were a
11   gloomy suite of rooms, in a lowering pile of a building,
12   old enough and dreary enough, for no one lived in it but
13   Scrooge, the other rooms being all let out as offices.
14   Scrooge had not given one thought to Marley since his
15   last mention of his seven-years-dead partner that
16   afternoon and, yet, having his key in the lock of his front
17   door, he suddenly saw in the knocker, without its
18   undergoing any intermediate process of change, not a
19   knocker, but Marley's face. To say that he was not startled
20   would be untrue. But he put his hand upon the key,
21   turned it sturdily, walked in, and lighted his candle. He
22   fastened the door, walked across the hall, and went up
23   the stairs slowly, trimming his candle as he went. Scrooge
24   did not mind the darkness, for darkness is cheap, and he
25   liked that. But before he shut his heavy door, he walked
26   through his rooms to see that all was right. He had just
27   enough recollection of the face on the knocker to do that.
28   Quite satisfied, he closed his door and locked himself
29   in — double-locked himself in, in fact, which was not his
30   custom. Thus secured against surprise, he took off his
31   cravat, put on his dressing gown and slippers and his
32   nightcap, and sat down before the low fire. *(SCROOGE*
33   *comes to life in his chair Down Center. Throughout all the*
34   *following narration, he pantomimes everything, hearing the*
35   *sounds, seeing the ghosts, etc.)* **As he threw his head back in**

1 his chair, his glance happened to rest upon a bell, a
2 disused bell *(See it)* that hung in the room, and
3 communicated with a chamber in the highest story of
4 the building. It was with great astonishment, and with
5 a strange, inexplicable dread, that, as he looked, he saw
6 this bell begin to swing. *(SOUND EFFECTS: Faint sound*
7 *of bell)* It swung so softly at the outset that it scarcely
8 made a sound; but soon it rang out loudly *(Increase volume*
9 *of the bell)*, and so did every bell in the house. *(Climactic*
10 *clanging of many bells; then stop suddenly.)* The bells ceased,
11 as they had begun, together. *(SOUND EFFECTS: Start*
12 *clanking of chains.)* They were succeeded by a clanking
13 noise, deep down below, as if some person were dragging
14 a heavy chain over the casks in the wine merchant's
15 cellar. The cellar door flew open with a booming sound
16 *(SOUND EFFECT: Door opening)*, and then he heard the
17 noise, much louder *(Increase volume of sound effect)*, on the
18 floors below; then coming up the stairs; then coming
19 straight to his door.
20 SCROOGE: *(Crying out)* It's humbug! I won't believe it!
21 NARRATOR: His color changed, though, when, without a
22 pause, it came on through the heavy door, and passed
23 into the room before his eyes. The same face, the very
24 same. It was not angry or ferocious, but looked at Scrooge
25 as Marley used to look. The hair was curiously stirred,
26 as if by breath or hot air, and though the eyes were wide
27 open, they were perfectly motionless. That, and its livid
28 color, made it horrible — but its horror seemed to be in
29 spite of the face, and beyond its control, rather than a
30 part of its own expression. The ghost wore a chain
31 clasped about it in the middle. It was long, and wound
32 about it like a tail; and it was made of cash boxes, keys,
33 padlocks, ledgers, deeds, and heavy purses wrought in
34 steel. The ghost's body was transparent; so that Scrooge
35 observing it, and looking through its waistcoat, could see

1   **the two buttons on its coat behind.** *(SCROOGE sees the*
2   *ghost Down Center between himself and the audience.)*
3 **MARLEY'S GHOST:** *(Just a voice, either from one of the chairs*
4   *Upstage or perhaps over a public address system, an unearthly,*
5   *hollow, sepulchral voice, or MARLEY may stand from his*
6   *Upstage chair and move Downstage if a "presence" is preferred.)*
7 **Scrooge.**
8 **SCROOGE:** How now! What do you want with me?
9 **MARLEY:** Much!
10 **SCROOGE:** Who are you?
11 **MARLEY:** Ask me who I *was.*
12 **SCROOGE:** Who *were* you then?
13 **MARLEY:** In life I was your partner, Jacob Marley.
14 **SCROOGE:** *(Uncertainly, hesitatingly)* Uh — can you — can
15   you sit down?
16 **MARLEY:** I can. *(Slight pause)* You don't believe in me.
17 **SCROOGE:** I don't.
18 **MARLEY:** What evidence would you have of my reality
19   beyond that of your senses?
20 **SCROOGE:** I — I don't know.
21 **MARLEY:** Why do you doubt your senses?
22 **SCROOGE:** Because a little thing affects them. A slight
23   disorder of my stomach makes them cheats. You may be
24   an undigested bit of beef, a blot of mustard, a crumb of
25   cheese, a fragment of an underdone potato. There's more
26   of gravy than of grave about you, whatever you are!
27   Dreadful apparition, why do you trouble me? Why do
28   spirits walk the earth, and why do they come to me?
29 **MARLEY:** It is required of every man that the spirit within
30   him should walk abroad among his fellow men, and travel
31   far and wide; and if that spirit goes not forth in life, it is
32   condemned to do so after death. I cannot tell you all I
33   would. A very little more is permitted me. I cannot rest,
34   I cannot stay, I cannot linger anywhere. My spirit never
35   walked beyond our countinghouse — mark me! — in life

1   my spirit never roved beyond the limits of our money-
2   changing hole; and weary journeys lie before me!
3   SCROOGE: Seven years dead. And traveling all the time? You
4   travel fast?
5   MARLEY: On the wings of the wind.
6   SCROOGE: You might have got over a great quantity of
7   ground in seven years.
8   MARLEY: O blind man, blind man! Not to know that ages of
9   incessant labor by immortal creatures for this earth must
10   pass into eternity before the good of which it is capable
11   is all developed. Not to know that any Christian spirit
12   working kindly in its little sphere, whatever it may be,
13   will find its mortal life too short for its vast means of
14   usefulness. Not to know that no space of regret can make
15   amends for one life's opportunities misused! Yet I was
16   like this man; I once was like this man!
17   SCROOGE: *(Falteringly)* But you were always a good man of
18   business, Jacob.
19   MARLEY: *(Crying out)* Business! Mankind was my business.
20   The common welfare was my business; charity, mercy,
21   forbearance, benevolence, were all my business. The
22   dealings of my trade were but a drop of water in the
23   comprehensive ocean of my business! O hear me, Scrooge!
24   Hear me! My time is nearly gone.
25   SCROOGE: I will. But don't be hard upon me, Jacob! Pray!
26   MARLEY: I am here tonight to warn you that you have yet a
27   chance and hope of escaping my fate. A chance and hope
28   that I got for you, Ebenezer.
29   SCROOGE: You were always a good friend to me. Thankee!
30   MARLEY: You will be haunted by three spirits.
31   SCROOGE: *(Taken aback)* Is that the chance and hope you
32   mentioned, Jacob? I — I think I'd rather not.
33   MARLEY: Without their visits, you cannot hope to shun the
34   path I tread. Expect the first tomorrow night when the
35   bell tolls one. Expect the second on the next night at the

1   same hour. The third, upon the next night when the last
2   stroke of twelve has ceased to vibrate. Look to see me no
3   more; and look that, for your own sake, you remember
4   what has passed between us. *(If MARLEY'S GHOST has*
5   *been suggested on stage in person, it will return to its Upstage*
6   *seat and freeze; SCROOGE freezes in his Down Center chair.)*
7   NARRATOR: The Ghost walked backward from him, and at
8   every step it took, the window raised itself a little so that
9   when the apparition reached it, it was wide open.
10   *(Transition)* After Marley's ghost faded on the wind,
11   Scrooge closed the window, and then examined the door
12   by which it had entered. It was still double-locked as he
13   had locked it with his own hands, and the bolts were
14   undisturbed. Scrooge tried to say, "Humbug!" but
15   stopped at the first syllable. And being, from the emotion
16   he had undergone, or the fatigues of the day, or his
17   glimpse of the invisible world, or the dull conversation
18   of the ghost, or the lateness of the hour, much in need of
19   rest, he went straight to bed without undressing, and fell
20   asleep at once. *(Transition)* When Scrooge awoke, it was
21   so dark that he could scarcely distinguish the
22   transparent window from the solid walls of his chamber.
23   Then, suddenly *(SOUND EFFECT: Church clock tolls one)*,
24   the church clock tolled a deep, dull, hollow, melancholy
25   one. *(GHOST OF CHRISTMAS PAST moves from chair*
26   *Upstage to area near SCROOGE.)* A strange figure
27   appeared — like a child, yet not so like a child as like an
28   old man diminished to a child's proportions.
29   SCROOGE: Are you the spirit, sir, whose coming was foretold
30   to me?
31   GHOST OF CHRISTMAS PAST: I am.
32   SCROOGE: Who and what are you?
33   GHOST OF CHRISTMAS PAST: I am the Ghost of Christmas
34   Past.
35   SCROOGE: Long past?

1 GHOST OF CHRISTMAS PAST: No. Your past. The things that
2 you will see with me are shadows of the things that have
3 been; they will not see or hear you and me.
4 SCROOGE: If I may be so bold as to ask, what business
5 brought you here to my rooms?
6 GHOST OF CHRISTMAS PAST: Your welfare. Come. Rise
7 and walk with me! We'll leave through the window.
8 SCROOGE: *(Frightened)* The window! But I am a mortal —
9 liable to fall.
10 GHOST OF CHRISTMAS PAST: Bear but a touch of my hand
11 upon your heart, and you shall be upheld in more than
12 this. *(GHOST touches the frightened SCROOGE on the heart;*
13 *then they move Down Right Center.)*
14 NARRATOR: As the words were spoken, they passed
15 through the window, and stood upon an open country
16 road, with fields on either hand. *(GHOST and SCROOGE*
17 *move to Down Right Center area.)* The darkness and the mist
18 had vanished with the city, and it was a clear, cold, winter
19 day, with snow upon the ground.
20 SCROOGE: Good heaven! I was bred in this place. I was a boy
21 here!
22 GHOST OF CHRISTMAS PAST: Your lip is trembling. And
23 what is that upon your cheek?
24 SCROOGE: The school. I went to school there.
25 GHOST OF CHRISTMAS PAST: The school is not quite
26 deserted. A solitary child, neglected by his friends, is left
27 there still.
28 SCROOGE: I know. *(Sobbing a bit)* I know it only too well.
29 GHOST OF CHRISTMAS PAST: What's the matter?
30 SCROOGE: Nothing, nothing. It's just — there was a boy
31 singing a Christmas carol at my door last night. I should
32 like to have given him something, that's all.
33 GHOST OF CHRISTMAS PAST: Let us see another Christ-
34 mas!
35 NARRATOR: The Ghost waved its hand, smiling thoughtfully,

1   and Scrooge's former self grew larger at the words. The
2   room in which they found themselves was a little dark
3   and dirty, and a boy was walking up and down
4   despairingly. *(The boy, EBENEZER, and his little sister, come*
5   *Downstage to Down Center for their scene.)* Scrooge looked at
6   the Ghost and with a mournful shaking of his head
7   glanced anxiously toward the door. It opened, and a little
8   girl, much younger than the boy, came darting in. *(FAN*
9   *comes Down Center.)*
10 FAN: I have come to bring you home, Ebenezer. Home for
11 good and all. Home for ever and ever!
12 EBENEZER: But father . . .
13 FAN: *(Interrupting him)* Father is so much kinder than he used
14 to be that home's like heaven! *(The two children resume their*
15 *seats.)*
16 GHOST OF CHRISTMAS PAST: Always a delicate creature,
17 whom a breath might have withered. But she had a large
18 heart!
19 SCROOGE: So she had. Little sister Fan.
20 GHOST OF CHRISTMAS PAST: She died a woman, and had,
21 I think, children.
22 SCROOGE: One child.
23 GHOST OF CHRISTMAS PAST: True. Your nephew, Fred.
24 SCROOGE: *(Thoughtfully)* Yes.
25 NARRATOR: While he spoke they left the school behind
26 them, passing through the thoroughfares of a city, where
27 the dressing of the shops and the lighted streets made
28 plain that it was Christmas time again. The Ghost
29 stopped at a warehouse door, and asked:
30 GHOST OF CHRISTMAS PAST: Do you know it?
31 SCROOGE: Know it! I was apprenticed here! Why, it's old
32 Fezziwig! Bless his heart, it's Fezziwig, alive again!
33 FEZZIWIG: *(Calling out in a comfortable, oily, rich, fat, jovial*
34 *voice)* Yo ho, there! Ebenezer! Dick! *(EBENEZER as a young*
35 *man and DICK come Down Left in answer to the call.)*

1   SCROOGE: Dick Wilkins, to be sure! My old fellow
2   apprentice, bless me, yes. There he is. He was very much
3   attached to me, was Dick. Poor Dick! Dear, dear!
4   FEZZIWIG: Yo ho, my boys! No more work tonight. Christmas
5   Eve, Dick. Christmas, Ebenezer! Let's have all the
6   shutters up, before a man can say "Jack Robinson." Clear
7   away, my lads, and let's have lots of room here.
8   EBENEZER: For dancing, Mr. Fezziwig?
9   FEZZIWIG: Ay, for dancing. And for feasting — and for
10   Christmas porter. Clear away!
11   NARRATOR: It was done in a minute. The floor was swept
12   and watered, the lamps were trimmed, fuel was heaped
13   upon the fire — and soon the warehouse was as snug and
14   as warm and dry and bright a ballroom as you would
15   desire to see on a winter night. In came a fiddler with a
16   music book. In came Mrs. Fezziwig, one vast substantial
17   smile. In came the three Miss Fezziwigs, beaming and
18   lovable. In came all the young men and women employed
19   in the business. Away they all went, many couples at
20   once, dancing to the lively fiddler. *(If desired, here a fiddler*
21   *and some period dancing can be inserted, remembered and*
22   *observed by SCROOGE.)* There were many dances, and
23   more dances, and there was cake, and there was punch,
24   and there was a great piece of cold roast, and there was
25   a great piece of cold boiled beef, and there were mince
26   pies, and plenty of beer. When the clock struck eleven
27   this domestic ball broke up.
28   GHOST OF CHRISTMAS PAST: *(As those in the scene return to*
29   *their seats to freeze)* A small matter to make these silly folks
30   so full of gratitude. He has spent but a few pounds of
31   your mortal money — three or four perhaps. Is that so
32   much that he deserves such praise?
33   SCROOGE: *(Heatedly, and speaking like his former self)* It isn't
34   that — it isn't that, Spirit. He had the power to render
35   us happy or unhappy; to make our service light or

1   burdensome; a pleasure or a toil. Say that his power lay

2   in words or looks; in things so slight and insignificant

3   that it was impossible to add and count 'em up: what

4   then? The happiness he gave was quite as great as if it

5   cost a fortune. *(Seeing the GHOST looking at him)*

6   **GHOST OF CHRISTMAS PAST:** What's the matter?

7   **SCROOGE:** Nothing particular.

8   **GHOST OF CHRISTMAS PAST:** Something, I think.

9   **SCROOGE:** No, no. I should like to be able to say a word or

10   two to my clerk just now. That's all.

11   **GHOST OF CHRISTMAS PAST:** My time grows short. Quick!

12   **NARRATOR:** Again Scrooge saw himself. He was older now,

13   a man in the prime of life. His face had not the harsh and

14   rigid lines of later years, but it had begun to wear the

15   signs of care and avarice. There was an eager, greedy,

16   restless motion in the eyes which showed the passion

17   that had taken root. *(SCROOGE sits in his chair Down Center;*

18   *BELLE moves her chair from Upstage to right of SCROOGE's,*

19   *and sits beside him.)* He was not alone, but sat by the side

20   of a fair young girl, in a mourning dress, in whose eyes

21   there were tears.

22   **BELLE:** *(Softly)* It matters little to you. Another idol has

23   displaced me; and if it can cheer and comfort you in time

24   to come, as I would have tried to do, I have no just cause

25   to grieve.

26   **SCROOGE:** What idol has displaced you?

27   **BELLE:** A golden one!

28   **SCROOGE:** But this is the dealing of the world! There is

29   nothing on which it is so hard as poverty, and there is

30   nothing it professes to condemn with such severity as

31   the pursuit of wealth!

32   **BELLE:** You fear the world too much. Our contract is an old

33   one, made when we were both poor. But you are changed.

34   When it was made, you were another man.

35   **SCROOGE:** I was a boy! But — have I sought release? Belle,

1   have I?

2   BELLE: In words, no. But in a changed nature, in an altered

3   spirit yes. Tell me, Ebenezer, would you seek me out and

4   try to win me now? Can I believe that you would choose

5   a dowerless girl, you who weigh everything by gain? Or,

6   if for one moment you were false to your own guiding

7   principle, do I not know that your repentance and regret

8   would surely follow? No, I release you, with a full heart,

9   for the love of him you once were! *(SCROOGE gets up, turns*

10   *to the GHOST. BELLE stays in chair Down Center and is joined*

11   *by her handsome husband and beautiful daughter.)*

12   SCROOGE: Spirit! Show me no more! Take me home. Why do

13   you delight to torture me?

14   GHOST OF CHRISTMAS PAST: One shadow more.

15   SCROOGE: No! No more, no more! Show me no more.

16   NARRATOR: But the relentless Ghost of Christmas Past

17   pinioned him in both his arms and forced him to look.

18   They were in another scene and place: a room, not very

19   large or handsome, but full of comfort. Near the fireplace

20   sat a beautiful young girl — at first Scrooge thought it

21   was his Belle again, until he saw her, now a comely

22   matron, sitting next to her daughter. The father entered

23   *(FATHER stands and comes Down Center to left of BELLE's*

24   *daughter)*, and joined the two at the fire.

25   DAUGHTER: *(Goes to her father to kiss him welcome.)* **Father,**

26   **how good that you got to come home early tonight on**

27   **Christmas Eve.**

28   BELLE: Hello, dear. *(As he kisses her and then sits beside her)*

29   Did you remember to bring home the packages I left at

30   your office?

31   HUSBAND: Yes, Belle. Oh, by the way, I saw an old friend of

32   yours this afternoon. I passed his office window, and as

33   it was not shuttered, and he had a candle inside, I could

34   scarely help seeing him. I hear his partner — Marley, I

35   think his name is — is upon the point of death, and there

1   **he sat alone. Quite alone in the world, I do believe.** *(The*
2   *three resume their Upstage seats.)*
3   **SCROOGE:**   **Spirit, remove me from this place. She might**
4   **have called me father, if I . . .**
5   **GHOST OF CHRISTMAS PAST:**   **I told you these were**
6   **shadows of the things that have been. That they are what**
7   **they are, do not blame me!**
8   **SCROOGE:**   **Remove me. I cannot bear it! Take me back!**
9   **Haunt me no longer!** *(SCROOGE returns to his Down Center*
10   *chair, and freezes.)*
11   **NARRATOR:**   **Scrooge was conscious of being exhausted, and**
12   **overcome by an irresistible drowsiness; and, further, of being**
13   **in his own bedroom. His hands relaxed; he barely had time**
14   **to pull up the covers before he sank into a heavy sleep.**
15   *(Transition)* **Awakening in the middle of a prodigiously tough**
16   **snore, and sitting up in bed to get his thoughts together,**
17   *(SCROOGE comes alive in his chair Down Center. SOUND*
18   *EFFECTS: Stroke of one)* **Scrooge did not have to be told that**
19   **the bell was once again upon the stroke of one. A ghostly**
20   **light was coming from the adjoining room. Scrooge got up**
21   **softly and shuffled to the door.** *(Cross to Down Right area*
22   *where the GHOST OF CHRISTMAS PRESENT has taken his*
23   *position)*
24   **GHOST OF CHRISTMAS PRESENT:**   **Come in — come in and**
25   **know me better, man! I am the Ghost of Christmas**
26   **Present. Look upon me! You have never seen the likes of**
27   **me before.**
28   **SCROOGE:**   **Never.**
29   **GHOST OF CHRISTMAS PRESENT:**   **You've never walked**
30   **forth with the younger members of my family; meaning**
31   **(for I am very young) my elder brothers born in these**
32   **later years?**
33   **SCROOGE:**   **I don't think I have — I'm afraid I haven't. Have**
34   **you had many brothers, Spirit?**
35   **GHOST OF CHRISTMAS PRESENT:**   **More than nineteen**

1   hundred and seventy-five.

2   SCROOGE: A tremendous family to provide for! Spirit,

3   conduct me where you will. Last night I learned a lesson

4   which is working now. Tonight, if you have anything to

5   teach me, let me profit by it.

6   GHOST OF CHRISTMAS PRESENT: Touch my robe.

7   NARRATOR: At once it was a clear, brisk, Christmas day.

8   Holly and mistletoe were everywhere. The voices of the

9   people rang with gaiety, joy, and merriment. Scrooge saw

10   all this and heard all this as he clutched the Spirit's robe.

11   And, in a twinkling, they were at the home of Scrooge's

12   clerk, Bob Cratchit. *(The CRATCHIT scene is played in a*

13   *wide Down Center area; SCROOGE and the GHOST OF*

14   *CHRISTMAS PRESENT observe it all.)*

15   MRS. CRATCHIT: What has ever got your precious father

16   then? And your brother, Tiny Tim! And Martha warn't as

17   late last Christmas day by half an hour!

18   MARTHA: Here's Martha, Mother! *(Coming down into the*

19   *scene, joining the two YOUNG CRATCHITS and MRS.*

20   *CRATCHIT.)*

21   TWO YOUNG CRATCHITS: Here's Martha, Mother! Hurrah!

22   There's *such* a goose, Martha. *(Not to be spoken in unison,*

23   *of course.)*

24   MRS. CRATCHIT: *(Kissing MARTHA several times)* Why, bless

25   your heart alive, my dear, how late you are.

26   MARTHA: We'd a deal of work to finish up last night, and had

27   to clear away this morning, Mother.

28   MRS. CRATCHIT: Well! Never mind so long as you are come.

29   Sit ye down before the fire, my dear, and have a warm,

30   Lord bless ye!

31   PETER CRATCHIT: No, no! There's Father coming.

32   SECOND YOUNG CRATCHIT: Hide, Martha, hide! *(MARTHA*

33   *hides behind MRS. CRATCHIT as BOB CRATCHIT enters the*

34   *scene with TINY TIM.)*

35   BOB CRATCHIT: Why, where's our Martha?

1　MRS. CRATCHIT:　Not coming.

2　BOB CRATCHIT:　Not coming! Not coming on Christmas

3　day!

4　*(Ad-lib greetings and laughter as MARTHA reveals herself, and*

5　*BOB CRATCHIT hugs and kisses his daughter.)*

6　MRS. CRATCHIT:　And how did little Tim behave?

7　BOB CRATCHIT:　As good as gold. Now, is our Christmas

8　dinner ready?

9　MRS. CRATCHIT:　Yes, just waiting for you and Tim.

10　BOB CRATCHIT:　Everyone, get the chairs to the table. *(Each*

11　*CRATCHIT takes a chair to the imaginary table except TINY*

12　*TIM; his father gets one for him next to him.)* **Here's a chair**

13　**for you, Tim.** *(As they seat themselves, ad-lib reactions to "such*

14　*a goose," applesauce, mashed potatoes, and "Mother made a*

15　*pudding, too.")* **Now, a toast!** *(General reactions of merriment)*

16　**A Merry Christmas to us all, my dears. God bless us!**

17　*(Which the family echoes, raising imaginary glasses high)*

18　TINY TIM:　*(The last of all)* **God bless us every one!**

19　BOB CRATCHIT:　Mr. Scrooge! I'll give you Mr. Scrooge,

20　the Founder of the Feast!

21　MRS. CRATCHIT:　The Founder of the Feast, indeed! I wish I

22　had him here. I'd give him a piece of my mind to feed

23　upon, and I hope he'd have a good appetite for it.

24　BOB CRATCHIT:　My dear, the children! Christmas day!

25　MRS. CRATCHIT:　It should be Christmas day, I am sure, on

26　which one drinks the health of such an odious, stingy,

27　hard, unfeeling man as Mr. Scrooge. You know he is,

28　Robert! Nobody knows it better than you do, poor fellow!

29　BOB CRATCHIT:　*(Mildly)* My dear, Christmas day.

30　MRS. CRATCHIT:　I'll drink his health for your sake and the

31　day's, not for his. Long life to him! A merry Christmas

32　and a happy New Year! He'll be very merry and very

33　happy, I have no doubt! *(The CRATCHITS return to their*

34　*Upstage positions, taking the extra chairs with them.)*

35　NARRATOR:　The Cratchits were not a handsome family; they

1	were not well dressed; their shoes were far from being
2	waterproof; their clothes were scanty. But they were
3	happy, grateful, pleased with one another, and contented
4	with the time; and when they faded, Scrooge had his eye
5	upon them, and especially on Tiny Tim, until the last. *(A*
6	*hearty laugh is heard.)* It was a great surprise to Scrooge
7	as this scene vanished to hear a hearty laugh. It was a
8	much greater surprise to Scrooge to recognize it as his
9	own nephew's, and to find himself in a bright, dry,
10	gleaming room, with the Spirit standing smiling by his
11	side, and looking at that same nephew. *(FRED and his*
12	*family come to a Down Left area for their scene.)*
13	FRED: *(Laughing)* He said that Christmas was a humbug, as I
14	live. He believed it, too!
15	FRED'S WIFE: More shame for him, Fred!
16	FRED: He's a comical old fellow, that's the truth; and not so
17	pleasant as he might be. However, his offenses carry their
18	own punishment, and I have nothing to say against him.
19	Who suffers by his ill whims? Himself, always. He loses
20	some pleasant moments, which could do him no harm. I
21	am sure he loses pleasanter companions than he can find
22	in his own thoughts, either in his moldy old office, or
23	his dusty chambers. I mean to give him the same chance
24	every year, whether he likes it or not, for I pity him. He
25	may rail at Christmas till he dies, but he can't help
26	thinking better of it — I defy him — if he finds me going
27	there, in good temper, year after year, and saying Uncle
28	Scrooge, how are you? Here he takes it into his head to
29	dislike us, and he won't come and dine with us. What's
30	the consequence? He doesn't lose much of a dinner.
31	FRED'S WIFE: Indeed, I think he loses a very good dinner.
32	FRED: *(Making a joke to which they laugh)* Well, I am very glad
33	to hear it because I haven't any great faith in these young
34	housekeepers. *(A hug and a kiss for his wife, the "young*
35	*housekeeper." Then they return Upstage to their seats.)*

1   NARRATOR: The whole scene passed off in the breath of
2   the last word spoken by Scrooge's nephew, Fred, and he
3   and the Ghost of Christmas Present were again upon
4   their travels. Much they saw, and far they went, and many
5   homes they visited, but always with a happy end.
6   Suddenly, as they stood together in an open place, the
7   bell struck twelve. *(SOUND EFFECTS: A cheerful bell tolls*
8   *twelve.)* Scrooge looked about him for the ghost, and saw
9   it no more. As the last stroke ceased to vibrate, he
10   remembered the prediction of Old Jacob Marley, and
11   lifting up his eyes, beheld a solemn phantom, draped and
12   hooded, coming like a mist along the ground toward him.
13   It was shrouded in a deep black garment which concealed
14   its head, its face, its form, and left nothing of it visible
15   save one outstretched hand.
16   SCROOGE: I am in the presence of the Ghost of Christmas Yet
17   to Come? Ghost of the Future? I fear you more than any
18   specter I have seen. But as I know your purpose is to do
19   me good, and as I hope to live to be another man from
20   what I was, I am prepared to bear you company, and do
21   it with a thankful heart. Will you not speak to me? No?
22   Then lead on! Lead on! The night is waning fast, and it is
23   precious time to me, I know. Lead on, Spirit!
24   NARRATOR: Scrooge recoiled in terror, for the scene had
25   changed, and now he saw a bed, a bare uncurtained bed
26   on which, beneath a ragged sheet, a covered up
27   something which, though it was dumb, announced itself
28   in awful sounds. The room was very dark, too dark to be
29   observed with any accuracy, though Scrooge glanced
30   round it in obedience to a secret impulse, anxious to know
31   what kind of a room it was. A pale light, rising in the
32   outer air, fell straight upon the bed; and on it, plundered
33   and bereft, unwatched, unwept, uncared for, was the
34   body of this unknown man.
35   SCROOGE: Spirit! This is a fearful place. In leaving it, I shall

1   not leave its lesson, trust me. Let us go!
2   NARRATOR: They scarcely seemed to enter the city, for the
3   city rather seemed to spring up about them. But there
4   they were in the heart of it, on the Exchange, among the
5   merchants. *(Several men gather in a small group Down Right.)*
6   FAT MAN: No, I don't know much about it either way. I only
7   know he's dead.
8   SECOND MAN: When did he die?
9   FAT MAN: Last night, I believe.
10   SECOND MAN: What was the matter with him? I thought
11   he'd never die.
12   FAT MAN: *(Yawning)* Goodness knows.
13   THIRD MAN: What has he done with his money?
14   FAT MAN: I haven't heard. I know he hasn't left it to me.
15   *(Chuckling)* That's all I know. Bye-bye. *(Return to Upstage*
16   *seat.)*
17   SECOND MAN: It's likely to be a very cheap funeral, for upon
18   my life I don't know anybody to go to it.
19   THIRD MAN: I heard he had a nephew.
20   SECOND MAN: Well, I don't mind going if a lunch is provided.
21   *(Return to Upstage seat.)*
22   NARRATOR: Scrooge and the ever-silent Spirit left this busy
23   city scene, and went into an obscure part of the town
24   where iron, old rags, bottles, bones, and rubbish were
25   bought. Into a low shop a woman with a heavy bundle
26   slunk. She had scarcely entered when another woman,
27   similarly laden, came in too; and she was closely followed
28   by a man in faded black. *(The three characters meet Down*
29   *Center, front.)* After a short period of blank astonishment,
30   they all three burst into a hearty laugh. *(All three laugh.)*
31   CHARWOMAN: Let the charwoman alone to be the first. Let
32   the laundress alone to be the second; and let the
33   undertaker's man alone to be the third! *(Again they all*
34   *laugh, turning to OLD JOE, the shop owner, who is seated in*
35   *the Down Center chair.)* Look here, Joe, here's chance! If

1   we haven't all three met here without meaning it!

2   OLD JOE: You couldn't have met in a better place. You were

3   made free of it long ago, you know; and the other two

4   ain't strangers. What've you got to sell? Hmmm, what've

5   you got this time?

6   LAUNDRESS: Half a minute's patience, Joe, and you shall

7   see.

8   CHARWOMAN: What odds then? What odds, Mrs. Dilber?

9   Every person has a right to take care of themselves. *He*

10   always did. Who's the worse for the loss of a few things

11   like these? Not a dead man, I suppose.

12   LAUNDRESS: No, indeed, Ma'am.

13   CHARWOMAN: If he wanted to keep 'em after he was dead,

14   a wicked old screw, why wasn't he natural in his lifetime?

15   If he had been, he'd have had somebody to look after him

16   when he was struck by death, instead of lying gasping

17   out his last there, alone by himself.

18   UNDERTAKER'S MAN: *(Unctuously)* It's the truest word that

19   ever was spoke, it's a judgment on him.

20   LAUNDRESS: I wish it was a little heavier judgment, and it

21   should have been, you may depend on it, if I could have

22   laid my hands on anything else. Open that bundle, old

23   Joe, and let me know the value of it. Speak out plain. I'm

24   not afraid to be the first, nor afraid for them to see it.

25   OLD JOE: *(Gets down on his knees as he pantomimes opening*

26   *the bundle and dragging out a heavy roll.)* What do you call

27   this? Bed curtains?

28   LAUNDRESS: Ah! Bed curtains! Blankets!

29   OLD JOE: *His* blankets?

30   LAUNDRESS: Whose else's do you think? He isn't likely to

31   take cold without 'em, I dare say. *(The others join her in a*

32   *laugh at this dark humor; OLD JOE picks up another item.)*

33   Ah! You may look through that shirt till your eyes ache,

34   but you won't find a hole in it, nor a threadbare place.

35   It's the best he had, and a fine one, too. They'd have

1   **wasted it by dressing him up in it, if it hadn't been for**

2   **me.** *(The others agree as they move back to their Upstage seats.)*

3   **SCROOGE:** *(In horror)* **Spirit! I see, I see. The case of this**

4   **unhappy man might be my own. My life tends that way,**

5   **now. Merciful heaven, what is this?**

6   **NARRATOR: The Ghost had conducted him to poor Bob**

7   **Cratchit's house — the dwelling he had visited before —**

8   **and found the mother and the children seated round the**

9   **fire.** *(Again the CRATCHITS have moved their chairs to the*

10   *Down Center area.)* **There was a vacant seat in the poor**

11   **chimney corner and a crutch without an owner, carefully**

12   **preserved. Tiny Tim was dead. The mother and daughter**

13   **were engaged in needlework, but surely they were very**

14   **quiet. Very quiet. The mother laid down her work, and**

15   **put her hand up to her face.**

16   **MRS. CRATCHIT: The color hurts my eyes. But they'll be**

17   **better soon again. It makes them weak by candlelight;**

18   **and I wouldn't show weak eyes to your father when he**

19   **comes home, for the world. It must be near his time, Peter.**

20   **PETER CRATCHIT: Past it rather. But I think he has walked**

21   **a little slower than he used to, these few last evenings,**

22   **Mother.**

23   **MRS. CRATCHIT: I have known him to walk with — I have**

24   **known him to walk with Tiny Tim upon his shoulder,**

25   **very fast indeed.**

26   **PETER CRATCHIT: And so have I, often.**

27   **SECOND YOUNG CRATCHIT: And so have I.**

28   **MRS. CRATCHIT: But he was very light to carry, and his**

29   **father loved him so, that it was no trouble — no trouble.**

30   **And there is your father at the door!** *(Ad-lib greetings;*

31   *MRS. CRATCHIT hugs and kisses her husband. As they take*

32   *their seats, she speaks.)* **You went today, then, Robert?**

33   **BOB CRATCHIT: Yes, my dear. I wish you could have gone.**

34   **It would have done you good to see how green a place it**

35   **is. But you'll see it often. I promised him that I would**

1   walk there on a Sunday. *(Breaks down all at once.)* **Oh Tim,**
2   **my little, little child! My tiny boy!** *(The CRATCHITS return*
3   *to their Upstage seats.)*
4   **SCROOGE:**   Specter, something informs me that our parting
5   moment is at hand. I know it, but I know not how. Tell
6   me what man that was, the man who died alone, the man
7   from whom those three stole the blankets, shirt, and all.
8   **NARRATOR:**   The Ghost of Christmas Yet to Come conveyed
9   Scrooge to a dismal, wretched, ruinous churchyard.
10   Standing among the graves, it pointed down to one.
11   Scrooge crept toward it, trembling as he went; and,
12   following the finger, read upon the stone of the neglected
13   grave his own name — EBENEZER SCROOGE.
14   **SCROOGE:**   Am I that man who died alone in bed? No, Spirit!
15   Oh no, no! Spirit, hear me! I am not the man I was. I will
16   not be the man I must have been but for this intercourse.
17   Why show me this, if I am past all hope? Assure me that
18   I yet may change these shadows you have shown me by
19   an altered life. I will honor Christmas in my heart, and
20   try to keep it all the year. I will live in the Past, the
21   Present, and the Future. The spirits of all three will strive
22   within me. I will not shut out the lessons that they teach.
23   Oh, tell me I may sponge away the writing on this stone!
24   **NARRATOR:**   Holding up his hands in one last prayer to have
25   his fate reversed, he saw an alteration in the phantom's
26   hood and dress. It shrunk, collapsed, and dwindled down
27   into a bedpost. *(Transition)* Yes, and the bedpost was his
28   own! The bed was his own, the room was his own. Best
29   and happiest of all, the time before him was his own, to
30   make amends in! And Scrooge repeated, as he scrambled
31   out of bed and rushed into his clothes:
32   **SCROOGE:**   I will live in the Past, the Present, and the
33   Future! The spirits of all three shall strive within me.
34   Oh, Jacob Marley! Heaven and the Christmas time be
35   praised for this! I say it on my knees, old Jacob, on my

1   knees! *(Laughing and crying in the same breath)* **I don't know**
2   **what to do! I'm as light as a feather; I am as happy as an**
3   **angel; I am as merry as a schoolboy. I am as giddy as a**
4   **drunken man. A merry Christmas to everybody! A happy**
5   **New Year to all the world! There's the door by which the**
6   **Ghost of Jacob Marley entered! There's the corner where**
7   **the Ghost of Christmas Present sat! There's the window**
8   **where I saw the wandering spirits! It's all right, it's all**
9   **true, it all happened. Let me open this window. Look! No**
10   **fog, no mist — just clear, bright, stirring, jovial cold! Oh,**
11   **glorious, glorious!** *(Calling to the street below)* **Boy, what's**
12   **today? What's today, my fine fellow?**
13 **BOY:**   *(Calling back from Upstage seat)* **Today? Why, Christmas**
14   **day!**
15 **SCROOGE:**   *(To himself)* **It's Christmas day! I haven't missed**
16   **it. The Spirits have done it all in one night. They can do**
17   **anything they like. Of course they can. Of course they**
18   **can!** *(Calling to the BOY again)* **Hallo, my fine fellow! Do**
19   **you know the poulterers in the next street but one? Do**
20   **you know whether they've sold the prize turkey that was**
21   **hanging there — not the little prize turkey, but the big**
22   **one? Go and buy it and tell 'em to bring it here, that I**
23   **may give them directions where to take it. Come back**
24   **with the man and I'll give you a shilling. Come back with**
25   **him in less than five minutes, and I'll give you half a**
26   **crown!**
27 **BOY:**   **You mean the one as big as me?**
28 **SCROOGE:**   **What a delightful boy! It's a pleasure to talk to**
29   **you! Yes, my buck!**
30 **BOY:**   **It's hanging there now.**
31 **SCROOGE:**   **Is it? Go and buy it.** *(To himself, rubbing his hands*
32   *and splitting with a laugh)* **I'll send it to Bob Cratchit's! He**
33   **shan't know who sends it. It's twice the size of Tiny Tim.**
34   **No one ever made such a joke as sending it to Bob's will be!**
35 **NARRATOR:**   **Scrooge dressed himself "all in his best," and at**

1   last got out into the streets. The people were by this time
2   pouring forth, as he had seen them with the Ghost of
3   Christmas Present, and Scrooge regarded everyone with
4   a delighted smile. In fact, he looked so irresistibly
5   pleasant that good-humoured folks said to him:
6   MAN: Good morning, sir! A merry Christmas to you.
7   NARRATOR: And Scrooge said often, afterward, that of all
8   the blithe sounds he had ever heard, those were the
9   blithest in his ears. He had not gone far when, coming
10   on toward him, he beheld the portly gentleman who had
11   walked with the other man into his countinghouse the
12   day before. Scrooge quickened his pace, and took the
13   portly old gentleman by both his hands.
14   SCROOGE: My dear sir, how do you do? I hope you
15   succeeded yesterday. It was very kind of you. A merry
16   Christmas to you, sir!
17   FAT MAN: Uh . . . Mr. Scrooge?
18   SCROOGE: Yes, that is my name, and I fear it may not be
19   pleasant to you. Allow me to ask your pardon. And will
20   you have the goodness . . . *(SCROOGE whispers in the FAT*
21   *MAN's ear.)*
22   FAT MAN: *(As if his breath was gone)* Lord bless me! My dear
23   Mr. Scrooge, are you serious?
24   SCROOGE: If you please, not a farthing less. A great many
25   back payments are included in it, I assure you. Will you
26   do me that favor?
27   FAT MAN: *(Shaking his hand)* My dear sir, I don't know what
28   to say to such munifi —
29   SCROOGE: *(Interrupting)* Don't say anything, please. Come
30   and see me. Will you come and see me?
31   FAT MAN: I will! I will!
32   SCROOGE: Thankee. I am much obliged to you. I thank you
33   fifty times. Bless you! *(To himself)* And now, to my nephew
34   Fred's.
35   NARRATOR: Scrooge passed his nephew's door a dozen

1 times before he had the courage to go up and knock. But
2 he made a dash, and did it.
3 SCROOGE: *(Meeting FRED Down Center)* **Fred!**
4 FRED: **Why, bless my soul! Who's that?**
5 SCROOGE: **It's I. Your Uncle Scrooge. I have come to dinner.**
6 **Will you let me in, Fred?**
7 NARRATOR: **Let him in! It is a mercy he didn't shake his**
8 **arm off. He was at home in five minutes. Nothing could**
9 **be heartier. And it was a wonderful party with wonderful**
10 **games, wonderful unanimity, wonderful happiness.**
11 *(Transition)* **But Scrooge was early at the office next**
12 **morning. If he could only be there first, and catch Bob**
13 **Cratchit coming late! That was the thing he had set his**
14 **heart upon. And he did it; yes, he did. The clock struck**
15 **nine.** *(SOUND EFFECTS: Clock strikes nine.)* **A quarter past.**
16 **No Bob. He was a full eighteen minutes and a half behind**
17 **his time. Scrooge sat with his door wide open, that he**
18 **might see him come into the tank. Cratchit rushed in and**
19 **was on his stool in a jiffy, driving away with his pen as**
20 **if he were trying to overtake nine o'clock.**
21 SCROOGE: *(Growling in his accustomed voice as near as he can*
22 *feign it)* **Hallo! What do you mean by coming here at this**
23 **time of the day?**
24 BOB CRATCHIT: **I am very sorry, sir. I *am* behind my time.**
25 SCROOGE: **You are? Yes, I think you are. Step this way, sir,**
26 **if you please.**
27 BOB CRATCHIT: *(Pleading)* **It's only once a year, sir. It shall**
28 **not be repeated. I was making rather merry yesterday,**
29 **sir.**
30 SCROOGE: **Now, I'll tell you what, my friend. I'm not going**
31 **to stand this sort of thing any longer. And therefore —**
32 **and therefore I am about to raise your salary!**
33 BOB CRATCHIT: *(Thinking SCROOGE has gone crazy)* **Mr.**
34 **Scrooge, I promise you . . .**
35 SCROOGE: *(Clapping CRATCHIT on the back)* **A merry**

1   Christmas, Bob! A merrier Christmas, Bob, my good
2   fellow, than I have given you for many a year! I'll raise
3   your salary, and endeavor to assist your family, and we'll
4   discuss your affairs this very afternoon over a Christmas
5   bowl of port wine — or smoking bishop, Bob! Make up
6   the fires, and buy another coal scuttle for your office
7   before you dot another i, Bob Cratchit! *(Readers freeze.)*
8 **NARRATOR:**   *(Comes Down Center to talk more intimately with the*
9   *audience.)* Scrooge was better than his word. He did it all,
10   and infinitely more. And to Tiny Tim, who did *not* die, he
11   was a second father. He became as good a friend, as good
12   a master, and as good a man, as the good old city knew.
13   Oh, some people laughed to see the change in him, but
14   he let them laugh, for he was wise enough to know that
15   nothing ever happened on this globe, for good, at which
16   some people did not have their fill of laughter in the
17   outset. His own heart laughed, and that was quite enough
18   for Scrooge. He had no further intercourse with spirits,
19   but lived upon the total abstinence principle, ever
20   afterward; and it was always said of Scrooge that he knew
21   how to keep Christmas well, if any man alive possessed
22   the knowledge. May that be truly said of us, and all of
23   us! *(Slight pause)* And so, as Tiny Tim observed, God Bless
24   Us, Every One!
25
26
27
28
29
30
31
32
33
34
35

THE GIFT OF THE MAGI*

by Arthur L. Zapel
Adapted from O. Henry

CAST OF CHARACTERS

READER 1: If performed in a school, this Reader could be the drama coach or the director. If performed in a church, the first speech of Reader 1 could be spoken by the church pastor to provide a lead-in. The remainder of the Reader 1 narration could be performed by an actor.

READER 2: If Reader 1 is a male, Reader 2 should be a female so that the viewpoints of both sexes are suggested by the Readers.

DELLA: Young. Pretty. About 21. Long brown hair, if possible.

JIM: Handsome. Conservative. A sense of humor at the end.

MADAME SOFRONIE: A dowdy, old frump. Very much business with very little compassion.

EXTRAS: (optional): During the shopping scene extras may be used pantomiming action with Della. Or Della may do all the pantomiming alone.

The staging of this play with both readers and actors is a unique theatrical approach that preserves as much of the original text as possible. Because this story is a classic the adapter chose to hold to O. Henry's style throughout letting the actors enact and speak only where O. Henry felt their dialog was more personal than his narrative.

We recommend that two readers be used speaking from both sides of the staging area. The script is written with alternative stage actions in the event that the play is not presented in a proscenium stage setting with curtains. An open stage is acceptable using only lights to change the scenes and indicate passages of time.

The diagram indicates one possible setting if you choose to create a total set. If presented open stage or in a church setting many of the props are unnecessary. They can be "imagined" by both the actors and the audience. If stage aprons are not available, any "Off-stage" area will be acceptable for the readers and the short scene with Madame Sofronie.

*Adapted for Readers Theatre by Arthur L. Zapel. Copyright © 1984 Meriwether Publishing Ltd. Amateur performance rights of this adaptation are granted with the purchase of this book.

187

The "before and after" business with Della's hair can be improvised with wigs or clever pinning to change the hairdo. The assumption is not that all of Della's hair is sold but only that much of its length is sacrificed for the sale.

This is definitely a period play and should be staged and costumed accordingly. The period is about 1915. Costumes for this era are not too hard to improvise. A tall stiff collar and dark coat for Jim and a long patterned dress for Della may be all that is necessary.

The details of stage action are covered on the right hand side of the pages of the scripts. Because synchronization with the narrative is important this format seemed to be the best way for the playwright to suggest the staging he envisioned. Your staging, of course, will vary from this according to your staging circumstances and the personalities and style of your actors. The director will find many opportunities to be creative with this style of adaptation.

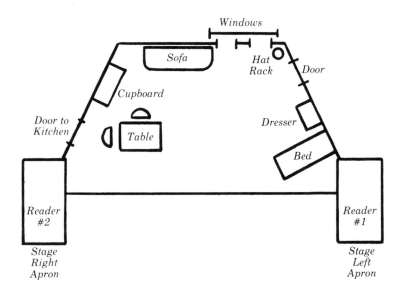

1   **READER 1:** *(From Stage Left apron)*
2   Every year new Christmas stories are written. In the past one
3   hundred years the total must be several thousand or more.
4   Most were forgotten after the first reading, others enjoyed a
5   brief flare of popularity for a few years and were lost to time.
6   But a very few really exceptional stories have endured and
7   very likely will continue to be with us for another hundred
8   years or more — the Santa Claus story; Rudolph, the red-nosed
9   reindeer; the legend about why the chimes rang and several
10   others. And, of course, the first story of Christmas — the story
11   of the Nativity — the beautiful story of how Christ came to be
12   born in a relatively small village in a faraway country almost
13   two thousand years ago. The story of how wise men came from
14   the East bearing valuable gifts for the baby Jesus destined to
15   be the Saviour. It was this part of the Nativity story that gave
16   us the wonderful custom of exchanging gifts at Christmas, a
17   custom we all enjoy because of the love giving and receiving
18   expresses. It is just this thought that inspired the imagination
19   of one of America's most popular short story writers at the
20   turn of the century. He wrote hundreds of stories, most of
21   which had surprise endings. He entertained people because
22   he knew people — he knew how they really were and how
23   they really acted and reacted. But even his many popular
24   stories are forgotten today, almost all of them except, perhaps,
25   one which seems to live on and on — "The Gift of the Magi."
26   From the title you might think it is a religious story but it's
27   not except for its message of true love. But decide for yourself.
28   May I present O. Henry's classic — "The Gift of the Magi."
29

30   **(NARRATION)**   **(STAGE ACTION)**

31   **READER 2:** *(Stage Right apron)*   *(Della is seated Stage Right at*
32   One dollar and eighty-seven   *a small table. She has just*
33   cents. That was all. And sixty   *emptied a ceramic vase of its*
34   cents of it was in pennies.   *contents of coins. Spreading*
35   Pennies saved one and two at a   *them out on the table, she*

1 time by bulldozing the grocer,	*proceeds to organize them into*
2 the vegetable man and the	*countable groups and she*
3 butcher until one's cheeks	*writes down the total. Then she*
4 burned with the silent	*throws down her pencil in*
5 imputation of parsimony that	*frustration.)*
6 such close dealing implied.	
7 Three times Della counted it.	
8 One dollar and eighty-seven	
9 cents. And the next day would	
10 be Christmas.	
11 There was clearly nothing to do	*(Della leaves table, walks in a*
12 but flop down on the shabby	*tight circle, expressing her*
13 little couch and howl. So Della	*frustration, then she throws*
14 did it, which instigates the	*herself down on a sofa at*
15 moral reflection that life is made	*Center Stage to cry and sob.)*
16 up of sobs, sniffles and smiles,	
17 with sniffles predominating.	
18	
19 **READER 1:** *(Stage Left)*	
20 In the vestibule below was a	*(Della ends her outburst but*
21 letter box into which no letter	*continues to lie face down on*
22 would go, and an electric button	*the sofa.)*
23 from which no mortal finger	
24 could coax a ring. Also	
25 appertaining thereunto was a	
26 card bearing the name "Mr.	
27 James Dillingham Young." The	
28 "Dillingham" had been flung to	
29 the breeze during a former	
30 period of prosperity when its	
31 possessor was being paid thirty	
32 dollars per week. Now when the	
33 income was shrunk to twenty	
34 dollars the letters of	
35 "Dillingham" looked blurred, as	

1 though they were thinking
2 seriously of contracting to a
3 modest and unassuming "D."
4 But whenever Mr. James
5 Dillingham Young came home
6 and reached his flat above he
7 was called "Jim" and warmly
8 hugged by Mrs. James
9 Dillingham Young, already
10 introduced to you as Della.
11
12   READER 2:
13 Della finished her cry and
14 attended to her cheeks with the
15 powder rag. She stood at the
16 window and looked out dully at
17 a gray cat walking a gray fence
18 in a gray backyard. Tomorrow
19 would be Christmas Day, and
20 she had only one dollar and
21 eighty-seven cents with which
22 to buy Jim a present. She had
23 been saving every penny she
24 could for months with this
25 result. Twenty dollars a week
26 doesn't go far. Expenses had
27 been greater than she
28 calculated. They always are.
29 Only one dollar and eighty-
30 seven cents to buy a present for
31 Jim. Her Jim. Many a happy
32 hour she had spent planning
33 something nice for him.
34 Something fine and rare and
35 sterling — something just a

(Della arises from the sofa wiping away the remaining moisture from her eyes and cheeks. She pushes her hair back into place, walks to the Upstage window, peeks out briefly, then begins to pace the room. She stops and looks at the small collection of coins on the table. She lifts a cardboard-mounted photo of him from a side table, paces and then returns it. She remains deeply preoccupied with her thoughts.)

1 little bit near to being worthy of
2 the honour of being Jim's wife.
3
4 There was pier glass between
5 the windows of the room.
6 Perhaps you have seen a pier
7 glass in an eight dollar flat. A
8 very thin and very agile person
9 may, by observing the reflection
10 in a rapid sequence of
11 longitudinal strips, obtain a
12 fairly accurate conception of
13 oneself's looks. Della, being
14 slender, had mastered the art.
15 Suddenly she whirled from the
16 window to find her hand mirror.
17 Her eyes were shining
18 brilliantly, but her face had lost
19 its color within twenty seconds.
20 Rapidly she pulled down her
21 hair and let it fall to its full
22 length.
23
24   **READER 1:**
25 Now, there were two possessions
26 of the James Dillingham Young's
27 in which they both took a
28 mighty pride. One was Jim's
29 gold watch that had been his
30 father's and his grandfather's.
31 The other was Della's hair. Had
32 the Queen of Sheba lived in a
33 flat across the airshaft, Della
34 would have let her hair hang out
35 the window some day to dry just

(Della, who had returned to look forlornly out the window, suddenly gets a flash idea. She whirls and steps across the room to the dresser and she takes up her hand mirror and a comb as she crosses to the table. She loosens her hair and it falls down along her back. Slowly she combs out the long strands of her hair as she studies her reflection in the hand mirror. Then she puts the hand mirror and comb down on the table and whirls again to look at her full image in the pier glass strips.)

1 to depreciate Her Majesty's
2 jewels and gifts. Had King
3 Solomon been the janitor, with
4 all his treasures piled up in the
5 basement, Jim would have
6 pulled out his watch every time
7 he passed, just to see him pluck
8 at his beard with envy.
9
10 **READER 2:**
11 **So now Della's beautiful hair fell**   *(In sequence with the narration*
12 **about her, rippling and shining**   *Della does up her hair after a*
13 **like a cascade of brownwaters.**   *pause or two for sad reflection.)*
14 **And then she did it up again**
15 **nervously and quickly. Once she**
16 **faltered for a moment and stood**
17 **still while a tear or two splashed**
18 **on the worn carpet. On went her**
19 **old jacket; on went her old**   *(Della resolutely slips on her*
20 **brown hat. With a whirl of skirts**   *old jacket and hat from a*
21 **and with the brilliant sparkle**   *clothes tree standing in the*
22 **still in her eyes, she fluttered out**   *corner. She whirls around and*
23 **the door and down the stairs to**   *disappears Off-stage. Lights*
24 **the street.**   *fade or curtain closes.)*
25
26   *(Spotlight appears on Stage*
27   *Right apron to the side of the*
28   *narrator. Beneath a sign*
29   *reading "Mme. Sofronie — Hair*
30   *Goods of All Kinds," a dowdy,*
31   *middle-age woman stands at a*
32   *table arranging the curls on a*
33   *wig resting on a wigstand*
34   *head. Della steps into the*
35   *scene.)*

1	**DELLA:**	
2	**Will you buy my hair?**	
3		
4	**MADAME:**	
5	**I buy hair. Take yer hat off and**	*(Della removes her hat and*
6	**let's have a sight at the looks of**	*releases her hair. Madame*
7	**it.** *(Pause)* **Twenty dollars, and**	*Sofronie walks around her,*
8	**that's it.**	*touching the hair in careful*
9		*appraisal.)*
10	**DELLA:**	*(Madame Sofronie is counting*
11	**Give it to me quick.**	*out the money from her cigar*
12		*box cache as the lights fade.)*
13		*(During the darkness the*
14		*actress portraying Della*
15		*quickly gathers up her hair*
16		*and pins it to appear short. She*
17		*may also put on a boy's cap.)*
18		
19	**MUSIC:**	
20	Busy music bridges the transition	
21	and continues under Reader 2's	
22	narration.	
23		
24		
25	**READER 2:**	
26	**And the next two hours tripped**	*(Moving spotlights criss-cross*
27	**by on rosy wings. She was**	*as Della is seen pantomiming*
28	**ransacking the stores for Jim's**	*the actions of a frenzied*
29	**present.**	*shopper moving from shop to*
30		*shop across the entire darkened*
31		*stage area or in front of closed*
32		*curtain.)*
33	**She found it at last. It surely had**	*(Spotlights stop moving as*
34	**been made for Jim and no one**	*Della stops at an imaginary*
35	**else. There was no other like it in**	*store counter Downstage*

1 any of the stores, and she had	*Center. She pantomimes*
2 turned all of them inside out. It	*looking at a fob chain which*
3 was a platinum fob chain simple	*she studies carefully, holding*
4 and chaste in design, properly	*it up to the light. Then she*
5 proclaiming its value by	*pantomimes Jim's action as if*
6 substance alone and not by flashy	*the fob were attached to his*
7 ornamentation — as all good	*watch and he was taking it*
8 things should do. It was even	*from his pocket to see the time.)*
9 worthy of The Watch. As soon as	
10 she saw it she knew it must be	
11 Jim's. It was like him. Quietness	
12 and value — the description	
13 applied to both.	
14 Twenty-one dollars they took	*(She pantomimes paying the*
15 from her for it and she hurried	*store clerk and receiving her*
16 home with the eighty-seven cents.	*change.)*
17	
18 **READER 1:**	
19 When Della reached home her	*(Della steps back Upstage as*
20 intoxication of joy gave way to	*lights again reveal the set or*
21 prudence and reason. She got	*the curtain opens. She removes*
22 out her curling irons, lighted the	*the boy's cap [if she's wearing*
23 gas and went to work repairing	*one] and goes to corner taking*
24 the ravages made by generosity	*up curling irons. She goes*
25 added to love which is always a	*through the motions of curling*
26 tremendous task, dear friends	*her hair into short, tight curls.)*
27 — a mammoth task. Within forty	
28 minutes her head was covered	
29 with tiny, close-lying curls that	
30 made her look wonderfully like	
31 a truant schoolboy.	
32	
33 **READER 2:**	
34 She looked at her reflection in	*(She takes up a hand mirror*
35 the mirror long, carefully and	*and studies her new hair style*

1   **critically and thought, "If Jim**   *from all angles.)*
2   **doesn't kill me before he takes**
3   **a second look, he'll say I look**
4   **like a Coney Island chorus girl.**
5   **But what could I do — what**   *(Lights fade down briefly and*
6   **could I do with a dollar and**   *up again slowly to indicate a*
7   **eighty-seven cents?"**   *passage of time.)*
8
9   **READER 1:**
10   **At seven o'clock the coffee was**   *(Della is seen looking out the*
11   **made and the frying pan was on**   *window. She turns, goes to the*
12   **the back of the stove. Jim was**   *table and sits on its corner*
13   **never late. Della doubled the fob**   *facing the door. She waits*
14   **chain in her hand and sat on the**   *expectantly.)*
15   **corner of the table near the door**
16   **he always entered. Then she**   *(She begins to squirm a little.*
17   **heard his step on the stair down**   *She quickly takes another peek*
18   **on the first flight and she turned**   *at her reflection in the hand*
19   **white for just a moment. She had**   *mirror, puts it down, then*
20   **a habit of saying little silent**   *resolutely faces the door.)*
21   **prayers about the simplest**
22   **everyday things, and now she**
23   **whispered to herself, "Please**
24   **God, make him think I am still**
25   **pretty."**
26
27   **READER 2:**
28   **The door opened and Jim**   *(Jim steps in, takes three steps,*
29   **stepped in. He looked thin and**   *sees Della and stops.)*
30   **very serious. Poor fellow, he was**
31   **only twenty-two — and to be**
32   **burdened with a wife. He**
33   **needed a new overcoat and he**
34   **was without gloves.**
35

1   **READER 1:**

2   **He stood as immovable as a**   *(Slowly without moving from*

3   **setter at the scent of quail. His**   *his place, without moving his*

4   **eyes were fixed upon Della and**   *head, he removes his overcoat*

5   **there was an expression in them**   *and lets it slide to the floor at*

6   **that she could not read, and it**   *his feet. His eyes are still fixed*

7   **terrified her.**   *on Della.)*

8   **It was not anger, nor surprise,**   *(Della smiles at him but she's*

9   **nor disapproval, nor horror, nor**   *afraid to approach him.*

10   **any of the sentiments that she**   *Awkwardly, she waves her*

11   **had prepared for. He simply**   *hand at Jim to try to break his*

12   **stared at her fixedly with that**   *fixed gaze or get some kind of*

13   **peculiar expression on his face.**   *movement or response. There is*

14   **Della wriggled off the table and**   *none.)*

15   **went for him.**

16

17   **DELLA:**

18   **Jim, darling, don't look at me**   *(At length she goes to Jim,*

19   **that way. I had my hair cut off**   *takes his arm, and kisses his*

20   **and sold it because I couldn't**   *hand. She steps back a step and*

21   **have lived through Christmas**   *pivots so Jim can see her new*

22   **without giving you a present.**   *style. She touches it with her*

23   **It'll grow out again — you won't**   *hand.)*

24   **mind, will you? I just had to do**

25   **it. My hair grows awfully fast.**

26   **Say "Merry Christmas!" Jim,**

27   **and let's be happy. You don't**

28   **know what a nice — what a**

29   **beautiful, nice gift I've got for**

30   **you.**

31

32   **JIM:**   *(Jim steps up close to her and*

33   *(Slowly, incredulous)* **You've cut**   *looks dumbfounded at her new*

34   **off your hair.**   *hair style. Then he walks about*

35   *the room looking blindly at*

1	**DELLA:**
2	*(As brightly as possible)* **Cut it off**
3	**and sold it. Don't you like me**
4	**just as well anyhow? I'm still me**
5	**without my hair.**
6	
7	**JIM:**
8	**You say your hair is gone?**
9	
10	**DELLA:**
11	**You needn't look for it, it's sold.**
12	**It's sold and gone, Jim. It's**
13	**Christmas Eve, honey. Be good**
14	**to me, for it went for you. Maybe**
15	**the hairs of my head were**
16	**numbered but nobody could**
17	**ever count my love for you, Jim.**
18	
19	**READER 2:**
20	**Out of his trance Jim seemed**
21	**quickly to wake. He enfolded his**
22	**Della. For ten seconds let us**
23	**regard with discreet scrutiny**
24	**some inconsequential object so**
25	**as not to intrude on their**
26	**privacy. Eight dollars a week or**
27	**a million a year — what is the**
28	**difference? A mathematician or**
29	**a wit would give you the wrong**
30	**answer. The Magi brought**
31	**valuable gifts, but that was not**
32	**among them. This dark**
33	**assertion will be illuminated**
34	**later on.**
35	**Jim drew a package from his**

Right column stage directions:

Line 1–2: *things, shaking his head in disbelief.)*

 (Jim pulls himself together, turns to Della with open arms. She enters into them laying her head blissfully on his chest. He raises her chin and kisses her. Both embrace each other.)

 (Jim releases Della, reaches to

198

1 overcoat pocket and threw it on
2 the table.
3

the floor for his overcoat and
takes a package from the pocket
which he throws on the table.)

4 JIM:
5 Don't make any mistake about
6 me, Dell. I don't think there's
7 anything in the way of a haircut
8 or a shave or a shampoo that
9 could make me love my girl any
10 less. But if you'll unwrap that
11 package you may see why I
12 acted as I just did.
13

(Turning again to Della, he
holds her at arm's length at the
shoulders. When he finishes
his speech he turns her to the
present and releases her.)

14 READER 1:
15 White fingers and nimble tore at
16 the string and paper. And then
17 an ecstatic reaction of joy; and
18 then, alas! A quick feminine
19 change to tears and wails,
20 necessitating the immediate
21 employment of all the
22 comforting powers of the lord of
23 the flat.
24

(Della tears open the package.
She gasps for joy as she studies
its contents. Then slowly her
beautiful smile wrinkles into
an outburst of tears as she puts
the package back on the table,
and she rushes into Jim's arms
again for comfort.)

25 READER 2:
26 For there lay The Combs — the
27 set of combs, side-by-side, that
28 Della had worshipped for a long
29 time in the Broadway shop
30 window. Beautiful combs, pure
31 tortoise shell, with jeweled
32 rims — just the shade to wear in
33 the beautiful vanished hair.
34 They were expensive combs, she
35 knew, and her heart had simply

(She pulls him over to the table
as she takes up the combs from
the box and holds them up to
Jim with a smile trying to find
its way through the tears.)

1 craved and yearned over them
2 without the least hope of
3 possession. And now, they were
4 hers, but the tresses that should
5 have adorned the coveted
6 adornments were gone.
7
8 **DELLA:**
9 **My hair grows so fast, Jim!** *(She impulsively breaks away*
10 *(Pause)* **Oh, oh! You haven't seen** *from Jim holding the combs up*
11 **your present from me, Jim.** *to her remaining hair as she*
12 *looks at them in the hand*
13 *mirror. Then, suddenly she*
14 *puts down the mirror and*
15 *quickly finds her present for*
16 *Jim.)*
17 **Isn't it a dandy, Jim? I hunted** *(She holds up the watch fob for*
18 **all over town to find it. You'll** *Jim to admire. Then she*
19 **have to look at the time a** *gestures for Jim to give her his*
20 **hundred times a day now. Give** *watch.)*
21 **me your watch. I want to see**
22 **how it looks on it.**
23
24 **JIM:**
25 **Dell. You know what? I have a** *(Jim takes the fob and the*
26 **great idea.** *combs and carefully puts them*
27 *aside. Again he takes Della in*
28 **DELLA:** *his arms.)*
29 **What, Jim?**
30
31 **JIM:**
32 **Well, it's that we put our**
33 **Christmas presents away and**
34 **keep 'em a while. They're too**
35 **nice to use just now.** *(Pause)* **You**

1 see, Dell, I sold my watch to get	*(She looks up at him with*
2 the money to buy your combs.	*incredulity, smiles, then they*
3 And now suppose we get busy	*begin laughing together as they*
4 and get our dinner started.	*proceed to get things ready for*
5	*dinner. Several times they stop,*
6	*point at each other and begin*
7	*the pantomime of laughter.)*
8	*(Continue actions under the*
9	*final narration until Reader 1's*
10	*final words, during which they*
11	*embrace once more as lights*
12	*fade or curtain closes.)*

13

14

15 **READER 1:**

16 The Magi, as you know were wise men — wonderfully wise
17 men — who brought gifts to the Babe in the manger. They
18 invented the art of giving Christmas presents. Being wise,
19 their gifts were no doubt wise ones, possibly bearing the
20 privilege of exchange in case of duplication.

21

22 **READER 2:**

23 And here we have lamely related to you the uneventful
24 chronicle of two foolish young lovers in a flat who most
25 unwisely sacrificed for each other the greatest treasures of
26 their house. But in a last word to the wise of these days let it
27 be said that of all who give gifts these two were the wisest.
28 Of all who give and receive gifts, such as they are wisest.

29

30 **READER 1:**

31 Everywhere they are wisest. They are the Magi.

32

33

34

35

THE EYES OF EL CRISTO

by George P. McCallum

CAST OF CHARACTERS

NARRATOR: A friendly voice.

TIO JUAN: Speaks with a bit of Mexican accent.

PABLOCITO: Speaks as a young boy.

MAMA: Everything that is a Mexican mama.

OLD LADY: Weariness and loneliness in her delivery.

This is a story told by a Narrator with warm moments of dialog and pantomime added. No props are required. The performers may indicate the presence of both props and place by their actions.

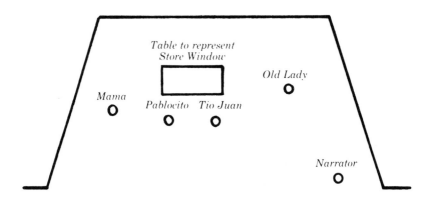

1   NARRATOR: Tio Juan, uncle to Pablocito, was lying on the
2   ground in Mama Conchita's back yard, leaning against
3   the Yucca tree. He had been there a long time, his hat
4   down over his eyes, dozing and being philosophical in
5   his thoughts. Occasionally there would be a puff of smoke
6   from his pipe, but he said nothing. Then, finally, he spoke:
7   TIO JUAN: It is good to be good.
8   NARRATOR: Pablocito, sitting near his uncle, said nothing,
9   but waited for Tio Juan to speak again. But to himself
10   he said:
11   PABLOCITO: It is nice to be here with Tio Juan, just sitting
12   in the sun, doing nothing, nothing at all.
13   NARRATOR: Once in a while Pablocito's uncle would puff
14   furiously on his pipe and emit huge clouds of smoke. That
15   was always a sign that he had reached some important
16   conclusion in his thoughts. Then he would reach up, take
17   his pipe from his mouth, push his hat back, and speak
18   what was on his mind — in as few words as possible, of
19   course. Just now there had been the cloud of smoke, and
20   Tio Juan removed his pipe, spat on the ground to his left,
21   and said, looking ahead and not at Pablocito:
22   TIO JUAN: Si, it is good to be good.
23   NARRATOR: Then he put his pipe back in his mouth, closed
24   his eyes, pulled his hat down, and began dozing again.
25   Pablocito wrinkled his small, otherwise unfurrowed
26   brow, as his uncle's philosophy gave him much food for
27   thought. He repeated to himself:
28   PABLOCITO: It is good to be good. I don't quite understand,
29   but if Tio Juan says so, it must be so. But when I am good,
30   I don't get anything for it. It is much more fun — and
31   much easier — to do as I please, just enjoy myself. When
32   I am good, no beautiful angel comes and says, "Fine work,
33   Pablocito. Here is a bagful of centavos." Nor when I am
34   bad does a devil come and carry me off to punish me.
35   *(Deciding)* No, Tio Juan is not right this time. It is not

1   necessarily good to be good. It is more fun just to take
2   life as it comes. It is not always good to be good.
3   **NARRATOR:**   Pulling his hat down over his eyes, Pablocito
4   assumed his uncle's position. He had hardly closed his
5   eyes when Mama Conchita came to the back door and
6   called:
7   **MAMA:**   Juan! Pablocito! Where are you? *(Looks around, and*
8   *then spots them under the Yucca tree.)* **Ah, just as I thought,**
9   you lazy ones! Come now! Get up!
10   **NARRATOR:**   Slowly the two rose, gradually aware of the din
11   of Mama Conchita's voice. Slowly they started toward
12   the house, Pablocito stumbling along a few feet behind
13   his uncle.
14   **MAMA:**   Fine ones you are! Half an hour it is now since I
15   asked you to go gather wood for me, and here you sit,
16   sleeping in the sun. How can you expect me to make
17   anything for you to eat if you do not bring me wood to
18   cook with? Now get along, both of you, and do not come
19   back until you have your arms full of wood! You hear me?
20   **NARRATOR:**   She turned without another word and went
21   into the house. Tio Juan blinked twice and looked at
22   Pablocito, who also blinked and stared at his uncle.
23   **TIO JUAN:**   Come Pablocito, I think we'd better do as your
24   mother says, and go after wood.
25   **PABLOCITO:**   Si, Tio Juan.
26   **TIO JUAN:**   She is right, your mother. If she has no wood,
27   she cannot cook anything for us to eat. Tomorrow is the
28   day of the Christmas fiesta, and she is cooking many
29   things for the celebration — the fiesta of La Navidad, si,
30   the birthday of the Christ child. It is a wonderful fiesta.
31   **PABLOCITO:**   Si, si! La Navidad, it's the best of all the fiestas!
32   **NARRATOR:**   The best of all the fiestas. Pablocito always looked
33   forward to it, counting the days and anticipating the good
34   times he would have. Always there were presents from
35   his mother, and even something from Tio Juan.

1   PABLOCITO: The presents! All the good things to eat! Dios
2   mio! Mother is the best cook in the world, and at
3   Christmas she makes better things than you can ever
4   think of! La Navidad is the most wonderful fiesta!
5   TIO JUAN: Let's cut across the village. There's a place on
6   the other side where we can get lots of wood. It isn't very
7   far. And we can look in the shop windows on the way
8   over, si?
9   PABLOCITO: Si!
10   NARRATOR: On their way through the village they stopped
11   at the many shops to gaze through the windows at the
12   good things inside. Some had all sorts of good things to
13   eat. Some had toys such as Pablocito had never seen
14   before. It was the shop window of Miguel Juarento that
15   caught their attention, however. Miguel's shop usually
16   was filled with all kinds of beautiful pictures, but now,
17   for the Christmas season, he had just one picture in his
18   display window, a portrait of Christ. Tio Juan and
19   Pablocito stopped and looked for a long while at the
20   picture. Christ was portrayed with a wreath of thorns
21   on his head, his eyes closed.
22   TIO JUAN: El Cristo. It is a beautiful picture of the Son of
23   the Blessed Virgin, verdad?
24   PABLOCITO: Ah, si. He looks so kind — and good.
25   TIO JUAN: It is one of the most famous portraits of Christ
26   ever painted.
27   PABLOCITO: Tio Juan, he looks sad, too. *(Seeing a card under*
28   *the picture)* What are the words under the picture?
29   TIO JUAN: *(Reading)* For those who are worthy and have the
30   faith, the Christ's eyes will open. *(Read in a halting fashion.)*
31   PABLOCITO: Those who are worthy?
32   TIO JUAN: It means those who are good and obey El Cristo's
33   teachings.
34   PABLOCITO: Oh. *(Stares at the picture.)* The eyes remain closed.
35   TIO JUAN: Come, Pablocito, we must hurry and get the wood,

1   or your mother will be very angry.

2   **PABLOCITO:** *(More to himself than to his uncle)* **The eyes did not**

3   **open. I must not be any good at all.**

4   **NARRATOR:** All of the rest of the way to the wood, and then

5   all of the way back home, his arms filled with sticks of

6   wood, Pablocito said nothing, thinking only of El Cristo

7   and the eyes which would not open for him. It made him

8   very sad to think they had remained closed. He would

9   give anything to have them open! Open for him!

10   *(Transition)* **The day of the fiesta La Navidad came.**

11   **MAMA:** Pablocito, eat your breakfast! Then go to the church

12   for mass. Don't forget to take your candle you saved your

13   pennies to buy, just for mass this morning.

14   **NARRATOR:** Of course he could have purchased a much

15   nicer one, but there had been those tempting candies in

16   Senora de Lara's sweet shop and the cakes in the bakery

17   which had cut down his small pile of pennies, so his

18   candle was not the majestic offering it might have been.

19   **MAMA:** Come right home after mass. We want to be all ready

20   for the fiesta when it begins.

21   **PABLOCITO:** When does it begin, Mama?

22   **MAMA:** This afternoon, right after we eat a bit. Tio Juan and

23   I went to early mass this morning so we can get

24   everything ready for fiesta, so remember — come right

25   home after mass.

26   **PABLOCITO:** Yes, Mama!

27   **NARRATOR:** The good Padre had a beautiful mass for the

28   birthday of El Cristo. Even to seven-year-old Pablocito,

29   it meant much: the story of the birth of our Saviour, the

30   three wise men, and the shepherds on the hill — the

31   Padre told the story simply and beautifully. Pablocito

32   thought it was the most beautiful story he had ever heard.

33   *(Transition)* **When mass was over, Pablocito started for**

34   **home, trotting along as fast as he could, because he lived**

35   **clear across the village, and it was getting late. As he**

1 dashed around the corner by Senora de Lara's sweet
2 shop, he almost ran into an old, old lady, loaded down
3 with bundles, trying to make her way along over the
4 rough, cobble-stoned road. Pablocito watched her. Every
5 few feet she would have to painfully bend down to pick
6 up one of the bundles which had dropped. His first
7 instinct was to help her.

8 PABLOCITO: But if I help her, I'll be late for the fiesta! I
9 don't want to miss the fun!

10 NARRATOR: Just then the old lady tripped on a protruding
11 stone and fell, her bundles flying every which way. There
12 was no alternative; Pablocito could do nothing but hurry
13 to her assistance.

14 OLD LADY: *(Moaning)* Ay! These packages have caused me
15 more trouble than they are worth.

16 PABLOCITO: *(Helping her to her feet)* Did you hurt yourself?

17 OLD LADY: No, no. I'm all right. *(Winces as bears down on left*
18 *foot.)* Maybe I did hurt my foot a little.

19 PABLOCITO: Let me pick up your bundles for you . . . and
20 help you to your home.

21 OLD LADY: Gracias a Dios. It is only a step to my house.
22 See, the little one between those two big ones, just over
23 there.

24 NARRATOR: She pointed down the street to a tiny house
25 squeezed in between two larger ones. In a few minutes
26 they were there and in the house, and the little old lady,
27 who told him her name was Senora Condora, was able
28 to rest her foot which had been turned but not badly
29 sprained.

30 OLD LADY: I'll be all right now.

31 PABLOCITO: *(Getting up to leave)* I hope so. I must go now, as
32 this afternoon . . .

33 OLD LADY: *(Interrupting)* Oh, please don't go. It's so nice to
34 have someone here to talk to. You see, I live here all by
35 myself, and sometimes I get so very lonely.

1   PABLOCITO: Well, all right — but just for a little while.

2   NARRATOR: He sat down again. Already the fiesta was

3   beginning, and he would miss part of it, but that was all

4   right. It was much better for him to be helping Senora

5   Condora, this little old lady who seemed to appreciate it

6   so much. *(Transition)* By the time Pablocito was able to

7   leave, the fiesta was nearly over. He had tried to get away

8   several times, but each time she had asked him to stay

9   just a little longer.

10   OLD LADY: Just a little longer. I'll make us some chocolate

11   — and I have some bizcochos we can share. Today is La

12   Navidad, and I am too old and tired to go — and now,

13   with my ankle. Please stay with me a little longer. It is

14   so good to have someone to talk to.

15   NARRATOR: Finally, Pablocito was able to leave. In a way

16   he was glad he had been able to help her, but the fiesta!

17   He had been looking forward to it for so long, and now

18   he would miss it all. He walked slowly down the street.

19   Now he would have to wait a whole year before the fiesta

20   of La Navidad. A whole year! At the window of Miguel

21   Juarento's shop, he stopped. In the window was the

22   wonderful picture of El Cristo.

23   PABLOCITO: El Cristo who would not open his eyes for me.

24   *(Face lights up.)* Si, it's true! The eyes are open. El Cristo

25   is looking at me — at me! Si, it's true, Tio Juan, it is good

26   to be good!

27   NARRATOR: All his troubles were forgotten — the fiesta he

28   had missed, his lost afternoon, everything!

29   PABLOCITO: For those who are worthy and have the faith,

30   the Christ's eyes will open.

31   NARRATOR: So it was true. He had been rewarded. The eyes

32   which opened only for the worthy, had opened for him!

33   What did he care for fiestas or anything else now? The

34   happiness which filled his very being as he again started

35   down the street toward home could not be equalled.

1   There was nothing like it!

2   PABLOCITO: Si, Tio Juan spoke the truth, just as he always

3   does; it is good to be good!

4

5

6

7

8

9

10

11

12

13

14

15

16

17

18

19

20

21

22

23

24

25

26

27

28

29

30

31

32

33

34

35

Folklore

ONE EYE, TWO EYES, AND THREE EYES*

From Grimm's Household Fairy Tales
Adapted for Readers Theatre by Melvin R. White, Ph. D.

CAST OF CHARACTERS

STORYTELLER: An effective narrator, man or woman.

ONE EYE: The youngest of three sisters; she has only one eye. A spoiled child, not very nice.

TWO EYES: The middle one of the three sisters; she has two eyes like everyone else. An abused child, very sweet.

THREE EYES: The oldest of the three sisters; she has three eyes, one in the middle between the other two. A spoiled child, not at all nice.

WISE WOMAN: A fairy godmother type, but without the magic wand, etc.

MOTHER: Not at all a motherly mother; she hates Two Eyes.

KNIGHT: A handsome young man.

This is an easily staged play, as there is no setting per se, and no properties (with the possible exception of one old blanket). All that is needed are six chairs or boxes, arranged as in the diagram below, a tall stool for the Narrator (and a lectern if desired), a short stool in the area of the pasture, and a not-too-tall ladder to represent a tree. Chairs 1 through 4 face the audience; chairs 5 and 6 face away from the audience.

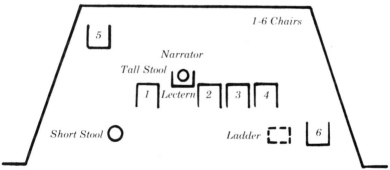

*Adapted for Readers Theatre by Melvin R. White. Amateur performance rights of this adaptation are granted with the purchase of this book.

All properties are imaginary: a table, food, apples, and all — including a goat. For the goat, it is suggested that the sound of a goat bleating be inserted after the line, "Billy goat, bleat!" each time it is used, as it adds fun for the young audience, although this suggestion is not included in the script. Use of the various properties is handled via pantomime.

Medieval fairy-tale costumes are not necessary, but should be provided if at all possible: Two Eyes in shabby, worn, and dirty attire, and the rest of the cast in more handsome dress. Make-up is necessary, but only to provide the necessary number of eyes for two of the three sisters. One requires a cover or patch of some kind to block out one of her eyes. A third eye must be painted in just above the nose of Three Eyes.

1   *(As the performance starts, the cast takes its designated seats,*
2   *relax their heads down slightly to "freeze," and the*
3   *STORYTELLER enters to start this Grimm fairy tale.)*
4 **STORYTELLER:** *(Takes her place atop a tall stool, slightly Up*
5   *Center.)* **Once upon a time there was a woman who had**
6   **three daughters.**
7 **ONE EYE:** *(Standing up from her seat #1)* **I am the youngest**
8   **daughter, and I am called Little One Eye because I have**
9   **only one eye, on one side of my forehead.**
10 **TWO EYES:** *(Standing up to introduce herself from seat #2)* **I am**
11   **the second daughter, and I am called Little Two Eyes.**
12   **This is because I have two eyes — just like everyone else.**
13 **THREE EYES:** *(Standing up, as her sisters did, from seat #3)* **I am**
14   **the oldest; I am called Little Three Eyes because I have**
15   **a third eye, right in the middle of my forehead between**
16   **my other two eyes.**
17 **MOTHER:** *(Standing up from seat #4)* **I am their mother. I love**
18   **Little One Eye and Little Three Eyes, but I can't stand**
19   **the sight of Little Two Eyes. She looks just like everyone**
20   **else.**
21 **ONE EYE:** *(To TWO EYES)* **You with your two eyes are no**
22   **better than anyone else.**
23 **THREE EYES:** **Yes. You do not belong to us. Go away. I can't**
24   **stand the sight of you! Like Mother said.**
25 **STORYTELLER:** **Her mother and sister knocked Little Two**
26   **Eyes about, hit her, made her dress in their old, worn-out**
27   **clothes, and even did not give her enough food to eat.**
28   **They made her go out into the hills to look after the goat.**
29   *(LITTLE TWO EYES crosses Down Right to the area of the field.*
30   *The others return to their seats and freeze, disappearing from*
31   *the scene. During the following narration, WISE WOMAN leaves*
32   *her seat #5 and crosses Down Right to TWO EYES.)*
33   **She was still very hungry because she had been**
34   **given only left-over scraps to eat. So she began to cry**
35   **and cry. But when she looked up she saw a woman standing**

1	beside her.
2	WISE WOMAN: Little Two Eyes, why are you crying?
3	TWO EYES: *(Sobbing)* Because I have two eyes, just like you,
4	like everyone else. So my mother and my sisters don't
5	like me. They make me do all the work, they don't give
6	me enough to eat, they make me wear dirty old clothes
7	like these. They even hit me and throw stones at me. I'm
8	so unhappy! *(Sobbing even more)*
9	WISE WOMAN: Little Two Eyes, listen to me. Now dry your
10	eyes and I'll tell you something so you won't ever be
11	hungry again.
12	TWO EYES: *(Drying her eyes)* Can you? Oh, tell me. What is it?
13	WISE WOMAN: All you have to do is say to your goat, "Billy
14	goat, bleat! I wish to eat."
15	TWO EYES: *(Puzzled)* "Billy goat, bleat! I wish to eat?"
16	WISE WOMAN: Yes. Then a table will appear before you,
17	filled with good things to eat. Then, when you have had
18	all you want, just say: "Billy goat, bleat! Clean it off neat."
19	And the table and the food will disappear. *(Returns to seat.)*
20	STORYTELLER: Then the wise woman went away, leaving
21	Little Two Eyes alone once again. Little Two Eyes
22	thought:
23	TWO EYES: I must do what she said right away, just to see if
24	it is true. Besides, I am so hungry, I can't wait! Billy goat,
25	bleat! I wish to eat. *(TWO EYES reacts in amazement to the*
26	*imaginary arrival of the table with its food piled high during*
27	*the following narration.)*
28	STORYTELLER: She had hardly finished saying the words
29	when a table appeared before her, piled high with hot
30	bread and butter, jam, a glass of milk, and all sorts of
31	good things to eat.
32	TWO EYES: Lord God, be our Guest at all times. Amen. *(TWO*
33	*EYES pantomimes taking a slice of bread and eating it, drinking*
34	*milk, etc.)* O, this is wonderful! Everything is so good —
35	even better than Mother makes for my sisters.

1 STORYTELLER: When she had eaten all she could, Two Eyes
2   thought a minute to remember what the wise woman had
3   told her to do and then said:
4 TWO EYES: Billy Goat, bleat! Clean it off neat. *(Sees all*
5   *disappear, then says:)* **This is an easy way of housekeeping.**
6   **Oh thank you, thank you, wise woman, whoever you are.**
7   *(Returns to her seat and freezes.)*
8 STORYTELLER: In the evening when Little Two Eyes
9   returned home with the goat, she found a small bowl of
10   crumbs and a bit of meat which her sisters had left for
11   her. But she did not touch it. She had already eaten all
12   she wanted of the good food on the table. The next day
13   she again went out with the goat, and when she returned
14   home, left the few crusts of bread left for her uneaten.
15   The first time and the second time this happened, the
16   sisters did not notice, but when the same thing happened
17   every day, they began to wonder. *(The MOTHER and*
18   *SISTERS stand.)*
19 MOTHER: Girls, have you noticed that Little Two Eyes does
20   not eat any of the food we leave for her?
21 ONE EYE: Yes, Mother.
22 THREE EYES: She never touches it anymore.
23 MOTHER: She always used to eat every last crumb we gave
24   her. I wonder —
25 ONE EYE: *(Interrupting)* She must be getting food somewhere
26   else.
27 MOTHER: Yes, but where?
28 THREE EYES: Mother, one of us should go with her to watch
29   over the goat. Then if someone brings her food, we'll see it.
30 MOTHER: That's a good idea. Tomorrow, Little One Eye, why
31   don't you go to the hills with Little Two Eyes when she
32   takes out the goat to graze.
33 ONE EYE: All right, Mother, I'll go — and I'll watch and see
34   what happens. *(MOTHER and THREE EYES return to their*
35   *seats as ONE EYE and TWO EYES cross Down Right to the*

1   *field area.)*

2   ONE EYE: I'm going with you today to help you watch over

3   the goat. We don't think you are taking proper care of

4   him, finding him good pasture.

5   STORYTELLER: But Little Two Eyes saw what Little One

6   Eye had in her mind, so after they found tall grass for

7   the goat, she said to her sister:

8   TWO EYES: Let's sit over here, Little One Eye. We don't need

9   to stand watching the goat.

10   ONE EYE: Is this all you do — just sit around and let the

11   goat eat?

12   TWO EYES: No, sometimes I sing to help pass the time. Do

13   you remember when we were babies? Mother used to

14   sing this lullaby to us. *(TWO EYES sings a lullaby, continues*

15   *to sing as she watches her sister to see for sure that she is sleeping.)*

16   Are you awake, Little One Eye? Are you asleep, Little

17   One Eye? *(Pause)* Little One Eye? Little One Eye? Yes,

18   she's asleep, so I think it is safe for me to eat now. Billy

19   goat, bleat! I wish to eat. *(Again, pantomime of table and*

20   *food)* Oh, good! Hot bread and jam and milk again — and

21   some meat, too! Thank you again, wise woman, wherever

22   you are.

23   STORYTELLER: So, once again, while Little One Eye was

24   sound asleep, Little Two Eyes almost cleaned the table

25   of the very best food imaginable, and when she was

26   satisfied, she said — oh, so quietly so she'd not awaken

27   her sister:

28   TWO EYES: Billy goat, bleat! Clean it off neat. *(Turning to her*

29   *sleeping sister)* Little One Eye, wake up. It is time to go

30   home. What a goat watcher you are, sleeping away the

31   day! He'd have run all over the world if I had not stayed

32   awake. Come, it's time to go home. *(The two return to their*

33   *seats where MOTHER and THREE EYES stand to meet ONE*

34   *EYE as TWO EYES seats herself and freezes.)*

35   MOTHER: Well, what happened? Who gave your sister food?

1   ONE EYE: Uh ... I didn't see anyone.

2   THREE EYES: What do you mean, you didn't see anyone?

3   Did she get something to eat?

4   MOTHER: Little One Eye, what is it?

5   ONE EYE: I'm sorry, Mother, but I fell asleep out there, so I

6   don't know whether someone brought Little Two Eyes

7   food or not. I'm sorry, Mother.

8   THREE EYES: Honestly, Little One Eye! Falling asleep, not

9   watching. Tomorrow, I'll go.

10   MOTHER: Yes, Little Three Eyes. You go with her tomorrow

11   — see if she eats, where she gets food. She never touches

12   anything we leave for her, and she must eat something,

13   somewhere. But where does she get it? You go tomorrow.

14   THREE EYES: Yes, Mother.

15   MOTHER: And don't fall asleep. Stay awake, watch her every

16   minute.

17   THREE EYES: Yes, Mother, I will. I'll not fall asleep.

18   STORYTELLER: So the next morning Little Three Eyes

19   joined Little Two Eyes as she led Billy goat out to pasture,

20   saying she would help her find a field with tall green

21   grass. *(The two stand and cross Down Right to the field area.)*

22   But Little Two Eyes knew that her sister had been sent

23   along to watch her, so after they found the tall grass for

24   the goat, she said:

25   TWO EYES: This looks like a good spot, lots of green grass.

26   Let's sit down here and rest a while and let Billy eat.

27   *(TWO EYES sits on a mound.)*

28   THREE EYES: *(Disagreeably)* Yes, I'm tired. Why did you bring

29   me so far, way up here on the hill? *(Sits near TWO EYES.)*

30   TWO EYES: Because this is where the best grass is.

31   THREE EYES: Now what do we do? Just sit here?

32   TWO EYES: Just about ... But we have to watch that Billy

33   does not move too far away. I usually sing in order to

34   pass the time. Shall I sing to you?

35   THREE EYES: I don't care. Oh, all right, sing if you want to.

1   *(TWO EYES sings a lullaby, watching to see if her sister is*
2   *falling asleep. When THREE EYES starts to doze, she changes*
3   *from the lullaby to:)*
4   **TWO EYES:** *(Still singing)*
5   **Three Eyes, are you awake?**
6   **Two Eyes, are you asleep?**
7   **STORYTELLER:**   **Little Two Eyes was thoughtless, made a**
8   **mistake. She meant to sing, "Three Eyes, are you asleep?"**
9   **but instead she had sung, "Two Eyes." So Three Eyes**
10   **closed two of her eyes but the third one did not go to**
11   **sleep, for that one was not included in the song. So Little**
12   **Three Eyes only pretended to go to sleep, and saw**
13   **everything her sister did. As soon as Little Two Eyes**
14   **thought she was asleep, she said her rhyme: "Billy goat,**
15   **bleat! I wish to eat."**
16   **As always, the little table appeared, loaded down**
17   **with lots of bread and butter and jam and meat and milk.**
18   **Little Three Eyes was amazed as she saw her sister eating**
19   **this feast — but she was careful not to let her sister see**
20   **that she was watching. So Little Two Eyes ate and ate**
21   **and ate until she simply could eat no more, and then**
22   **recited her verse once again:**
23   **TWO EYES:**   **Billy goat, bleat! Clean it off neat. Oh, that was**
24   **good — and I am so full. Now I'll wake up Little Three**
25   **Eyes, and we can go home.** *(Giggles at the thought.)* **I think**
26   **both Billy goat and I have had plenty to eat.** *(Goes to her*
27   *sister and shakes her a little.)* **Sister! Little Three Eyes, wake**
28   **up! It's time to go home. What a helper you are, sleeping**
29   **all the time.**
30   **THREE EYES:** *(Pretending)* **I'm sorry. I guess I was just too**
31   **tired from walking way up here.**
32   **TWO EYES:**   **That's all right, but now it's time to take Billy**
33   **home. Come on.** *(Two two girls return to their chairs. TWO*
34   *EYES freezes in hers. ONE EYE and MOTHER stand to greet*
35   *THREE EYES.)*

1 MOTHER: Well, what happened? Tell us! What did you see?

2 ONE EYE: Or did you fall asleep like I did?

3 THREE EYES: I know why she never eats here at home.
4   You'll never guess!

5 MOTHER: Don't be stupid! Tell us! What did she do? Did
6   someone come and bring her food?

7 THREE EYES: *(Enjoying herself)* Well, when we got to the
8   pasture, we sat down to rest. Then Two Eyes started to
9   sing — and I pretended to fall asleep.

10 MOTHER: Go on, go on!

11 THREE EYES: When she thought I was asleep, she said to the
12   goat, "Billy goat, bleat! I wish to eat."

13 ONE EYE: Yes? Yes?

14 MOTHER: And then?

15 THREE EYES: Then, a table appeared like magic, all covered
16   with food — much better than we have here at home —
17   and when she ate all she wanted, she said, "Billy goat,
18   bleat! Clear the table off neat," or something like that.

19 MOTHER: And?

20 THREE EYES: Everything disappeared.

21 ONE EYE: That's impossible! You fell asleep and dreamed it!

22 THREE EYES: I did not! I saw it all! She sang two of my eyes
23   asleep, but I kept my middle one awake. I did *not* dream it.

24 MOTHER: *(Angrily)* Does she think she can fare better than
25   we do? No! I'll kill the goat!

26 STORYTELLER: The mother in her anger seized a butcher-
27   knife, drove it into the heart of the goat, and he fell dead.
28   *(TWO EYES stands and runs Down Right.)* When Little Two
29   Eyes saw this, she ran out into the field, sat down on a
30   mound, and cried and cried. *(WISE WOMAN unfreezes to*
31   *cross Down Right to TWO EYES.)* Presently the wise woman
32   stood beside her once again.

33 WISE WOMAN: What's the matter, Little Two Eyes? Why are
34   you crying?

35 TWO EYES: How can I help it? My mother killed Billy goat.

1   **WISE WOMAN:**   Why did she do that?

2   **TWO EYES:**   She had my sister spy on me. But I thought Little
3   Three Eyes was asleep, so when I got hungry, I spoke to
4   the goat as you told me to do. Three Eyes was only
5   pretending to be asleep, and saw the table and the food
6   and everything — and now I'll be hungry again. *(Sobbing*
7   *away)*

8   **WISE WOMAN:**   Little Two Eyes, I'll give you some good
9   advice again. Just go home and ask your sisters for the
10   heart of the goat. Then bury it somewhere near the front
11   door of your house, and you will have good luck.

12   **TWO EYES:**   What will happen? Will I get food to eat again, or
13   what?

14   **WISE WOMAN:**   Just do what I told you to do, and then see
15   what happens. *(Returns to her seat and freezes.)*

16   **STORYTELLER:**   Little Two Eyes was very curious, so she
17   hurried home as fast as she could, hoping that her mean
18   sister would share the goat with her — at least give her
19   the heart to bury. *(TWO EYES crosses to center where she is*
20   *met by the two sisters.)*

21   **TWO EYES:**   Dear sisters, will you share some of the goat
22   meat with me?

23   **ONE EYE:**   With you? Why should we give you any of it? You
24   did not share your good food with us when you had the
25   goat to get it for you.

26   **THREE EYES:**   That's right, Little Two Eyes. No meat for you.

27   **TWO EYES:**   Please, just a little piece of my goat. Not a good
28   part — just the heart. *(Sisters laugh at her.)*

29   **ONE EYE:**   You want the heart? No one eats the heart of a
30   goat. Can you imagine, Little Three Eyes, she wants the
31   heart. *(Laugh heartily)* Shall we let her have it?

32   **THREE EYES:**   Why not? I don't want it. You don't want it, do
33   you?

34   **ONE EYE:**   I certainly don't. All right, if that's all you want,
35   you may have it. *(The three sisters return to their seats and freeze.)*

222

1   STORYTELLER: She took the heart, and that night when
2   everyone was asleep, she buried it near the front door
3   as the wise woman had told her. She waited and waited,
4   and nothing happened, so finally she gave up and went
5   to bed. The next morning she was awakened by her
6   sisters, yelling in the front yard. *(The two SISTERS cross*
7   *Down Left to the area of a short stepladder.)*
8   THREE EYES: Look! Look! A tree, a beautiful tree! Right in
9   our yard. Mother! Mother! *(MOTHER stands and comes out.)*
10   ONE EYE: It's all silver and gold. *(Calling, as her sister did)*
11   Mother come here! Wait till you see! *(To her SISTER)* Little
12   Three Eyes, it's an apple tree, but the apples are gold!
13   Gold!
14   THREE EYES: Yes, it's the most beautiful thing I've ever
15   seen — and it's ours. Oh, Mother, isn't it fabulous?!
16   MOTHER: Yes, fabulous. I wonder how it came to grow on
17   our lawn — but since it did, it is ours. But I wonder how
18   it came there.
19   STORYTELLER: Two Eyes alone knew how the tree had
20   come there, as it had grown from the earth right where
21   she had buried the heart of her goat. And she seemed to
22   know that the tree was *hers,* and not her sisters' — or her
23   mother's. But she heard her mother saying:
24   MOTHER: Climb up, Little One Eye, and pick some fruit from
25   the tree for us.
26   ONE EYE: All right, Mother. *(Climbing up the ladder, reaching*
27   *for apples)* Mother, the branches spring away from me; I
28   can't reach an apple, not a single one. *(Tries again and*
29   *again.)*
30   MOTHER: *(Irritated)* Oh, come down from that tree, and let
31   your sister, Little Three Eyes pick the fruit. You never
32   could do anything I asked you to do, silly girl. Little Three
33   Eyes, you climb the tree; you have three eyes, and can
34   see better than Little One Eye.
35   THREE EYES: Yes, Mother. Hurry up, come down. Let me

1   **up there; I'll get us some apples.** *(May push her sister.)*

2   **ONE EYE:**   **Wait a minute! Let me get down first! Stop pushing**

3   **me!**

4   **THREE EYES:** *(Climbs the ladder, tries to pick fruit, but can get*

5   *none, although she leans and grabs and grabs.)* **Oh, this tree**

6   **is horrible! I can't get a single apple. It's like the branches**

7   **jump away from me — like you said, sister.**

8   **MOTHER:** **You girls are spoiled. I should never ask you to do**

9   **anything. Here, let me do it.** *(THREE EYES and MOTHER*

10   *exchange places, and MOTHER tries, but to no avail. Finally,*

11   *LITTLE TWO EYES, who has been watching all of this, speaks*

12   *up.)*

13   **TWO EYES:** **Mother, would you like me to try? Perhaps I'll**

14   **succeed better.**

15   **THREE EYES:** **You with your two eyes! What can you do?**

16   **ONE EYE:** **Don't be stupid! If we can't pick the apples, you**

17   **can't either.**

18   **TWO EYES:** **Let me try — please.**

19   **MOTHER:** *(Getting down from the ladder)* **Oh, all right — try.**

20   *(TWO EYES climbs the ladder, picks fruit, and tosses one or*

21   *two apples down to each of the other three — all of this in*

22   *pantomime, of course, timing each toss and each catch perfectly.)*

23   **TWO EYES:** **Here, Mother, a nice big apple for you . . . and**

24   **for you, Little One Eye . . . and for you, Little Three Eyes.**

25   **And one for me, too.** *(All freeze in their positions near the tree*

26   *during the narration.)*

27   **STORYTELLER:** **When Little Two Eyes climbed the tree, the**

28   **branches seemed to bend toward her, and the apples**

29   **almost fell into her hands as she reached toward them.**

30   **The mother and sisters took them from her, but instead**

31   **of being grateful for them, and treating Little Two Eyes**

32   **better, they did not even thank her for the apples. In fact,**

33   **they were all so envious because she alone could pick**

34   **the fruit from the tree, they hated her even more, and**

35   **were even more mean and unkind to her.** *(Transition)*

1   One day they were all in the yard near the tree, and
2   Little Two Eyes was picking apples for them. Just as she
3   finished and came down from the ladder, they saw a
4   handsome young man, a knight, approaching. *(KNIGHT*
5   *rises from chair #6 Down Left.)*
6 THREE EYES: Quick, Two Eyes, get out of sight. Go into the
7   house where he can't see you.
8 ONE EYE: It's too late. Here, get under this old blanket, hide
9   yourself so we don't have to be ashamed of you, you and
10   your two eyes. *(It may add to the fun for younger audiences*
11   *to use a real blanket here. TWO EYES does as she is told,*
12   *huddling on her elbows and knees under the blanket.)*
13 KNIGHT: *(Who has approached and has been admiring the silver*
14   *and gold tree)* Tell me, to whom does this beautiful tree
15   belong? I've never seen one like it. Gold apples on it, but
16   with silver leaves. Beautiful!
17 THREE EYES: It's our tree.
18 ONE EYE: Yes, ours.
19 KNIGHT: May I have an apple? I'd like to taste one, as I've
20   never seen a more perfect apple.
21 ONE EYE: I'll get you one.
22 THREE EYES: No, let me. I have three eyes; I can see better
23   than you with your one eye.
24 STORYTELLER: The sisters each tried to pick an apple for
25   the knight, but as before, the branches drew away from
26   their hands, and they could not reach a single one. Yet
27   they insisted that the tree belonged to them. Finally the
28   knight said:
29 KNIGHT: It's rather strange that the tree should belong to
30   you, and yet neither of you can get me a single apple.
31   Very strange. *(TWO EYES wiggles under the blanket a bit,*
32   *and the KNIGHT notices the movement.)* What's this? What
33   do you have hidden under this old blanket?
34 ONE EYE: It's our sister, Little Two Eyes. We're ashamed of
35   her, so we hid her when we saw you coming.

1   KNIGHT: Little Two Eyes, come here.

2   TWO EYES: Yes, sir.

3   KNIGHT: Why, you are beautiful, very beautiful — like this

4   tree. Tell me, do you know who owns this tree?

5   TWO EYES: Yes, I do, and I'll show you. Let me get you an

6   **apple.** *(Climbing ladder to pick one, coming back down and*

7   *handing it to KNIGHT)* **You see, I can do that easily, for**

8   the tree belongs to me.

9   KNIGHT: Why did your sisters lie to me?

10   TWO EYES: Because they hate me. You see, I have two eyes

11   like everyone else.

12   KNIGHT: Like I have, too. What shall I give you for this apple,

13   Little Two Eyes?

14   TWO EYES: Oh, I need so much. I am often hungry and thirsty,

15   as my Mother gives me only leftover scraps. I have to do

16   all of the housework. I guess most of all I need someone

17   to take me away from here. Yes, then I could be happy.

18   KNIGHT: Come with me to my father's castle. There I shall

19   give you beautiful dresses — and you can eat and drink

20   as much as you like. *(They cross Down Left and freeze, standing*

21   *with their backs to the audience.)*

22   ONE EYE: Everything good happens to Little Two Eyes. I

23   hate her! *(Crying)*

24   THREE EYES: Don't cry, sister. We still have the wonderful

25   tree.

26   ONE EYE: But we can't get any of the fruit from it!

27   THREE EYES: Maybe not. But everyone who passes here

28   will stop to admire it. And who knows what good fortune

29   may come to us — just like it did to Little Two Eyes. *(Turn*

30   *away from the audience and freeze.)*

31   STORYTELLER: *(Leaving her stool to come Down Center to talk*

32   *with the audience very personally)* **But the next morning the**

33   tree had disappeared, and with it went their hopes. What

34   happened to the silver and gold tree? It followed Little

35   Two Eyes! Yes, when she looked out of her window in the

1 **castle the next morning, she saw to her great joy that**
2 **her lovely tree had followed her!** *(Transition)*
3 **The knight loved Little Two Eyes dearly, and when**
4 **she grew up they were married amid great rejoicing —**
5 **and of course, they lived happily ever after.** *(The cast may*
6 *unfreeze at this point, and come down to take a bow before*
7 *exiting.)*
8
9
10
11
12
13
14
15
16
17
18
19
20
21
22
23
24
25
26
27
28
29
30
31
32
33
34
35

URASHIMA TARO*

A Japanese folktale
Adapted for Readers Theatre by Melvin R. White, Ph.D.

CAST OF CHARACTERS

STORYTELLER: An effective narrator. Man or woman.

URASHIMA: A young boy, a fisherman; matures during the script, and becomes an old man at the end.

BOYS 1, 2 & 3: All bad boys.

TORTOISE: A man; described as having a deep but soft voice; stately and somewhat measured in speech.

PORTER (A Fish): A tall, good-looking man.

FISHERMAN 1: A man, middle-aged or older.

FISHERMAN 2: Man, any age.

NOTE: If more women than men are available, the boys, tortoise, and fisherman can be played by women.

To stage this charming folktale requires much imagination. The characters are all Japanese, but may be interpreted by readers of any nationality. It is best to keep the production as simple as possible, using the audience's imagination rather than attempting any sets, lights, costumes, make-up or properties.

It is suggested that the stage be divided into four playing areas:

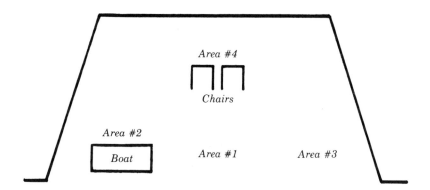

Place a short bench or two stools in Area #4 and, if desired, a platform or object shaped like a small boat in Area #2, although this is not necessary. Unlike the usual custom of keeping all cast members on stage throughout a show, if it is possible, let them enter from Offstage as needed in a scene and leave at the end of the scene in this production. For example, the three bad boys enter for their Area #1 scene, and leave the stage as it ends, taunting Urashima as they run off. These various entrances and exits should be timed as dictated by the storyteller's narration. The storyteller, however, remains on stage, perhaps sitting on a stool or chair when not narrating, but taking stage as needed.

As the performance starts, the storyteller enters, walks Down Center, and starts the story of "Urashima Taro," moving away from the center spot as the boys make their entrance, continuing to narrate Down Left.

1   STORYTELLER: A long, long time ago on the seacoast of
2   Japan, a young boy, a fisherman, by the name of Urashima
3   Taro, lived in a small village. Of all the fishermen in the
4   village, he was the best. He was also the most
5   kindhearted. If someone else didn't have a good catch,
6   he always shared his fish with him. But above all, he
7   could not stand to see any creature teased or tormented.
8   *(Transition. The seashore scene is played Down Center, Area*
9   *#1. The BAD BOYS and URASHIMA enter here, and cross to*
10   *Down Center.)*
11   One evening when Urashima was on his way home
12   to his father's cottage, he saw some bad boys teasing a
13   tortoise. One boy was throwing rocks at it, another was
14   hitting it, and a third was poking at the tortoise with a
15   stick. This made Urashima very angry.
16   URASHIMA: Stop that! You're mean! What's that poor
17   tortoise done to you? Don't you know that unless you put
18   it back in the sea it'll die? *(The following three lines may*
19   *overlap each other.)*
20   BOY 1: What of it? It's just a stupid tortoise.
21   BOY 2: Who cares if it dies?
22   BOY 3: We don't care.
23   URASHIMA: Will you give me your tortoise?
24   BOY 3: No.
25   BOY 1: Of course not. Why should we give it to you?
26   BOY 2: It's ours. We want it.
27   URASHIMA: Listen. If you won't give it to me, maybe you'll
28   sell it. Uh ... I'll give you my week's wages, all the money
29   I have. *(BOYS ad-lib negative responses.)* Think what you
30   can buy with this money, what fun you can have with it.
31   Much better things than this tortoise.
32   BOY 1: What do you think? Shall we sell?
33   BOY 2: Why not? Who wants a silly tortoise anyway!
34   BOY 3: Yes. Let's take the money and give Urashima the
35   tortoise.

1   STORYTELLER: So the three boys took Urashima's few
2   coins, and ran off, laughing and jumping, making fun of
3   Urashima for buying the tortoise from them. The fisher
4   boy was left alone with his purchase. He stroked its tan-
5   colored head . . .
6   URASHIMA: Poor old fellow. I wonder if it's true that you
7   tortoises live for a thousand years or more. Maybe you're
8   still young and have nine hundred and ninety years left
9   to live. Anyhow, I'm going to put you back into the sea.
10   And my advice to you, my friend, is not to let anyone
11   catch you again. *(Lifts the tortoise, puts it back into the water,*
12   *Down Center.)* **There you go. That's right, swim away from**
13   the shore, out where no one can catch you.
14   STORYTELLER: *(May take Center Stage here.)* **He watched it**
15   swim away, but it seemed to him that the tortoise kept
16   looking back at him every once in a while — and this
17   made him happy. *(URASHIMA crosses Down Right.)* **The**
18   next morning Urashima got up early, as he knew he had
19   to work extra hard to make up for the money he had
20   given the bad boys for their tortoise. It was a beautiful
21   morning, the sea was as smooth as glass, a deep blue,
22   reflecting the color of the cloudless sky. *(The ocean scene*
23   *is played Down Right, Area #2.)* **He left the shore with the**
24   other and older fishermen, but his slender boat soon left
25   those of the others far behind. Then, suddenly, he heard
26   a soft voice calling him.
27   TORTOISE: Urashima Taro! Urashima!
28   STORYTELLER: Urashima stood up in his boat, shaded his
29   eyes with his hand, but he couldn't see anyone.
30   TORTOISE: Urashima!
31   STORYTELLER: The voice came from the sea. Looking
32   down, he saw a tortoise swimming beside his boat . . . and
33   it looked just like the one he had befriended the day
34   before. He was a little frightened, but he decided to see
35   if he really was hearing the tortoise talk.

1	URASHIMA:	*(Politely)* Mr. Tortoise, did you call me just now?
2	TORTOISE:	Yes, I did. Don't you remember me? You saved
3		me from those bad boys yesterday, and I have come to
4		thank you.
5	URASHIMA:	That's kind of you; I was glad to help you. Would
6		you like to come into my boat and sun yourself? I know
7		you tortoises like to do that sometimes.
8	TORTOISE:	Thank you. But you'll have to help me in.
9	URASHIMA:	Yes, of course. Swim right up here, close to the
10		boat! There you are.
11	TORTOISE:	Thank you. *(Slight pause)* Tell me, have you ever
12		seen the palace of the King of the Sea?
13	URASHIMA:	*(Shaking his head "no")* We've all heard of that
14		palace, but none of us has ever seen it.
15	TORTOISE:	Would you like to? I can show you the way there.
16	URASHIMA:	Oh, yes! *(Then, remembering)* But I'm just a boy, a
17		human. I can swim, but not like you — and I can't swim
18		very far, either.
19	TORTOISE:	Swim? Why should you swim? I can carry you on
20		my back easily.
21	URASHIMA:	But I'm heavy, maybe heavier than you think.
22	TORTOISE:	Let me climb over the edge and slip into the
23		water. Now, try me. Perhaps I am larger than you think,
24		Urashima! *(Pause a moment as URASHIMA hesitates)* Come
25		on, get on my back!
26	URASHIMA:	All right. Here I come. Don't let me fall off! Why,
27		this is great! But don't swim so fast! And don't dive down!
28		If you do, I'll drown.
29	TORTOISE:	I'm going to dive. But don't worry. You won't be
30		drowned. Here we go, so hang on, don't fall off!
31	STORYTELLER:	*(Stands to narrate to the audience again.)* And
32		down, down, down the two of them went through the
33		clear blue water. To his surprise, Urashima could breathe
34		as well under the sea as he could above it. And it was
35		wonderful! Fishes of all sizes and all colors swam above

1	his head and all around him, and seaweed and anemones
2	grew like flowers on the bottom of the sea. Soon, in the
3	distance, Urashima saw a huge gate, and beyond the gate,
4	magnificent buildings all shining with blue and green
5	tiles. *(The gate scene is played Down Center in Area #1.)* **As**
6	**they approached the gate the tortoise swam faster and**
7	**faster, and in no time at all stopped at the gate which**
8	**was guarded by a porter, a large and very handsome fish.**
9	**He opened the gate for them.**
10	TORTOISE: This is the honorable Mr. Urashima Taro from
11	the land of Japan. He has come to visit the palace of the
12	King of the Sea.
13	PORTER: Mr. Taro, you are very welcome.
14	URASHIMA: What a beautiful place! Look at those flowers
15	... and the trees ... Why, it's just like the Emperor's
16	palace in Tokyo!
17	TORTOISE: But this is different. To the east it is always
18	spring, the fruit trees are always in bloom, and the spring
19	flowers. To the south it is perpetual summer, and in the
20	west it is autumn, the maples in ruddy gold and red and
21	yellow, and the chrysanthemums shine like fire.
22	URASHIMA: In the north, winter?
23	TORTOISE: That's right, winter. The fir trees are always
24	white with snow, and the streams under the red bridges
25	frozen solid.
26	URASHIMA: It all takes my breath away. *(LADY OTOHIME*
27	*enters, crossing to Down Center.)* **But who is that lady**
28	**approaching us? She's the most beautiful person I have**
29	**ever seen.**
30	TORTOISE: That's Lady Otohime, the daughter of the
31	**Dragon-King of the Sea.** *(URASHIMA falls to his knees, bows*
32	*his head to the ground.)*
33	OTOHIME: Welcome and greetings, Urashima Taro.
34	URASHIMA: *(Not raising his head)* **Most humbly do I thank**
35	**your honorable ladyship.**

233

1   **OTOHIME:** It is I who must thank you, Urashima Taro. You
2   will not understand why, perhaps, so listen while I tell
3   you. Once a year, as we immortals count years, my father,
4   the King of the Sea, wills that I take on the form of some
5   sea creature, and allow myself to be caught by some
6   mortal's net or snare. If that mortal be merciful, his
7   reward is to be a great one. But if he is cruel, his
8   punishment will be great. Urashima Taro, arise. *(He does*
9   *so.)* Fear nothing, my friend. I was that tortoise you
10   rescued from the bad boys who were making me suffer
11   so much pain. Come with me. We'll go to the garden where
12   it is always spring, enjoy rice and sake under the cherry
13   trees, and listen to the musicians play for us. *(They cross*
14   *Up Center to Area #4.)*
15   **STORYTELLER:** Urashima and Lady Otohime went into the
16   garden. Days passed, and Urashima found favor in the
17   eyes of the lady, and, with the approval of the King of
18   the Sea, before long they were married. Urashima was
19   very happy with his royal bride in the depths of the sea,
20   and for a long time he forgot about his father and mother
21   and his old home on the craggy coast of Japan. But, one
22   day, Otohime noticed that her husband was looking
23   thoughtful and sad.
24   **OTOHIME:** What is the matter, Urashima? You have
25   changed. You do not look happy.
26   **URASHIMA:** I find myself thinking of my father and mother,
27   of my home in Japan. They're old. I try not to worry about
28   them, but if I don't see them again soon, I may never see
29   them again. And they must cry for me, wonder what
30   happened to me. I'm sure they think I drowned at sea,
31   that I'll never return.
32   **OTOHIME:** Oh, Urashima, you do not love me! Are you no
33   longer happy with me? With life in the palace?
34   **URASHIMA:** But I do still love you. I'll always love you. But I
35   miss my father and mother so much. I can never be really

1   happy again until I see them. I'm ashamed that I forgot
2   them for so long. Let me go to them, even if it's just for
3   one day. Then I'll return to you.
4   OTOHIME: *(Weeping)* **If you wish to leave, I cannot keep you**
5   here. Go, if you must. But take with you this golden
6   lacquer casket. I have tied it securely, as it has in it
7   something very rare, very precious. Take it with you, my
8   husband, wherever you go. But remember. You must not
9   open it. If you do, evil will befall you.
10 URASHIMA: I promise. I'll never open the box you have
11   given me. Now I must go. *(Looking around)* I'll miss all of
12   this, the gardens and flowers — and most of all, I'll miss
13   you. But I'll return to you soon.
14 OTOHIME: Goodbye, Urashima. Remember always that I
15   love you. But go now since you must. You'll find a tortoise
16   at the gate to take you to your home once again.
17 STORYTELLER: The tortoise swam steadily, Urashima on
18   his back. At last the blue peaks of Japan appeared on the
19   horizon. Urshima's heart began to beat faster. He
20   recognized the coastline, the craggy shore. Soon he would
21   see his old home again, and kneel down before his father
22   and mother and beg their forgiveness. *(URASHIMA to*
23   *Down Center)* He was so impatient he jumped from the
24   tortoise's back and waded ashore. Coming toward him
25   was an old man he thought was his father. A moment
26   later he realized his mistake, and ran in the direction
27   where his father's house had stood. It was not there. The
28   little hut was gone, and a larger house was in its place.
29   A man came out of the house, and Urashima spoke to him
30   politely.
31 URASHIMA: Honorable Sir, can you tell me if the parents of
32   Urashima Taro still live here?
33 FISHERMAN 1:   Who are you, stranger?
34 URASHIMA: I'm Urashima Taro.
35 FISHERMAN 1:   *(Laughing)* You? Young Taro? Why, he's been

1   dead for more than three hundred years!

2   URASHIMA: No, no. I am he. I know I've been gone a long

3   time — I don't know how long — maybe a year or even

4   two, but I have come home because I want to see my

5   father and mother before they die.

6   FISHERMAN 1:   You're three hundred years too late. Why,

7   the Taro house was pulled down in my great-

8   grandfather's time, and even then it was many years since

9   that fisher-lad vanished at sea that fine morning. So

10   you're joking — or you're a ghost.

11   URASHIMA: *(Stamping his feet)* I am not a ghost! You know

12   ghosts have no feet! See, I have feet! I am as much alive

13   as you are. I am Urashima Taro!

14   FISHERMAN 1:   Urashima lived three hundred years ago. It's

15   all written in the town records in the temple. Why do you

16   keep on joking as you are?

17   STORYTELLER: Urashima turned slowly away, and walked

18   along the shore. At every step he saw changes which

19   proved the man was right, and that not one year, or two,

20   but three centuries had come and gone since he had left

21   home.

22   URASHIMA: Everyone I knew and loved in Japan has long

23   ago died. Now there is no reason for me to stay here. I

24   must go back at once to the beautiful land of the

25   immortals, and to my wife, my lovely Lady Otohime. But

26   how do I return? The tortoise who brought me here is

27   gone. I wonder, what about this casket she gave me? It's

28   all I have in this world — and I promised not to open it,

29   ever. But I'm sure she'll forgive me if I break my promise,

30   because I think it may show me how to return to my wife.

31   I'll untie the cords, see what is in the casket. Why, it's

32   empty! There's nothing in it. But ... but ... what's this?

33   A thin purple cloud is coming out of the box ...

34   STORYTELLER: The faint purple cloud gathered around

35   Urashima's head, stayed there for just a moment, and

1	then floated away across the sea. As he watched the cloud
2	disappear, the strong, dark-haired, well-built lad began
3	to change. His bright eyes grew dim, his hair turned to
4	white, his strong legs withered and bent. *(URASHIMA, as*
5	*an old man, lets out a cry of despair, falls upon his knees, and*
6	*then face down on the ground.)* **The next morning some**
7	**fishermen going down to the sea with their nets found**
8	**an old man lying dead beside a casket of golden lacquer.**
9	FISHERMAN 1: Look, the old man is dead.
10	FISHERMAN 2: I wonder what's in that casket.
11	FISHERMAN 1: Open it and see.
12	FISHERMAN 2: It's empty. There's nothing in it. By the way,
13	is this the man you told me spoke to you yesterday?
14	FISHERMAN 1: Oh, no, that was a strong young man who
15	tried to make me believe he was Urashima Taro.
16	
17	
18	
19	
20	
21	
22	
23	
24	
25	
26	
27	
28	
29	
30	
31	
32	
33	
34	
35	

THE GLASS IN THE FIELD

by James Thurber
Adapted for Readers Theatre by Joan Steen Silberschlag

CAST OF CHARACTERS

NARRATOR (Man): Storytelling style.

NARRATOR (Woman): Storytelling style.

GOLDFINCH: He's still hurting.

SEAGULL: A good friend.

EAGLE: Pompous.

HAWK: Accommodating.

SWALLOW: Cautious.

As with the style of all of Thurber's stories, this brief tale should also be staged with the utmost simplicity. The Narrators can speak from the stage apron (Stage Right). As the story opens, the four birds at the club should be facing Upstage. When the Goldfinch enters on cue from the Narrators the four birds turn and pantomime appropriate actions as the story unfolds.

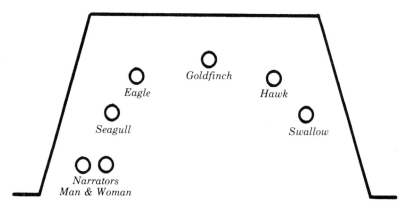

1   NARRATOR (Man):   A short time ago some builders, working
2   on a studio in Connecticut, left a huge square of plate
3   glass standing upright in a field one day.
4   NARRATOR (Woman):   A goldfinch flying swiftly across the
5   field struck the glass and was knocked cold. When he
6   came to, he hastened to his club, where an attendant
7   bandaged his head and gave him a stiff drink.
8   SEAGULL: What happened?
9   NARRATOR (Woman):   asked a seagull.
10   GOLDFINCH: I was flying across a meadow when all of
11   a sudden the air crystallized on me,
12   NARRATOR (Woman):   said the goldfinch.
13   NARRATOR (Man):   The seagull and a hawk and an eagle all
14   laughed heartily. *(Laughter)*
15   NARRATOR (Woman):   A swallow listened gravely.
16   EAGLE: For fifteen years, fledgling and bird, I've flown this
17   country,
18   NARRATOR (Woman):   said the eagle,
19   EAGLE: and I assure you there is no such thing as air
20   crystallizing. Water, yes; air, no.
21   HAWK: You were probably struck by a hailstone,
22   NARRATOR (Man):   the hawk told the goldfinch.
23   SEAGULL: Or he may have had a stroke,
24   NARRATOR (Man):   said the seagull.
25   SEAGULL: What do you think, swallow?
26   SWALLOW: Why, I — I think maybe the air crystallized on
27   him.
28   NARRATOR (Woman):   The large birds laughed so loudly
29   that the goldfinch became annoyed and bet them each a
30   dozen worms that they couldn't follow the course he had
31   flown across the field without encountering the hardened
32   atmosphere.
33   NARRATOR (Man):   They all took his bet. The swallow went
34   along to watch.
35   NARRATOR (Woman):   The seagull,

1   NARRATOR (Man):   the eagle,

2   NARRATOR (Woman):   and the hawk

3   NARRATOR (Man):   decided to fly together over the route

4   the goldfinch indicated.

5   SEAGULL, HAWK, and EAGLE: You come, too,

6   NARRATOR (Woman):   they said to the swallow.

7   SWALLOW: I — I — well, no — I don't think I will.

8   NARRATOR (Woman):   So the three large birds took off

9   together and they hit the glass together and they were

10   all knocked cold.

11   NARRATOR (Man):   Moral: He who hesitates is sometimes

12   saved.

13

14

15

16

17

18

19

20

21

22

23

24

25

26

27

28

29

30

31

32

33

34

35

Children's Classics

THE WIND IN THE WILLOWS*

By Kenneth Grahame
Adapted for Readers Theatre by Melvin R. White, Ph.D.

CAST OF CHARACTERS

THE RAT: Ratty, ". . . brown and small with whiskers. Grave and round, with neat ears and silky hair." A good-natured water rat, replete with a twinkle in his eye.

THE MOLE: Moley, black-furred, with a long snout. Has a "candid nature."

THE TOAD: Toady, ". . . a fat animal with short legs who is thoroughly good-hearted and affectionate," yet "headstrong and willful." "All conceit and boasting and vanity," "all self-praise and gross exaggeration."

THE BADGER: Taller and bigger than the small animals — "Nobody interferes with him." Shy ("Simply hates society"). Too large and serious to support a nickname; has a dry manner, ". . . has never been a very smart man."

STORYTELLER: An effective narrator, man or woman.

The Wind in the Willows may be produced very simply without any special theatrical costuming, settings, and such. However, it has been done with animal costumes, with masks, with cutouts of a caravan, a car, and various locales, and even with printed signs such as "Private. No Landing Allowed at Toad Hall."

A series of platforms of various heights establishes areas and allows for variety in composition. In one production, these were arranged with Platform 4 higher than the others to represent the gypsy caravan in this manner: *(See page 244 for staging diagram.)*

---

*Adapted for Readers Theatre by Melvin R. White. Amateur performance rights of this adaptation are granted with the purchase of this book.

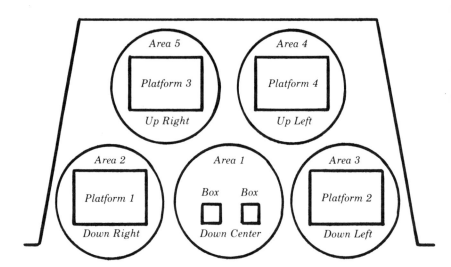

Production suggestions included in this adaptation follow the above stage arrangement. But in Readers Theatre, "theatre of the imagination," none of this is necessary. The actors assuming the characters of the various animals will suffice, making the audience, young or old, see the small creatures, envision the locales, and participate in the action.

1 **ACT I**

2

3 **SETTING:**   As the production starts, the RAT is sitting on a box or

4 mound of dirt Downstage Center, in Area 1, singing a little

5 song he has just made up. The MOLE is standing, back to

6 audience, on Platform 2 in Area 3, Down Left, with the

7 STORYTELLER Down Right, on Platform 1, also back to

8 audience. TOAD is seated above Platform 1, back to audience,

9 frozen.

10

11 RAT: *(Singing)* **"All along the backwater, through the rushes**

12 **tall,**

13 **Ducks are a-dabbling, up tails all!**

14 **Ducks' tails, drakes' tails, yellow feet a-quiver,**

15 **Yellow bills all out of sight, busy in the river!"**

16 MOLE: *(Unfreezing, crossing toward RAT)* **Ratty, if you please . . .**

17 RAT: **"Slushy green underneath where the roach swim —**

18 **Here we keep our larder, cool and full and dim."**

19 MOLE: *(Again trying to interrupt)* **Ratty, I want to . . .**

20 RAT: *(Ignoring him — almost)* **Every one for what he likes!**

21 **"We like to be heads down, tails up, dabbling free!"**

22 MOLE: *(More insistently)* **If you please, I want to ask you a**

23 **favor!**

24 RAT: *(Determined to finish his song)* **"High in the blue above,**

25 **swifts whirl and call —**

26 **We are down a-dabbling up tails all!"**

27 MOLE: *(Cautiously)* **I don't know that I think so very much of**

28 **that little song, Rat.**

29 RAT: *(Cheerfully)* **Nor don't the ducks neither. They say, "Why**

30 **can't fellows be allowed to do what they like, when they**

31 **like, and as they like, instead of other fellows sitting on**

32 **banks and watching them all the time and making**

33 **remarks, and poetry and things about them? What**

34 **nonsense it all is!" That's what the ducks say.**

35 MOLE: *(With great heartiness)* **So it is, so it is.**

1   **RAT:** *(Indignantly)* **No, it isn't!**

2   **MOLE:** *(Soothingly)* **Well then, it isn't, it isn't. But what I**

3   **wanted to ask you was, won't you take me to call on Mr.**

4   **Toad? I've heard so much about him, and I do so want to**

5   **make his acquaintance.**

6   **RAT:** *(Jumping to his feet)* **Why, certainly. We'll go up there to**

7   **Toad Hall at once. It's never the wrong time to call on**

8   **Toad. Early or late he's always the same fellow. Always**

9   **good-tempered, always glad to see you, always sorry**

10   **when you go.** *(They start toward Area 2, Down Right, as the*

11   *STORYTELLER, who has been listening and observing, moves*

12   *toward the Down Center position, and TOAD turns in toward*

13   *the audience but remains frozen.)*

14   **MOLE:**   **He must be a very nice animal.**

15   **RAT:**   **He is, indeed, the best of animals. So simple, so good-**

16   **natured, and so affectionate. Perhaps he's not very**

17   **clever — we can't all be geniuses; and it may be that he**

18   **is both boastful and conceited. But he has got some great**

19   **qualities, has Toady.**

20   **STORYTELLER:**   **Rounding a bend in the river, Mole and Rat**

21   **came in sight of a handsome, dignified old house of**

22   **mellowed red brick, with well-kept lawns reaching down**

23   **to the river's edge.**

24   **RAT:**   **There's Toad Hall, and that creek where the notice**

25   **board says, "Private. No Landing Allowed," leads to his**

26   **boathouse. The stables are over there. Toad is rather rich,**

27   **you know, and this is really one of the nicest houses in**

28   **these parts, though we never admit as much to Toad.**

29   **MOLE:**   **Toad does a lot of boating?**

30   **RAT:**   **I understand boating is played out. He's tired of it, and**

31   **done with it. I wonder what new fad he has taken up**

32   **now? Come along and let's look him up. We shall hear all**

33   **about it quite soon enough. Oh, there's Toady now.**

34   **TOAD:** *(Who has heard them and looked around, jumps up and*

35   *crosses Downstage on Platform 1 to greet them)* **Hooray! This**

1   **is splendid!** *(Shaking their paws, slapping them on the back,*
2   *ignoring the fact that he has not met MOLE)* **How kind of you!**
3   **I was just going to send a boat down the river for you,**
4   **Ratty, with strict orders that you were to be fetched up**
5   **here at once, whatever you were doing. I want you**
6   **badly — both of you. Now, what will you take? Come**
7   **inside and have something! You don't know how lucky**
8   **it is, your turning up just now!**
9   **RAT:** *(Sitting on the edge of the platform, where MOLE joins him)*
10   **Let's sit quiet a bit, Toady!**
11   **MOLE:** *(Trying to make conversation)* **Mr. Toad, you have a**
12   **delightful residence.**
13   **TOAD:** *(Boisterously)* **Finest house on the whole river — or**
14   **anywhere else, for that matter.** *(RAT and MOLE glance at each*
15   *other, and TOAD sees them. He laughs.)* **All right, Ratty. It's only**
16   **my way, you know. And it's not such a very bad house, is it?**
17   **You know you rather like it yourself.** *(Back to subject)* **Now,**
18   **look here. Let's be sensible. You are the very animals I**
19   **wanted. You've got to help me. It's most important!**
20   **RAT:** *(Innocently)* **It's about your rowing, I suppose. You're**
21   **getting on fairly well, though you splash a good bit still.**
22   **With a great deal of patience, and some more coaching,**
23   **you may —**
24   **TOAD:** *(In disgust, sits.)* **Oh, pooh! Boating! Silly boyish**
25   **amusement. I've given that up long ago. Sheer waste of**
26   **time, that's what it is. It makes me downright sorry to**
27   **see you fellows, who ought to know better, spending all**
28   **your energies in that aimless manner. No, I've discovered**
29   **the real thing, the only genuine occupation for a lifetime.**
30   **I propose to devote the remainder of mine to it, and can**
31   **only regret the wasted years that lie behind me,**
32   **squandered in trivialities.** *(Stands.)* **Come with me, dear**
33   **Ratty, and your amiable friend also, if he will be so very**
34   **good, just as far as the stable yard, and you shall see**
35   **what you shall see!** *(Leads them Upstage to Area 4, Up Left,*

1   *where the three group themselves below the platform.)*

2 **STORYTELLER:** *(Crosses Downstage to talk with the audience.)*

3   **Mr. Toad led the way to the stable yard, and there, they**

4   **saw a gypsy caravan, shining with newness, painted a**

5   **canary yellow picked out with green, and red wheels. Mr.**

6   **Toad expanded himself:**

7 **TOAD:** *(Crying out proudly)* **There you are! There's real life for**

8   **you, embodied in that little cart.** *(Indicates it on the*

9   *platform.)* **The open road, the dusty highway, the heath,**

10   **the common, the hedgerows, the rolling downs! Camps,**

11   **villages, towns, cities! Here today, up and off to**

12   **somewhere else tomorrow! Travel, change, interest,**

13   **excitement! The whole world before you, and a horizon**

14   **that's always changing! And mind, this is the very finest**

15   **cart of its sort that was ever built, without any exception.**

16   **Come inside and look at the arrangements.** *(Stepping up*

17   *on Platform 4)* **Planned 'em all myself, I did.** *(MOLE,*

18   *interested and excited, follows him; RAT snorts and stays where*

19   *he is. TOAD points everything out as he talks.)* **See, compact**

20   **and comfortable. Sleeping bunks ... a little table that**

21   **folds up against the wall, a cooking stove, lockers,**

22   **bookshelves —**

23 **MOLE:** **A birdcage with a bird in it!**

24 **TOAD:** **Yes, and pots, pans, jugs, kettles, all complete.**

25   *(Triumphantly)* **Look in this locker: biscuits, potted**

26   **lobster, sardines — everything you can possibly want.**

27   **Soda water here — 'baccy there — writing paper —**

28   **bacon, jam, cards and dominoes — well, you'll find that**

29   **nothing whatever has been forgotten** *(Stepping down from*

30   *platform with MOLE following)* **when we make our start this**

31   **afternoon.**

32 **RAT:** *(Slowly)* **I beg your pardon, but did I hear you say**

33   **something about "we" and "start" and "this afternoon"?**

34 **TOAD:** *(Imploringly)* **Now, you dear good old Ratty, don't**

35   **begin talking in that stiff and sniffy sort of way, because**

1   you know you've got to come. I can't possibly manage

2   without you, so please consider it settled, and don't

3   argue — it's the one thing I can't stand. You surely don't

4   mean to stick to your dull, fusty old river all your life,

5   and just live in a hole in a bank, and boat? I want to show

6   you the world! I'm going to make an animal of you, my

7   boy!

8 RAT: *(Doggedly)* I don't care, I'm not coming, and that's flat.

9   And I am going to stick to my old river, and live in a hole,

10   and boat, as I've always done. And what's more, Mole's

11   going to stick to me and do as I do, aren't you, Mole?

12 MOLE: *(Loyally)* Of course, I am. I'll always stick to you, Rat,

13   and what you say is to be — has got to be. *(Wistfully)* All

14   the same, it sounds as if it might have been — well, rather

15   fun, you know. *(TOAD has been watching them closely.)*

16 TOAD: *(Diplomatically)* Come along in and have some lunch,

17   and we'll talk it over. We needn't decide anything in a

18   hurry. Of course, I don't really care. I only want to give

19   pleasure to you fellows. "Live for others." That's my motto

20   in life. *(They turn, backs to audience, and freeze as the*

21   *STORYTELLER takes over.)*

22 STORYTELLER: During luncheon — which was excellent, of

23   course — Toad simply let himself go, painting the

24   prospects of the trip and the joys of the open road in

25   such glowing colors that Mole could hardly sit in his chair

26   for excitement. Somehow it soon seemed taken for

27   granted by all three that the trip was a settled thing.

28   After luncheon the now triumphant Toad led his

29   companions to the paddock to get the old grey horse

30   harnessed, and they set off, all talking at once. Late in

31   the evening, tired and happy and miles from home, they

32   drew up beside the road, turned the horse loose to graze,

33   and ate their simple supper sitting on the grass by the

34   side of the cart. *(The three unfreeze to sit on or near Platform*

35   *4, MOLE and RAT next to each other.)*

1   TOAD: Well, good night, you fellows! This is the real life for a
2   gentleman! Talk about your old river!
3   RAT: I don't talk about my river. You know I don't, Toad.
4   *(Pathetically)* **But I think about it. I think about it all the**
5   **time!** *(TOAD turns his back, curling up to sleep. MOLE gives*
6   *RAT's hand a squeeze and whispers:)*
7   MOLE: I'll do whatever you like, Ratty. Shall we run away
8   tomorrow morning, quite early — very early — and go
9   back to our dear old hole on the river?
10   RAT: *(Whispers back.)* No, no, we'll stick it out. Thanks awfully,
11   but I ought to stick by Toad till this trip is ended. It
12   wouldn't be safe for him to be left to himself. It won't
13   take very long. His fads never do. Good night!
14   MOLE: All right. Whatever you say. Good night, Rat. *(They,*
15   *too, curl up to sleep.)*
16   STORYTELLER: The end was, indeed, nearer than even Rat
17   suspected. The next day they had a pleasant ramble over
18   grassy downs and along narrow by-lanes. In the
19   afternoon, they came out on their first main road. There
20   disaster, fleet and unforeseen, sprang out on them. Far
21   behind them they heard a faint warning hum. Glancing
22   back, they saw a small cloud of dust, with a dark center
23   of energy, advancing on them at incredible speed. *(The*
24   *three pantomime this scene.)* **From out the dust a faint "poop-**
25   **poop"** *(Imitating an auto horn)* **wailed like an uneasy animal**
26   **in pain. Then, in an instant (as it seemed), it was upon**
27   **them!** *(The three throw themselves aside and to the ground,*
28   *violently.)* **The "poop-poop" rang with a brazen shout in**
29   **their ears. They had a moment's glimpse of the**
30   **magnificent motorcar, immense, with its pilot tense and**
31   **hugging the wheel, as it flung a cloud of dust that blinded**
32   **and enwrapped them utterly, and then dwindled to a**
33   **speck in the far distance. The horse, terrified, reared and**
34   **plunged. There was a heart-rending crash — and the**
35   **canary-colored cart, their pride and joy, lay on its side**

1   **in the ditch, an irredeemable wreck.** *(The three gather*
2   *themselves up, RAT and MOLE standing, but TOAD sits on the*
3   *front edge of Platform 4, staring into the distance, a placid,*
4   *satisfied expression on his face.)*
5   **RAT:** *(Jumping up and down with passion)* **You villains!** *(Shaking*
6   *his fists)* **You scoundrels! You highwaymen! You — you —**
7   **road hogs! I'll have the law on you! I'll report you! I'll**
8   **take you through all the courts! Villains! Road hogs!**
9   **TOAD:** **Poop-poop!**
10   **MOLE:** **Look at the cart! It's wrecked! Windows smashed . . .**
11   **axles bent . . . that wheel off . . . everything scattered all**
12   **over! Let's see if we can right the cart.**
13   **TOAD:** **Poop-poop!**
14   **RAT:** **Let me help you, Mole. Hi! Toad! Come and bear a hand,**
15   **can't you?**
16   **TOAD:** *(Still with a happy smile on his face, eyes fixed on the*
17   *distance)* **Poop-poop!**
18   **RAT:** *(Shaking him by the shoulder)* **Are you going to help us,**
19   **Toad?**
20   **TOAD:** **Glorious, stirring sight! The poetry of motion! The**
21   **real way to travel! The only way to travel. Poop-poop!**
22   **Here today — in next week tomorrow! Villages skipped,**
23   **towns and cities jumped — always somebody else's**
24   **horizons! Oh bliss! Oh poop-poop! Oh my! Oh my!**
25   **MOLE:** *(Shaking him by the other shoulder)* **Oh stop being an ass,**
26   **Toad.**
27   **TOAD:** *(Dreamily)* **And to think I never knew! All those**
28   **wasted years that lie behind me, I never knew, never**
29   **even dreamt! But now** *(Standing as he builds his excitement)*
30   **— but now that I know, now that I fully realize! Oh what**
31   **a flowery track lies spread before me, henceforth! What**
32   **dust clouds shall spring up behind me as I speed on my**
33   **reckless way! What carts I shall fling carelessly into the**
34   **ditch in the wake of my magnificent onset! Horrid little**
35   **carts — common carts — canary-colored carts! Poop-**

1   poop! Poop-poop!

2 MOLE: What are we to do with him?

3 RAT: *(Firmly)* **Nothing at all. Because there is really nothing**

4   **to be done. You see, I know him from of old. He is now**

5   **possessed. He's got a new craze, and it always takes him**

6   **that way, in its first stage.** *(TOAD does not even hear them.)*

7 MOLE: First stage?

8 RAT: Yes. **He'll continue like that for days now, like an**

9   **animal walking in a happy dream, quite useless for all**

10   **practical purposes. Never mind him. Let's see what can**

11   **be done about the cart.**

12 MOLE: I don't think it can ever travel again.

13 RAT: You're right. The axles are hopeless.

14 MOLE: That wheel is in pieces. And I don't think we can right

15   it anyway!

16 RAT: *(Grimly)* **Come on! It's five or six miles to the nearest**

17   **town, and we'll just have to walk it. The sooner we make**

18   **a start the better.**

19 MOLE: What about Toad? We can't leave him here, sitting

20   in the middle of the road all by himself, not in the state

21   he's in! It's not safe. Supposing another *thing* were to

22   come along?

23 RAT: **Oh bother Toad. I've done with him!** *(RAT and MOLE*

24   *cross toward Area 1, Down Center. TOAD sees them leaving,*

25   *and hurries after them.)*

26 MOLE: Here he comes, Rat.

27 RAT: *(Sharply)* **Now look here, Toad, as soon as we get to the**

28   **next town, you'll have to go straight to the police station,**

29   **and see if they know anything about that motorcar and**

30   **who it belongs to, and lodge a complaint against it.**

31 MOLE: And then you'll have to go to a blacksmith's or

32   wheelwright's and arrange for the cart to be fetched and

33   mended and put to rights. It'll take time, but it's not quite

34   a hopeless smash.

35 RAT: **Meanwhile, Mole and I will go to an inn and find**

1   comfortable rooms where we can stay till the cart's ready,

2   and till your nerves have recovered from their shock.

3   TOAD: *(Dreamily)* **Police station! Complaint! Me complain of**

4   **that beautiful, that heavenly vision that has been**

5   **vouchsafed me!**

6   RAT: *(Firmly)* **Yes!**

7   TOAD: **Mend the cart! I've done with carts forever. I never**

8   **want to see the cart, or hear of it again. Oh, Ratty! You**

9   **can't think how obliged I am to you for consenting to**

10   **come on this trip! I wouldn't have gone without you, and**

11   **then I might never have seen that — that swan, that**

12   **sunbeam, that thunderbolt! I might never have heard**

13   **that entrancing sound — poop-poop — or smelt that**

14   **bewitching smell! I owe it all to you, my best of friends!**

15   RAT: *(In despair, turning to MOLE)* **You see what it is? He's**

16   **quite hopeless. I give it up — when we get to the town,**

17   **we'll go to the railway station, and with luck we may pick**

18   **up a train there that'll get us back to River Bank tonight.**

19   **And if you ever catch me going a-pleasuring with this**

20   **provoking animal again!** *(Snorts)* **Let's go. Help me with**

21   **Toad!** *(The three move Upstage Center, dragging TOAD with*

22   *them, the two each holding one of TOAD's arms. They freeze,*

23   *backs to audience, Up Center.)*

24   STORYTELLER: **Eventually, a slow train having landed**

25   **them at a station not too far from Toad Hall, Mole and**

26   **Rat deposited Toad at his door.** *(MOLE and RAT plunk*

27   *TOAD down, his back to audience, on Platform 1, Down Right,*

28   *and cross to Platform 2, Down Left, seating themselves facing*

29   *front.)* **Then they walked along the river home, and at a**

30   **very late hour sat down to supper in their own cozy**

31   **riverside parlor, to the Rat's great joy and contentment.**

32   *(STORYTELLER moves to a Down Right position as MOLE*

33   *crosses to Down Center to sit on a box.)* **The following evening**

34   **Mole, who had risen late and taken things very easy all**

35   **day, was sitting on the bank fishing** *(Does so in pantomime)*

1   **when Rat** *(Crosses from Down Left to MOLE, Down Center)*,
2   **who had been looking up his friends and gossiping, came**
3   **strolling along to find him.**
4 **RAT:** **Heard the news?**
5 **MOLE:** **What news?**
6 **RAT:** **There's nothing else being talked about, all along the**
7   **river bank. Toad went up to town by an early train this**
8   **morning. He has ordered a large and very expensive**
9   **motorcar!** *(If a curtain is being used, it can be drawn at this*
10   *time to mark the end of Act I, "The Open Road." If not, MOLE,*
11   *RAT, and TOAD may turn, backs to audience, freeze for a*
12   *moment, and then exit, followed by STORYTELLER. If desired,*
13   *this may be the end of the performance. If not, it is an intermission*
14   *before Act II during which the boxes Down Center in Area 1 are*
15   *replaced by one bench long enough to serve as a bed for TOAD.)*
16
17   **ACT II**
18
19 *SETTING:*   BADGER, RAT and MOLE are found On-stage, Down
20   Center, as the curtain opens, or, if no front curtain is used, they
21   enter and take seats Down Center. STORYTELLER follows
22   them in, and observes the scene from his usual Down Right
23   position.
24
25 **BADGER:** *(Heartily)* **Now then! Tell us the news from your**
26   **part of the world. How's old Toad going on?**
27 **RAT:** *(Gravely)* **From bad to worse.**
28 **MOLE:** *(Mournfully)* **Yes, from bad to worse.**
29 **RAT:** **Another smashup only last week, and a bad one. You**
30   **see, he will insist on driving himself, and he's hopelessly**
31   **incapable. If he'd only employ a decent, steady, well-**
32   **trained animal, pay him good wages, and leave**
33   **everything to him, he'd get on all right. But no; he's**
34   **convinced he's a heaven-born driver, and nobody can**
35   **teach him anything; and all the rest follows.**

1   MOLE: All the rest follows.

2   BADGER: *(Gloomily)* How many has he had?

3   RAT: Smashes, or machines? Oh, well, after all, it's the same
4   thing — with Toad. This is the seventh. As for the
5   others — you know that coach house of his? Well, it's piled
6   up — literally piled to the roof — with fragments of
7   motorcars, none of them bigger than your hat! That
8   accounts for the other six — so far as they can be
9   accounted for.

10 MOLE: *(Eager to participate)* He's been in the hospital three
11   times, and as for the fines he's had to pay, it's simply
12   awful to think about.

13 RAT: Yes, and that's part of the trouble. Toad's rich, we all
14   know; but he's not a millionaire. And he's a hopelessly
15   bad driver, and quite regardless of law and order. Killed
16   or ruined — it's got to be one of the two things, sooner
17   or later, Badger! We're his friends — oughtn't we to do
18   something?

19 BADGER: *(Thinking)* Now look here! Of course you know I
20   can't do anything now?

21 MOLE: *(Not understanding)* Now?

22 RAT: *(Understanding)* Of course, of course, not now, winter
23   season.

24 BADGER: Very well then! But, when once the year has really
25   turned, and the nights are shorter, and halfway through
26   them one rouses and feels fidgety and wanting to be up
27   and doing by sunrise, if not before — you know!

28 RAT: Yes, yes, we know!

29 MOLE: Oh yes, we do know.

30 BADGER: Well, then, we — that is, you and me and our
31   friend the Mole here — we'll take Toad seriously in hand.
32   We'll stand no nonsense whatever. We'll bring him back
33   to reason, by force if need be. We'll make him be a sensible
34   Toad. We'll — *(Sees RAT has dozed off to sleep)* you're asleep,
35   Rat!

1   **RAT:** *(Waking up with a jerk)* **Not me!**
2   **MOLE:** *(Laughing)* **He's been asleep two or three times since**
3   **supper.**
4   **BADGER:** **Well, it's time we were all in bed. Come along, you**
5   **two, and I'll show you your quarters.** *(Standing to lead RAT*
6   *and MOLE Upstage Center, where they all freeze, backs to*
7   *audience.)* **And take your time tomorrow morning —**
8   **breakfast at any hour you please!** *(STORYTELLER stands*
9   *to cross Down Center. As he does this, RAT and MOLE cross*
10 *Down Left to Platform 2 and freeze. BADGER remains Up*
11 *Center.)*
12 **STORYTELLER:** **Winter is over, and the animals are no**
13 **longer hibernating. It is a bright morning in early**
14 **summer, and Mole and Rat have been up since dawn,**
15 **very busy on matters connected with boats and the**
16 **opening of the boating season. Now they've just finished**
17 **breakfast in their little parlor and are eagerly discussing**
18 **their plans for the day when a heavy knock sounds on**
19 **the door.** *(Sound effect of heavy knocking as BADGER moves*
20 *Down Center to the area of Platform 2.)*
21 **RAT:** **Bother! See who it is, Mole, like a good chap, since**
22 **you're finished eating.** *(MOLE crosses to open an imaginary*
23 *door at the center edge of Platform 2.)*
24 **MOLE:** **Mr. Badger!**
25 **RAT:** **Badger, what a surprise! Come in, come in!** *(BADGER*
26 *takes an Upstage position between and above RAT and MOLE.)*
27 **BADGER:** *(With great solemnity)* **The hour has come!**
28 **RAT:** *(Uneasily)* **What hour?**
29 **BADGER:** **Whose hour, you should rather say. Why, Toad's**
30 **hour! The hour of Toad! I said I would take him in hand**
31 **as soon as the winter was well over, and I'm going to take**
32 **him in hand today!**
33 **MOLE:** *(Delightedly)* **Toad's hour, of course. Hooray! I**
34 **remember now! We'll teach him to be a sensible Toad!**
35 **BADGER:** **This very morning, I have learned, another new**

1   and exceptionally powerful motorcar will arrive at Toad
2   Hall on approval of return. At this very moment, perhaps,
3   Toad is busy arraying himself in those hideous
4   habiliments so dear to him — his driving gear — which
5   transforms him from a comparatively good-looking Toad
6   into an object which throws any decent-minded animal
7   that comes across it into a violent fit. We must be up and
8   doing, ere it is too late.
9 RAT: Yes, yes!
10 MOLE: Oh, my, yes!
11 BADGER: You two animals will accompany me instantly to
12   Toad Hall, and our work of rescue shall be accomplished.
13 RAT: *(Standing up)* Right you are! We'll rescue the poor
14   unhappy animal! We'll convert him. He'll be the most
15   converted Toad that ever was before we're done with
16   him. *(The three cross to Platform 1, Down Right, timing their*
17   *arrival there with the STORYTELLER's narration and TOAD's*
18   *entrance.)*
19 STORYTELLER: They set off on their mission of mercy in a
20   proper and sensible animal manner, single file, Badger
21   leading the way. They reached the carriage drive of Toad
22   Hall to find, as the Badger had anticipated, a shiny new
23   motorcar of great size, painted a bright red (Toad's
24   favorite color), standing in front of the house. As they
25   neared the door it was flung open, and Mr. Toad, arrayed
26   in goggles, cap, gaiters, and enormous overcoat, came
27   swaggering down the steps, drawing on his gauntleted
28   gloves.
29 TOAD: *(Catching sight of them)* Hello! Come on, you fellows!
30   You're just in time to come with me for a jolly — to come
31   for a jolly — for a — er — jolly — *(Falters as he sees their*
32   *unbending and solemn looks.)*
33 BADGER: *(Sternly)* Take him inside. *(RAT and MOLE do so,*
34   *TOAD struggling and protesting. BADGER turns to speak to*
35   *the imaginary salesman in charge of the new motorcar.)* I'm

1   **afraid you won't be wanted today. Mr. Toad has changed**
2   **his mind. He will not require the car. Please understand**
3   **that this is final. You needn't wait.** *(Turns to follow the others*
4   *inside, Platform 1, pantomiming opening and closing the door*
5   *as he enters.)* **Now, then! First of all, take those ridiculous**
6   **things off!**
7   **TOAD:**   *(With great spirit)* **Shan't! What is the meaning of this**
8   **gross outrage? I demand an instant explanation!**
9   **BADGER:**   **You knew it must come to this, sooner or later,**
10   **Toad. You've disregarded all the warnings we've given**
11   **you, you've gone on squandering the money your father**
12   **left you, and you're getting us animals a bad name in the**
13   **district by your furious driving and your smashes and**
14   **your rows with the police. Independence is all very well,**
15   **but we animals never allow our friends to make fools of**
16   **themselves beyond a certain limit; and that limit you've**
17   **reached.**
18   **RAT:**   **True, true!**
19   **BADGER:**   **Now, you're a good fellow in many respects, and I**
20   **don't want to be too hard on you. I'll make one more**
21   **effort to bring you to reason. You'll come with me into**
22   **the sitting room, and there you will hear some facts about**
23   **yourself; and we'll see whether you come out of that room**
24   **the same Toad that you went in.** *(BADGER takes TOAD*
25   *firmly by the arm and propels him to an area Up Left of Platform*
26   *1 where, if desired, BADGER can be seen, back to audience,*
27   *gesturing and "telling off" TOAD — or they may simply freeze,*
28   *backs to audience.)*
29   **RAT:**   *(Contemptuously)* **That's no good! Talking to Toad'll**
30   **never cure him. He'll say anything.**
31   **MOLE:**   **You're probably right, but if anyone can talk him**
32   **into being sensible, Badger can do it.**
33   **RAT:**   **I doubt it. But let's sit down and wait, see what**
34   **happens.** *(They do so, and freeze.)*
35   **STORYTELLER:**   **After some three-quarters of an hour, the**

1	door opened and the Badger reappeared, solemnly
2	leading by the paw a very limp and dejected Toad. His
3	legs wobbled, and his cheeks were furrowed by the tears
4	so plentifully called forth by Badger's moving discourse.
5	*(RAT and MOLE rise to meet BADGER and TOAD as they*
6	*return to Platform 1.)*
7	BADGER: Sit down there, Toad. *(TOAD takes a seat.)* **My**
8	friends, I am pleased to inform you that Toad has at last
9	seen the error of his ways. He is truly sorry for his
10	misguided conduct in the past, and he has undertaken
11	to give up motorcars entirely and forever. I have his
12	solemn promise to that effect.
13	MOLE: *(Gravely)* That is very good news.
14	RAT: *(Dubiously)* Very good news, indeed, if only — if only —
15	BADGER: There's only one more thing to be done. Toad, I
16	want you to solemnly repeat, before your friends here,
17	what you fully admitted to me in the sitting room just
18	now. First, you are sorry for what you've done, and you
19	see the folly of it all.
20	TOAD: *(A long pause as TOAD looks around. Then, sullenly but*
21	*stoutly)* No! I'm not sorry. And it wasn't folly at all! It was
22	simply glorious!
23	BADGER: *(Scandalized)* What? You backsliding animal,
24	didn't you tell me just now, in there —
25	TOAD: *(Impatiently)* Oh, yes, yes, in there. I'd have said
26	anything in there. You're so eloquent, dear Badger, and
27	so moving, and so convincing, and put all your points so
28	frightfully well — you can do what you like with me in
29	there, and you know it. But I've been searching my mind
30	since, and going over things in it, and I find that I'm not
31	a bit sorry or repentant really, so it's no earthly good
32	saying I am, now is it?
33	BADGER: Then you don't promise never to touch a motorcar again?
34	TOAD: *(Emphatically)* Certainly not! On the contrary, I
35	faithfully promise that the very first motorcar I see, poop-

1   **poop, off I go in it!**

2   **RAT:** *(To MOLE)* **Told you, didn't I?**

3   **BADGER:** *(Firmly)* **Very well, then, since you won't yield to**

4   **persuasion, we'll try what force will do. I feared it would**

5   **come to this all along. You've often asked us three to**

6   **come and stay with you, Toad, in this handsome house**

7   **of yours; well, now we're going to. When we've converted**

8   **you to a proper point of view we may quit, but not before.**

9   **Take him, you two, and lock him up in his bedroom, while**

10   **we arrange matters between ourselves.**

11   **RAT:** **It's for your own good, Toady, you know.** *(RAT and*

12   *MOLE haul TOAD to Down Center area as he kicks and*

13   *struggles.)* **Think what fun we shall all have together, just**

14   **as we used to, when you've got over this — painful attack**

15   **of yours!**

16   **MOLE:** **We'll take great care of everything for you till you're**

17   **well, Toad. And we'll see your money isn't wasted, as it**

18   **has been.**

19   **RAT:** **No more of those regrettable incidents with the police,**

20   **Toad.**

21   **MOLE:** **And no more weeks in the hospital, being ordered**

22   **about by female nurses.** *(TOAD sits Down Center, back to*

23   *audience, as RAT and MOLE return to Platform 1, Down Right.)*

24   **BADGER:** *(Sighing)* **But it's going to be a tedious business.**

25   **I've never seen Toad so determined. However, we'll see**

26   **it out. He must never be left an instant unguarded. We'll**

27   **have to take turns to be with him, till the poison has**

28   **worked itself out of his system. We'll take turns sleeping**

29   **in Toad's room at night, and divide up the days between**

30   **us.** *(BADGER and MOLE may leave the stage, or turn backs to*

31   *audience and freeze. TOAD lies down on the bench which has*

32   *been placed Down Center during the intermission, and RAT*

33   *moves Down Center to stand above the bench to talk down to*

34   *TOAD in the next scene.)*

35   **STORYTELLER:** **Which is exactly what the three friends did.**

1 At first Toad was very trying to his careful guardians. As
2 time passed, however, these temperamental outbursts
3 grew gradually less frequent, and his friends tried to
4 divert his mind to channels other than motorcars. But
5 Toad's interest in other matters did not seem to revive,
6 and he grew daily more languid and depressed. One fine
7 morning Rat took his turn in the bedroom with Toad.

8 **RAT:** *(Cheerfully as he approaches TOAD's bedside)* **How are you**
9 **today, old chap?**

10 **TOAD:** *(Feebly, making believe he is very sick)* **Thank you so**
11 **much, dear Ratty. So good of you to inquire! But first tell**
12 **me how you are yourself, and the excellent Mole?**

13 **RAT:** **Oh, we're all right. Mole is going out for a run round**
14 **with Badger. They'll be gone till luncheon time, so you**
15 **and I will spend a pleasant morning together, and I'll do**
16 **my best to amuse you. Now jump up, there's a good fellow,**
17 **and no moping on a fine morning like this!**

18 **TOAD:** *(Murmuring)* **Dear, kind Rat, how little you realize my**
19 **condition, and how very far I am from jumping up now —**
20 **if ever! But do not trouble about me. I hate being a burden**
21 **to my friends, and I do not expect to be one much longer.**
22 **Indeed, I almost hope not.**

23 **RAT:** *(Heartily)* **Well, I hope not, too. You've been a fine bother**
24 **to us all this time, and I'm glad to hear it's about to stop.**
25 **And in weather like this, and the boating season just**
26 **beginning! It's too bad of you, Toad! It isn't the trouble**
27 **we mind, but you're making us miss such an awful lot.**

28 **TOAD:** *(Languidly)* **I'm afraid it is the trouble you mind,**
29 **though. I can quite understand it. It's natural enough.**
30 **You're tired of bothering about me. I mustn't ask you to**
31 **do anything further. I'm a nuisance, I know.**

32 **RAT:** **You are, indeed. But I tell you, I'd take any trouble on**
33 **earth for you, Toady, if only you'd be a sensible animal.**

34 **TOAD:** *(More feebly than ever)* **If I thought that, Ratty, then I**
35 **would beg you — for the last time, probably — to step**

1 round to the village as quickly as possible — even now
2 it may be too late — and fetch the doctor. But don't you
3 bother. It's only a trouble, and perhaps we may as well
4 let things take their course.
5 RAT: *(Coming closer and examining TOAD)* Why, what do you
6 want a doctor for?
7 TOAD: Surely you have noticed of late — but no, why should
8 you? Noticing things is only a trouble. Tomorrow, indeed,
9 you may be saying to yourself, "Oh, if only I had noticed
10 sooner! If only I had done something!" But no; it's a
11 trouble. Never mind — forget that I asked.
12 RAT: *(Getting alarmed)* Look here, old man, of course I'll fetch
13 a doctor for you, If you really think you want him. But
14 you can hardly be bad enough for that yet. Let's talk
15 about something else.
16 TOAD: *(With a sad smile)* I fear, dear friend, that talk can do
17 little in a case like this — or doctors either, for that
18 matter; still, one must grasp at the slightest straw. And,
19 by the way — while you are about it — I hate to give you
20 additional trouble, but I happen to remember that you'll
21 pass the door — would you mind at the same time asking
22 the lawyer to step up? It would be a convenience to me,
23 and there are moments — perhaps I should say there is
24 a moment — when one must face disagreeable tasks, at
25 whatever cost to exhausted nature!
26 RAT: A lawyer! Oh, you must be really bad. It's best to be on
27 the safe side. I'll go; it won't take very long! *(RAT hurries*
28 *Off-stage, or moves to a remote part of the stage to freeze, back*
29 *to audience. TOAD hops lightly out of bed, laughing heartily,*
30 *and talking to himself.)*
31 TOAD: Smart piece of work that. *(Chuckling)* Brain against
32 brute force — and brain came out on top — as it's bound
33 to do. Poor old Ratty! My! Won't he catch it when Badger
34 gets back! A worthy fellow, Ratty, with many good
35 qualities, but very little intelligence and absolutely no

1   education. **I must take him in hand some day, and see if**
2   **I can make something of him.** *(Crosses Down Left and sits,*
3   *back to audience, freezing.)*
4   STORYTELLER: *(Taking Center Stage)* **Toad dressed rapidly,**
5   **filled his pockets with cash from a small drawer in his**
6   **dressing table, and next, knotting the sheets from his bed**
7   **together and tying one end of the improvised rope to the**
8   **bed, scrambled out the window and slid lightly to the**
9   **ground. Shortly, gay and irresponsible, he was walking**
10   **briskly along the high road, some miles from home. When**
11   **he reached a little town, he entered "The Red Lion" there**
12   **to enjoy a hearty breakfast. He was about halfway**
13   **through his meal when he heard "poop-poop" and a car**
14   **drew up outside the tavern. Presently the party entered**
15   **the coffee room, hungry and talkative, bragging of the**
16   **merits of the car that had brought them there. Toad could**
17   **stand it no longer. He slipped out of the room quietly,**
18   **paid his bill at the bar, and sauntered round quietly to**
19   **the car.** *(TOAD crosses Down Center, using the bench which*
20   *had been his bed as a car. He walks slowly around it, inspecting,*
21   *musing deeply.)*
22   TOAD: **There can't be any harm in my just looking at it.**
23   **Hmmmh, red, my favorite color! And look at that polished**
24   **brass! What a shine — and leather seats! I wonder if this**
25   **car starts easily? I'll just try it.** *(Takes hold of the crank and*
26   *turns it.)* **Oh, listen to that motor.** *(Climbs into the driver's*
27   *seat, adjusts equipment, takes the wheel, and drives away,*
28   *wiggling up and down, clasping and turning the wheel.)* **Great,**
29   **great! I'm Toad once more, Toad at my best. Toad the**
30   **terror, the traffic queller, the lord of the lone trail! Ho,**
31   **ho! I am The Toad, the handsome, the popular, the**
32   **successful Toad!** *(Breaks into conceited song.)*
33   **"The world has held great heroes, as history books have**
34   **showed;**
35   **But never a name to go down to fame compared with that**

1　　　　　of Toad!
2　　　The clever men at Oxford know all that there is to be
3　　　　　knowed
4　　　But they none of them know one half as much as intelligent
5　　　　　Mr. Toad!
6　　　The animals sat in the ark and cried, their tears in
7　　　　　torrents flowed.
8　　　Who was it said, 'There's land ahead?' Encouraging Mr.
9　　　　　Toad!
10　　The army all saluted as they marched along the road.
11　　Was it the King? Or Kitchener? No. It was Mr. Toad!
12　　The Queen and her ladies-in-waiting sat at the window
13　　　　and sewed.
14　　She cried, 'Look! Who's that handsome man?' They
15　　　　answered, 'Mr. Toad.' "
16　　*(At the end of the song, TOAD turns back to audience and freezes,*
17　　*and STORYTELLER resumes his narration.)*
18　**STORYTELLER:**　Did Mr. Toad get away with stealing the
19　　car? Not for long. He was caught shortly, tried, and
20　　sentenced to many years in prison. He did escape — and
21　　finally, back in Ratty's hole in the ground, told of his
22　　adventures.
23　**TOAD:**　*(Turning front as RAT seats himself near him.)* Oh,
24　　Ratty! I've been through such times since I saw you last,
25　　you can't think! Such trials, such sufferings, and all so
26　　nobly borne! Then such escapes, such disguises, such
27　　subterfuges, and all so cleverly planned and carried out!
28　　Been in prison — got out of it, of course! Been thrown
29　　into a canal — swam ashore! Stole a horse — sold him for
30　　a large sum of money! *(Puffing up more and more as he brags)*
31　　Humbugged everybody — made 'em all do exactly what
32　　I wanted! Oh, I am a smart Toad, and no mistake!
33　**RAT:**　Toady, now stop swaggering and bragging! Now I
34　　don't want to give you pain, after all you've been through
35　　already; but seriously, don't you see what an awful ass

1   you've made of yourself? On your own admission you've
2   been handcuffed, imprisoned, starved, chased, terrified out
3   of your life, insulted, jeered at, and ignominiously flung
4   into the water! What's the amusement in that? Where does
5   the fun come from? And all because you must needs go and
6   steal a motorcar. You know that you've never had anything
7   but trouble from motorcars from the moment you first set
8   eyes on one. But if you will be mixed up with them — as
9   you generally are, five minutes after you've started — why
10   steal them? Be a cripple, if you think it's exciting; be a
11   bankrupt, for a change, if you've set your mind on it; but
12   why choose to be a convict? When are you going to be
13   sensible, and think of your friends, and try to be a credit
14   to them? Do you suppose it's any pleasure to me, for
15   instance, to hear animals saying, as I go about, that I'm
16   the chap that keeps company with jailbirds?
17 TOAD: Quite right, Ratty! How sound you always are! Yes,
18   I've been a conceited ass, I can quite see that; but now
19   I'm going to be a good Toad, and not do it anymore. As
20   for motorcars, I've not been at all so keen about them
21   since my last ducking in that river of yours. I've had
22   enough of adventures. I shall lead a quiet, steady,
23   respectable life, pottering about my property, and
24   improving it, and doing a little landscape gardening at
25   times. There'll always be a bit of dinner for my friends
26   when they come to see me; and I shall keep a pony cart
27   to jog about the country in, just as I used to in the good
28   old days, before I got restless, and wanted to do things.
29   Come along, walk me home to Toad Hall now. *(As they*
30   *walk off together, arm in arm, TOAD sings:)*
31   "The motorcar went poop-poop-poop, as it raced along the
32   road.
33   Who was it steered it into a pond? Ingenious Mr. Toad!"
34   *(The two may laughingly repeat the tune together on the curtain*
35   *call.)*

AESOP'S FABLES

Adapted for Readers Theatre by Melvin R. White, Ph.D.

Aesop's Fables are animal stories told over 2500 years ago by a Greek slave. Each of these fables is a play unto itself, but all make a delightfully humorous longer program when played in sequence, the cast making transitional pauses and movements from one fable to the next. The length of the program depends on how many of the stories are acted out. Seven readers can perform all of them, or a larger cast is possible if it is decided to have different players in each fable. If this is done, one cast will take a bow and move off as the next cast moves on, bringing with them whatever staging devices are needed.

---

*Adapted for Readers Theatre by Melvin R. White. Amateur performance rights of this adaptation are granted with the purchase of this book.

Most of these fables can be presented without special staging. A few such as "The Hen and the Fox" and "The Cock and the Fox" benefit if a stepladder is used, but even these can be done effectively on a totally bare stage. The success of these fables depends on effective characterizations and well-planned and executed mime, and suggesting the various animals vocally and physically can be great fun, not only for the actor/readers, but for audiences of all ages.

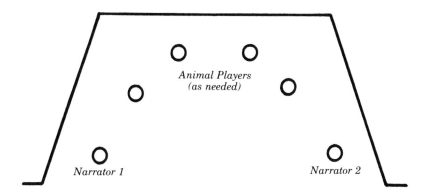

1	**THE QUACK FROG**
2	
3	*CHARACTERS:* Narrators 1 and 2, Frog, Fox, Jackass, Goat, Hare,
4	Sheep
5	
6	**1ST NARRATOR:** **In these stories we meet the ants and foxes**
7	**and goats — and a few humans and some pagan gods.**
8	**Too, we always learn a moral, and find it to be as true**
9	**today as it ever was. For example,** *The Quack Frog.*
10	**2ND NARRATOR:** **One day a frog came out from his home in**
11	**a muddy swamp and announced to all the animal world:**
12	**FROG:** **I can cure every disease there is!** *(JACKASS, GOAT,*
13	*FOX, HARE and SHEEP gather around him.)*
14	**FOX:** **What did you say? You can cure every disease?!**
15	**FROG:** *(Puffing up in pride from the attention)* **Yes. Here, come**
16	**and see! You're looking at the greatest physician in the**
17	**world. Not even Jove's court doctor —**
18	**JACKASS:** *(Braying loudly, interrupting)* **Hee-haw! Hee-haw!**
19	**You, Frog, a physician? Hee-haw! Hee-haw!**
20	**GOAT:** *(Baaa-ing in disdain)* **Baaa-baaa!** *(Several times as if*
21	*laughing)*
22	**FOX:** **How dare you set yourself up to heal others? Why don't**
23	**you first try to heal your own limping gait?**
24	**HARE:** *(Excited)* **Yes . . . and your wrinkled and blotchy skin?!**
25	**SHEEP:** *(In bleating voice)* **And your bulgy and ugly eyes?!**
26	**2ND NARRATOR:** *(As the animals all laugh him to scorn)* **At this**
27	**the quack frog drew in his head and hopped rapidly away**
28	**back to the swamp from whence he had come while all**
29	**the animals laughed him to scorn.**
30	**1ST NARRATOR:** **Moral: Physician, heal thyself!**
31	
32	
33	
34	
35	

1 **THE HOUSE DOG AND THE WOLF**
2
3 ***CHARACTERS:*** Narrator, Wolf, Dog
4
5 NARRATOR: The moon was shining very brightly one night
6   when a thin, half-starved wolf, his ribs almost sticking
7   out through his skin, met a fat, plump, overfed house
8   dog. They sized each other up, exchanged greetings, and
9   then chatted a bit:
10 WOLF: Cousin dog, how come you are so well-fed, fat and
11   contented? I hunt and hunt, try ever so hard, but I can't
12   find enough food to keep from starving. Look how skinny
13   I am.
14 DOG: Cousin wolf, I fear you do not work steadily as I do.
15   You lead too irregular a life, running around as you do,
16   night and day.
17 WOLF: I'd be happy to work steadily if only I could find a job.
18 DOG: That's easy. I'll tell you — why don't you come with me
19   to my master's house? You can help me keep away thieves
20   at night.
21 WOLF: Great! Living in the woods as I do, I have an awful
22   time. To have a roof over my head and a belly full of food
23   always! Let's go now; I'm starving.
24 DOG: Follow me.
25 WOLF: Uh — what's that mark on your neck? What caused
26   that?
27 DOG: Oh, that's not much of anything. I guess my collar was a
28   little too tight.
29 WOLF: Collar?
30 DOG: Yes, my collar where my chain is fastened.
31 WOLF: *(Surprised)* Chain? You mean you're not free to run
32   loose as you wish?
33 DOG: *(Shamefacedly)* Well, not exactly. You see, my master
34   thinks I'm a bit fierce, so he ties me up in the daytime.
35   But he lets me run free every night. It's really convenient

269

1   for everybody. I get plenty of sleep during the day so I

2   can watch better at night. I really am a great favorite at

3   the house. My master feeds me off his own plate

4   sometimes, and in the kitchen the servants are always

5   offering me handouts. *(Pause)* But wait, where are you

6   going?

7   WOLF: Back to the woods. Good night to you, my poor friend.

8   You're welcome to your food and your shelter — and your

9   chains. As for me, I'll take my freedom to your fat.

10   NARRATOR: Moral: Lean freedom is better than fat slavery.

11

12

13

14

15

16

17

18

19

20

21

22

23

24

25

26

27

28

29

30

31

32

33

34

35

1	<div align="center">**THE HORSE AND THE STAG**</div>
2	
3	*CHARACTERS:* Narrator, Horse, Hunter
4	
5	**NARRATOR:** A bitter quarrel arose between the stag and the
6	horse back in the old days when they both ran wild in
7	the forest. The horse came to a hunter and said to him:
8	**HORSE:** The stag and I have been fighting. Will you take my
9	side in our quarrel?
10	**HUNTER:** Yes, I will. But if I am to help you to punish the
11	stag, you must let me put this bit in your mouth and this
12	saddle on your back.
13	**HORSE:** That's fine with me as long as I can win the
14	argument with the stag.
15	**NARRATOR:** Soon the horse was bridled and saddled. The
16	hunter climbed into the saddle, and together the hunter
17	and the horse put the stag to flight.
18	**HORSE:** Now, hunter, if you get off my back and take out
19	this bit and take off the saddle, I'll go. I won't need your
20	help any longer.
21	**HUNTER:** Not so fast, friend horse. I have you under bit and
22	spur, and from now on you'll be the slave of man.
23	**NARRATOR:** Moral: Liberty is too high a price to pay for
24	revenge.
25	
26	
27	
28	
29	
30	
31	
32	
33	
34	
35	

1   **THE HEN AND THE FOX**

2

3   *CHARACTERS:*   Narrator, Fox, Hen

4

5   **NARRATOR:**   **A fox, very hungry, was out looking for a late**
6   **supper. He came to a henhouse, and through the open**
7   **door he saw a hen far up on the highest perch, safe from**
8   **his reach.**

9   **FOX:**   *(To himself)* **Here is a case for diplomacy — either that,**
10   **or not get this hen for my supper. Now, let me see, how**
11   **can I approach this high-perched meal?** *(To HEN who is*
12   *perched atop a folding ladder or some other high spot available*
13   *in the performance area)* **Hello up there, friend hen. Where**
14   **have you been? I haven't seen you around recently.**
15   **Somebody told me you had a sick spell, and I was very**
16   **worried about you. Do you know, you look as pale as a**
17   **ghost!**

18   **HEN:**   *(Clucking a bit)* **I do?**

19   **FOX:**   **Yes. Why don't you come down here? I'll take your**
20   **pulse — and look at your tongue. I'm afraid you're in for**
21   **quite a siege.**

22   **HEN:**   **You never said a truer word, cousin fox. It'll have to**
23   **be a siege, for I'm in such a state that if I were to climb**
24   **down to where you are, I'm afraid it'd be the death of me.**

25   **NARRATOR:**   **Moral: Beware of the insincere friend!**

26

27

28

29

30

31

32

33

34

35

1   **THE FARMER AND THE NIGHTINGALE**
2
3   ***CHARACTERS:***   Narrator, Farmer, Bird
4
5   **NARRATOR: After a day of hard work, a farmer went to bed**
6   **early.** *(Sound: nightingale singing)* **But he could not go to**
7   **sleep because of the beautiful song of a nightingale. It**
8   **kept him awake all night — but the song of the bird**
9   **pleased him so he decided the next night to set a trap**
10   **for it.**
11   **FARMER: Ah, my beautiful nightingale, now that I have**
12   **caught you, you shall hang in my cage and sing just for**
13   **me every night.**
14   **BIRD: But we nightingales never sing in a cage. If you put me**
15   **in a cage, I shall become sick and die — and then you'll**
16   **never hear my song again.**
17   **FARMER: All right. Then I'll put you in a pie and eat you.**
18   **I've heard that nightingale pie is delicious, the most**
19   **delicious pie there is.**
20   **BIRD:** *(Begging)* **Please do not kill me. If you'll set me free,**
21   **I'll tell you three great truths that will be worth much**
22   **more to you than my poor and small body.**
23   **FARMER:** *(Reluctantly)* **Well, all right. There, I've set you**
24   **loose. Now, what are the three great truths? Tell me,**
25   **nightingale.**
26   **BIRD:** *(Trills a few happy notes.)* **First, never believe a**
27   **captive's promise. Second, keep what you have. And**
28   **third, never sorrow over what is lost forever.**
29   **NARRATOR: Then the songbird flew away. Moral: A bird in**
30   **the cage is worth two on the branch.**
31
32
33
34
35

THE MILLER, HIS SON, AND THEIR DONKEY

CHARACTERS: Narrator, Girls 1 and 2, Men 1 and 2, Women 1 and 2.

NARRATOR: A miller and his son were driving their donkey to a fair to sell him. They had gone only a short distance when some girls saw them and started to laugh.

1ST GIRL: Look there!

2ND GIRL: *(Laughing)* Look at that man and his son, walking on foot when they could be riding on the donkey!

1ST GIRL: Such fools! I can't believe it!

NARRATOR: So the miller put his son on the donkey, and they went on their way to the fair. Soon they came to two men who were arguing.

1ST MAN: There! That proves exactly what I'm saying. No one has any respect for old age anymore. Look at that boy riding while his poor old father has to walk. *(To boy)* Get down, you lazy lout! Let the old man ride!

NARRATOR: So the miller made his son get down from the donkey, and got on in his place. In this manner they proceeded on their way to the fair until they met some women.

1ST WOMAN: Why, shame on you, old man! How can you ride when that poor little boy can hardly keep up with you?!

2ND WOMAN: Shame on you.

NARRATOR: So the miller, trying to please everyone, reached down, picked up his son, and put him on the donkey behind him. But, just as they were reaching the fair, a man saw them, two on the back of the one not-too-large donkey.

2ND MAN: Two of you on that one small donkey? I've a mind to report you to the police for treating that poor beast so shamefully. You two big fellows could more easily carry the donkey than he can carry the two of you!

274

1 NARRATOR: So, getting down, the miller and his son
2 managed to tie the beast's legs together, and with a pole
3 across their shoulders, started to carry the donkey to the
4 fair. They had to cross a bridge to get into the fair, and
5 it was such a funny sight, the two men carrying a donkey
6 on a pole, crowds came out to see it. How they laughed
7 and hooted and howled! This frightened the poor animal,
8 so he struggled and managed to free himself. The miller
9 and his son tried to catch him, the crowd started to help,
10 and in the middle of the turmoil, the donkey fell off the
11 bridge into the water and was drowned. Moral: Try to
12 please everyone and you end up not pleasing anyone.
13
14
15
16
17
18
19
20
21
22
23
24
25
26
27
28
29
30
31
32
33
34
35

1   **THE COCK AND THE FOX**

2

3   **CHARACTERS:** Narrator, Fox, Cock

4

5   *(Sound: COCK crowing several times. Should be on top of a*

6   *ladder or table.)*

7   **NARRATOR: A fox was passing a farmyard early one**

8   **morning when he heard a cock crowing. Looking about,**

9   **he spotted the rooster perched high in a tree, far above**

10   **the reach of anyone who might be thinking of having**

11   **him for breakfast.**

12   **FOX: Why, cousin cock, what a pleasure it is to see you! Why**

13   **don't you come down and let me greet you properly?**

14   **COCK: I would love to, but, as you know, there are some**

15   **animals who'd like nothing better than to grab me and**

16   **eat me.**

17   **FOX: Oh, my dear cousin, you mean you haven't heard the**

18   **news?**

19   **COCK: What news?**

20   **FOX: That all the animals have agreed to live in peace with**

21   **one another.** *(COCK is craning his neck as if he is watching*

22   *something very interesting in the distance.)* **Uh — cousin —**

23   **what in the world do you see up there that is so**

24   **interesting?**

25   **COCK: Oh, nothing much. Just a pack of dogs headed in**

26   **this direction — and coming at a fast run.**

27   **FOX:** *(Nervously)* **Please excuse me. I just — uh — thought of**

28   **something I had forgotten.**

29   **COCK: What's your hurry? I was just coming down for a talk.**

30   **You don't mean to say that you've anything to be afraid**

31   **of, now that you know about the wonderful peace plan?**

32   **FOX:** *(As he runs off)* **Well, maybe those hounds haven't heard**

33   **about it yet!**

34   **NARRATOR: Moral: The best liars often get caught in their**

35   **own lies.**

1   **THE LION AND HIS THREE COUNSELORS**
2

3 *CHARACTERS:*   Narrator, Lioness, Lion, Sheep, Wolf, Fox
4

5 **NARRATOR: The king of beasts was in an irritable mood.**
6   **That morning his mate had said to him:**

7 **LIONESS: Your breath is very unpleasant!**

8 **NARRATOR: After roaring around a lot to prove that he was**
9   **king, he decided to call his counselors.**

10 **LION: Friend sheep, would you say that my breath smells**
11   **bad?**

12 **SHEEP:**   *(Smells breath.)* **You want an honest answer?**

13 **LION: Of course!**

14 **SHEEP: Your breath is very unpleasant.** *(LION roars.)*

15 **NARRATOR: The king of beasts bit her head off. Then he**
16   **called the wolf and asked him the same question.**

17 **LION: Friend wolf, would you say that my breath smells bad?**

18 **NARRATOR: The wolf, catching sight of the carcass of the**
19   **sheep, said:**

20 **WOLF: Why, your majesty, you have a breath as sweet as**
21   **the blossoms of spring!**

22 **NARRATOR: The wolf had hardly finished when he was torn**
23   **to pieces as a flatterer. At last the lion called the fox and**
24   **put the question to him. The fox gave a hollow cough,**
25   **then cleared his throat:**

26 **FOX:**   *(Clearing his throat and coughing a bit, he whispered:)* **Your**
27   **majesty, I have such a cold in my head, I can't smell at all.**

28 **NARRATOR: Moral: In dangerous times wise men say**
29   **nothing.**

30

31

32

33

34

35

1   **THE HEN AND THE CAT**

2

3   ***CHARACTERS:***   Goose, Turkey, Cat, Narrator, Hen

4

5   **GOOSE:**   Have you heard, the hen is indisposed.

6   **TURKEY:**   Indisposed?

7   **GOOSE:**   Not well.

8   **CAT:**   Is that so? I think I shall pay her a visit of condolence.

9   **TURKEY:**   Condolence?

10   **CAT:**   Visit of — well, tell her I am sorry she is not feeling well.

11   **NARRATOR:**   Creeping up to the hen's nest, the cat in a most

12   sympathetic voice said:

13   **CAT:**   How are you, my dear friend? I was so sorry to hear of

14   your illness. Is there anything I can bring you to cheer

15   you up, help you feel yourself again?

16   **HEN:**   Thank you. Please be good enough to leave me in

17   peace, and I have no fear that I shall soon be well.

18   **NARRATOR:**   Moral: Uninvited guests are often most

19   welcome when they are gone.

20

21

22

23

24

25

26

27

28

29

30

31

32

33

34

35

1   THE PORCUPINE AND THE SNAKES
2
3   *CHARACTERS:*   Porcupine, Snakes 1 and 2, Narrator
4
5   PORCUPINE: I think this'll be a very comfortable cave for
6   me to use as my home. Just the right size for a porcupine.
7   SNAKE 1:   But we snakes already live here. This is our home!
8   PORCUPINE: Well, couldn't I just use one corner of your
9   cave this winter?
10   SNAKE 1:   All right. I guess it'll be all right. It is larger than
11   we need.
12   PORCUPINE: Thank you. I'll just curl up in a ball and take a
13   nap.
14   NARRATOR: So, he moved in, curled up, and stuck out all
15   his prickly quills. He was settled down for the winter.
16   But it was not long before the snakes realized they had
17   made a mistake.
18   SNAKE 1:   Every time I move I prick myself on one of that
19   porcupine's quills!
20   SNAKE 2:   Me, too. The children are full of sores. When they
21   play, they forget to be careful. What'll we do?
22   SNAKE 1:   We'll just have to complain, I guess. I hate to but . . .
23   cousin porcupine, cousin porcupine, wake up!
24   PORCUPINE: *(Sleepily)* Yes? You want me? What is it?
25   SNAKE 1:   We find there just isn't room for all of us in this
26   cave. We keep bumping into your quills — and they are
27   sharp and painful.
28   PORCUPINE: That's just too bad. I'm most comfortable here.
29   But if you snakes aren't satisfied, why don't you move
30   out?
31   NARRATOR: And he curled up once more, stuck out his
32   quills, and resumed his nap. Moral: It is safer to know
33   one's guest before offering him hospitality.
34
35

279

1   **THE WOLF AND THE LAMB**

2

3   ***CHARACTERS:***   Narrator, Wolf, Lamb

4

5   **NARRATOR:**   A wolf was drinking water at the head of a

6   **brook when he spied a lamb paddling his feet in the water**

7   **some distance down the stream. He said to himself:**

8   **WOLF:**   *(To himself)* **A tender young lamb! That's my supper.**

9   **But what excuse can I give to attack such a harmless**

10   **creature? I know what I'll do!** *(Shouting)* **Little lamb, how**

11   **dare you stir up the water I am drinking and make it**

12   **muddy!**

13   **LAMB:**   *(Bleating back)* **Cousin wolf, you must be mistaken.**

14   **How can I be spoiling your water since it runs from you**

15   **to me and not from me to you?**

16   **WOLF:**   *(Snapping)* **Don't argue. I know you. You're the one**

17   **who was saying those ugly things about me behind my**

18   **back a year ago.**

19   **LAMB:**   *(Trembling)* **Oh, sir, a year ago I was not even born.**

20   **WOLF:**   *(Snarling)* **Well, if it was not you, then it was your**

21   **father, and that amounts to the same thing. Besides, I'm**

22   **not going to have you argue me out of my supper.**

23   **NARRATOR:**   **Without another word, he fell upon the**

24   **helpless lamb and tore her to pieces. Moral: Any excuse**

25   **will serve a tyrant.**

26

27

28

29

30

31

32

33

34

35

MERCURY AND THE SCULPTOR

CHARACTERS: Mercury, Sculptor, Narrator

MERCURY: At times when I am not busy running errands here on Olympus, I yearn to know whether I am still held in high esteem by mankind. I think I'll go down to earth to see. I'll disguise myself as a traveler and visit that sculptor's studio, the one who does images of the gods. "Sir, how much are you asking for this odd piece?"

SCULPTOR: That image of Jupiter? I'll let you have that one cheap. It's one of our less popular numbers. One drachma.

MERCURY: *(A bit amused that Jupiter's image is so cheap)* Uh — how much for this stout lady here?

SCULPTOR: Juno? We have to get a little more for females.

MERCURY: I see you have a very handsome statue there of Mercury. How high do you value that excellent likeness?

SCULPTOR: On that I'm willing to make you a bargain. If you'll pay me the price I quoted you on the other two statues — Juno and Jupiter — I'll throw this one of Mercury in free.

NARRATOR: Moral: He who seeks a compliment sometimes discovers the truth.

281

1   **THE LARK AND HER YOUNG ONES**
2
3   *CHARACTERS:*   Lark, Narrator, Farmer
4
5   LARK: Now, my babies, I must leave you here in the nest
6   while I go out to hunt for food. But you'll be safe here in
7   the wheat field.
8   NARRATOR: And they were safe, and the mother lark left
9   them every day to find food. But as the wheat ripened
10   she knew the reapers would be coming, so she told her
11   growing babies:
12 LARK: Be sure to listen to anything you can hear, and report
13   to me all the news you learn.
14 NARRATOR: One day while she was absent, the farmer came
15   to check his crops. He said to his son:
16 FARMER: It is high time that our wheat is cut. Go, tell all our
17   neighbors to come early in the morning to help us reap it.
18 NARRATOR: The little larks were very frightened, and when
19   their mother came home they told her what they had
20   heard, begging her to move them to a safe place.
21 LARK: Don't worry, my children. There's plenty of time. If a
22   farmer waits for his neighbors to help him, there's no
23   danger of the grain being harvested tomorrow.
24 NARRATOR: The next day the owner came again, and
25   finding the day warmer and the wheat dead-ripe, said to
26   his son:
27 FARMER: There's not a moment to be lost. We cannot
28   depend upon our neighbors; we must call in all of our
29   relatives. You run now and call all your uncles and
30   cousins and tell them to be here bright and early
31   tomorrow morning to begin the harvest.
32 NARRATOR: In greater fear than before, the young larks
33   repeated to their mother the farmer's words when she
34   came home to her nest.
35 LARK: Is that all? Then do not be frightened, for relatives

282

1   always have harvesting of their own to do. But I want
2   you to listen very carefully to what you hear the next
3   time, and be sure to tell me exactly what the farmer says.
4   NARRATOR: The next day while she was away, the farmer
5   came as before, and finding the grain almost ready to fall
6   to the ground from overripeness, and still no one at work,
7   called to his son:
8   FARMER: We can't wait for our neighbors and relatives any
9   longer. You and I are going to the barn right now and
10   sharpen our sickles. At dawn tomorrow morning we shall
11   get to work and harvest the grain ourselves.
12   NARRATOR: When the young larks told their mother what
13   the farmer had said, she cried:
14   LARK: Get ready! We must move the nest. It is now time to
15   be off. Indeed, if the farmer has made up his mind to do
16   the work himself, the grain really will be cut!
17   NARRATOR: Moral: If you want a task well done, do it
18   yourself!
19
20
21
22
23
24
25
26
27
28
29
30
31
32
33
34
35

RIKKI-TIKKI-TAVI*

By Rudyard Kipling
Adapted for Readers Theatre by Melvin R. White, Ph.D.

Rudyard Kipling knew India well, and wrote exciting stories about life there, often with talking animals. One of his thrilling tales is about a young mongoose, a mammal that is born to fight snakes. This story relates, step by step, how Rikki-Tikki battled his way to victory with the help of Darzee, a tailorbird, Chuchundra, a muskrat, and a young boy's father. One of the advantages of Readers Theatre is that the roles of the mongoose, the birds, the muskrat, and the snakes, characters that intrigue children, may be portrayed by humans. No sets, lights, or special costumes are required, as children have vivid imaginations.

CAST OF CHARACTERS

Five men, three women, three either men or women. (Four are humans, with seven either snakes, birds, or mammals.)

NARRATOR: An effective storyteller, man or woman.

TEDDY: A small boy of five or six.

MOTHER: Alice; in her mid-thirties or younger.

FATHER: A bit older than Alice.

RIKKI-TIKKI-TAVI: A young male mongoose, a slender, brownish, small carnivore of India; noted especially for its ability to kill cobras.

DARZEE: A tailorbird, a feather-brained little fellow, excitable. Tailorbirds stitch leaves together to form and conceal their nests.

DARZEE'S WIFE: More sensible than her husband, Darzee.

NAG: A big black cobra some six feet long. Has the ability to flatten his neck into a hoodlike form when disturbed. In this story, he is the villain.

KARAIT: A dusty brown or gray snakeling that lives by choice on the dusty earth. Very small, but is as deadly as the cobra; may be a man or a woman.

*Adapted for Readers Theatre by Melvin R. White. Amateur performance rights of this adaptation are granted with the purchase of this book.

CHUCHUNDRA: A timid muskrat, male or female, given to tears; always frightened.

NAGAINA: Not as long as her husband, Nag, but just as mean and deadly.

In casting, consider giving contrast by the heights of your readers, making your humans tall, with the nonhumans short, probably children, and small except for Nag, who is six feet long, as is his wife, Nagaina. Choose readers who can *be* the characters, vocally and physically. The muskrat chatters, the snakes hiss, the mongoose is quick in his movements and a bit too proud and confident, etc.

A suggested stage/platform arrangement is for three chairs, stools, or boxes at Stage Right, four at Stage Left, with one short and two tall stools Upstage at the back, and perhaps a stool or chair Down Right for the Narrator.

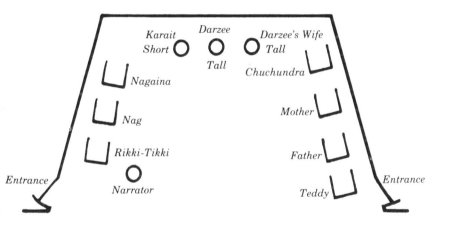

Diagram of the stage area

Costuming? None is necessary — but it does add to the production if you at least help your readers when possible. Thus the cobra and his wife may be dressed in black; the muskrat, brown or gray; the birds, bright colors; Rikki-Tikki-Tavi, some shade of brown; the snakeling, dusty brown. Try light-colored somewhat light and tropical clothes for the parents, with short pants for Teddy. You might even go so far as to provide the two birds with colorful feather boas, even as you remember you are only *suggesting* costumes, not providing them.

If there is a curtain, the cast may take its assigned seats before it is opened. If there is no curtain, the readers may file out from both Off-stage Left and Off-stage Right to take seats.

1   NARRATOR: This is the story of the great war that Rikki-
2   Tikki-Tavi fought single-handedly, through the bathrooms
3   of the big bungalow in Segowlee, a lonely country place
4   in India where the nearest neighbor lived miles away. It
5   takes place in the days when England governed India,
6   and many English families lived in India. Rikki-Tikki-
7   Tavi was a mongoose, named after the sound he made
8   when he was ready to fight. Darzee, the tailorbird, helped
9   him in his battles, and Chuchundra gave him advice —
10   Chuchundra was a muskrat, but Rikki-Tikki did the real
11   fighting. *(Transition)* **One day, a high summer flood
12   washed him out of the burrow where he lived with his
13   father and mother, and carried him, kicking and
14   clucking, down a roadside ditch. He found a bunch of
15   grass floating there, and clung to it until he passed out.
16   When he revived, he found himself lying in the middle
17   of a garden path, very draggled indeed, and a small boy
18   was saying:** *(NARRATOR crosses Down Left. TEDDY leaves
19   his seat, crosses Down Center.)*
20   TEDDY: Mother, here's a dead mongoose! Let's have a
21   funeral.
22   MOTHER: *(Follows the boy to Down Center.)* **No, let's take him
23   in and dry him. Perhaps he's not really dead.** *(The two
24   cross toward Down Left, where FATHER meets them.)*
25   FATHER: No, he's not dead, just half-drowned. We'll wrap
26   him in cotton wool and warm him. *(RIKKI-TIKKI sneezes,
27   still in his seat.)* **See, he's not dead; he's still alive! Now
28   don't frighten him, and we'll see what he'll do.**
29   TEDDY: *(Pantomime that RIKKI-TIKKI has come to him, and is
30   climbing up his leg.)* **Father, he's climbing up my leg!**
31   FATHER: Don't be frightened, Teddy. That's his way of
32   making friends.
33   TEDDY: *(Continue pantomime near neck.)* **Ouch! He's tickling
34   under my chin!**
35   MOTHER: Good gracious, be careful. That's a wild creature.

1   I suppose he's so tame because we've been kind to him.
2   FATHER: All mongooses are like that. If Teddy doesn't pick
3   him up by the tail, or try to put him in a cage, he'll run
4   in and out of the house all day — and all night, too. Let's
5   give him something to eat, some small pieces of raw meat.
6   MOTHER: I'll boil an egg for him. I think he'll like that.
7   TEDDY: I'll get him a banana. May I hold him, Father?
8   FATHER: I think it'll be all right.
9   MOTHER: I don't think so. He may bite the child.
10 FATHER: No, he won't bite. Teddy's safer with that little
11   beast than if he had a bloodhound to watch him. If a
12   snake came into his room now . . .
13 MOTHER: Snakes?! Snakes coming into the house! I won't
14   think of such an awful thing! Oh, all right, let's feed him —
15   if we must! *(They return to their seats, and NARRATOR rises,*
16   *comes Down Center.)*
17 NARRATOR: The   next   morning,   Rikki-Tikki,   always
18   curious, went out into the garden to see what was to be
19   seen. It was a large garden with bushes as big as small
20   houses, clumps of bamboo, and lots of thick grass. *(Moving*
21   *Down Right as RIKKI-TIKKI rises and crosses Up Center.)*
22   Rikki-Tikki licked his lips.
23 RIKKI-TIKKI: This is a splendid hunting ground. I'll find lots
24   of things here to keep me from being hungry. *(Birds ad-lib*
25   *a few "Oh dears!" and "What'll we do?", and RIKKI-TIKKI*
26   *hears them as they turn around to face front on their stools.)*
27   What's the matter? Who are you?
28 DARZEE: I'm Darzee, a tailorbird, and this is my wife. We
29   made this beautiful nest by pulling two leaves together
30   and stitching them up the edges with fibers . . .
31 DARZEE'S WIFE: And filling the hollow with cotton and
32   downy fluff. *(She is crying.)*
33 RIKKI-TIKKI: So what's the matter? Why are you crying?
34 DARZEE: One of our babies fell out of the nest yesterday,
35   and Nag ate him.

1   **RIKKI-TIKKI:**   That's very sad — but I'm a stranger here.
2   **Who is Nag?** *(Birds cry even more. Sound of loud hissing as*
3   *NAG rises and crosses to the left of the birds.)*
4   **DARZEE:**   Nag is a big black cobra.
5   **DARZEE'S WIFE:**   He's five feet long!
6   **NAG:**   Who is Nag? I am Nag. Look, and be afraid!
7   **RIKKI-TIKKI:**   Well, big or not big, do you think it is right to
8   eat baby tailorbirds who fall out of the nest?
9   **NAG:**   Let us talk. You eat eggs. Why shouldn't I eat birds?
10   **DARZEE:**   *(In terror)* **Behind you! Look behind you!** *(All freeze,*
11   *back to audience, during the narration.)*
12   **NARRATOR:**   Rikki-Tikki knew better than to waste time in
13   staring. He jumped up in the air as high as he could go,
14   and just under him whizzed by the head of Nagaina, Nag's
15   wife. The mongoose came down almost across her back.
16   He bit, but didn't bite long enough, and he jumped clear
17   of the whisking tail, leaving Nagaina hurt and angry. The
18   two cobras tried to catch Rikki-Tikki, but couldn't. And
19   they tried to knock down the nest of the tailorbirds, but
20   it was too high; they could not reach it. Defeated, Nag
21   and Nagaina disappeared into the grass. Just then, Teddy
22   came running down the path. *(TEDDY rises, crosses toward*
23   *RIKKI-TIKKI as KARAIT rises to cross down to the group.)*
24   **KARAIT:**   Be careful. I am death! My bite is as dangerous as
25   the cobra's. But I'm so small, nobody thinks of me, so I
26   do more harm to people. *(TEDDY enters the scene.)*
27   **RIKKI-TIKKI:**   You must not harm my family. I must kill you,
28   Karait.
29   **TEDDY:**   *(Shouts.)* **Come look! Look here! Our mongoose is**
30   **killing a snake! Bring a stick or your gun! Help!**
31   **RIKKI-TIKKI:**   What's the use of that? I've settled it all.
32   Karait is dead, I'll carry him away, and then take a
33   dustbath under the castor-oil bushes. *(RIKKI-TIKKI may*
34   *drag KARAIT away as the two of them return to their seats.*
35   *NARRATOR crosses Down Center to talk with the audience.)*

1   NARRATOR: That night, after dinner, Teddy carried Rikki-
2   Tikki off to bed, but as soon as Teddy was asleep, he went
3   off for his nightly walk around the house. In the dark he
4   ran into Chuchundra, the muskrat, creeping oh so
5   timidly around by the wall. *(CHUCHUNDRA enters,*
6   *timidly.)*
7   CHUCHUNDRA: Don't kill me. *(Almost weeping)* Don't kill me.
8   Rikki-Tikki, don't kill me.
9   RIKKI-TIKKI: *(Scornfully)* Do you think a snake-killer kills
10   muskrats?
11 CHUCHUNDRA: Those who kill snakes get killed by snakes.
12   And can I be sure that Nag won't mistake me for you
13   some dark night?
14 RIKKI-TIKKI: There's not the least danger; Nag is in the
15   garden, and I know you don't go there.
16 CHUCHUNDRA: My cousin Chua, the rat, told me — *(Stops*
17   *suddenly.)*
18 RIKKI-TIKKI: Told you what?
19 CHUCHUNDRA: Shhhh! Nag is everywhere, Rikki-Tikki.
20   You should have talked to Chua in the garden.
21 RIKKI-TIKKI: I didn't — so you must tell me. *(Menacingly)*
22   Quick, Chuchundra, or I'll bite you.
23 CHUCHUNDRA: *(Sobbing)* I'm a very poor man. I've never
24   had nerve enough even to run out into the middle of the
25   room. H'sh! I mustn't tell you anything. Can't you hear,
26   Rikki-Tikki?!
27 RIKKI-TIKKI: *(Listening. Then sotto voce into CHUCHUNDRA's*
28   *ear)* I hear a faint scratch-scratch. That's Nag or Nagaina,
29   crawling into the bathroom's sluice. You're right,
30   Chuchundra, I should have talked to Chua. But listen —
31   maybe we can hear them.
32 CHUCHUNDRA: No, not me. I'm frightened. I'm getting
33   away from here! *(CHUCHUNDRA returns rapidly to his seat.*
34   *RIKKI-TIKKI moves close to NAG and NAGAINA who have*
35   *stood up, and now face each other. They whisper to each other,*

1   *or use sotto voce.)*

2   **NAGAINA:** When the house is empty of people, *he* will have

3   to go away. Then the garden will be ours again. Go in

4   quietly, and remember that the big man who helped

5   Rikki-Tikki is the first one to bite. Then come back out

6   and tell me, and we'll hunt that mongoose together.

7   **NAG:** But are you sure there's anything to be gained by

8   killing the people?

9   **NAGAINA:** Everything. When there were no people in the

10   house, did we have any mongoose in the garden? When

11   the house is empty, we're king and queen of the garden;

12   and remember that as soon as our eggs in the melon-bed

13   hatch — as they may tomorrow — our children will need

14   room and quiet.

15   **NAG:** I hadn't thought of that. I'll go, but there is no need for

16   us to hunt Rikki-Tikki. I'll kill the big man and his wife . . .

17   **NAGAINA:** *(Interrupting)* **And the boy if you can . . .**

18   **NAG:** . . . and come away quietly. Then the house will be

19   empty, and Rikki-Tikki will go away. I'm going into the

20   bathroom now through the sluice. *(Moves across to the left;*

21   *NAGAINA returns to her seat. RIKKI-TIKKI moves Upstage to*

22   *listen and watch.)*

23   **NAG:** *(Looking about, sees the imaginary big water jar, peers into*

24   *it.)* **Here's a big water jar. I need a drink.** *(Leans over jar*

25   *to take a few sips.)* **That's good. Now, when Karait was**

26   **killed, the big man had a stick. He may have that stick**

27   **yet — and his gun, but when he comes in to bathe in the**

28   **morning, he'll not have his stick or his gun. I'll wait here**

29   **until he comes. Nagaina, do you hear me? I'll wait here**

30   **in the cool until he comes. Nagaina?** *(Listens a moment.)* **I**

31   **guess she's gone.**

32   **RIKKI-TIKKI:** *(Moves into the scene.)* **Now, if I kill Nag here,**

33   **Nagaina will know. If I fight him on the open floor, the**

34   **odds are in his favor. What am I to do? Well, at least**

35   **Nagaina seems to have gone away. Nag's coiling himself**

1   **around the bottom of the water jug.** *(NAG lies on the floor*
2   *in a circle. Then he closes his eyes in sleep.)* **He is going to**
3   **sleep. I wonder what part of his back I should get a hold.**
4   **If I don't break his back at my first jump, he can still**
5   **fight, and if he fights — O, Rikki! It must be the head, his**
6   **head above his cobra hood. When I am once there, I must**
7   **not let go, no matter what Nag does!** *(RIKKI-TIKKI runs*
8   *to NAG, puts arms around his neck, climbs onto his back, and*
9   *holds on. NAG tires to shake him off, and the two roll around*
10   *on the floor as violently as possible. RIKKI appears to be biting*
11   *the back of NAG's neck; NAG yells and protests. FATHER enters*
12   *carrying a stick, and beats NAG, who sags to the floor and dies.*
13   *MOTHER, awakened by the noise, enters.)*
14   **FATHER: There, Rikki-Tikki, I think we've killed him. You**
15   **saved our lives!**
16   **MOTHER: What's going on? What happened? So much noise!**
17   **FATHER: Alice, it's our mongoose again. The little chap**
18   **saved our lives!**
19   **RIKKI-TIKKI:** *(As the others return to their seats; well pleased*
20   *with himself)* **Now I have Nagaina to settle with, and she'll**
21   **be worse than five Nags — and there's no knowing when**
22   **her eggs will hatch. Goodness! I must go see Darzee.**
23   *(Crosses Up Center as DARZEE turns front on stool.)*
24   **DARZEE: Nag is dead! Nag is dead!**
25   **RIKKI-TIKKI:** *(Angrily)* **Oh, you stupid tuft of feathers! Is this**
26   **the time to sing?**
27   **DARZEE: Nag is dead — is dead — is dead! The valiant**
28   **Rikki-Tikki caught him by the head and held fast. The**
29   **big man brought the stick, and Nag fell in two pieces! He**
30   **will never eat my babies again.**
31   **RIKKI-TIKKI: All that's true enough, but where's Nagaina?**
32   **DARZEE: Nagaina went to the bathroom sluice and called**
33   **for Nag, but Nag came out on the end of a stick — the**
34   **sweeper picked him up on the end of a stick and threw**
35   **him on the rubbish heap. Let us sing about the great, the**

1   red-eyed Rikki-Tikki!

2 RIKKI-TIKKI: *(Angrily)* If I could get up to your nest, I'd roll

3   all of your babies out! You don't know when to do the

4   right thing at the right time. You're safe enough in your

5   nest there, but it's war for me down here. Stop singing a

6   minute, Darzee!

7 DARZEE: For the great, the beautiful Rikki-Tikki's sake, I'll

8   stop. What is it, O killer of the terrible Nag?

9 RIKKI-TIKKI: Where is Nagaina, for the third time?

10 DARZEE: On the rubbish heap by the stables, mourning for

11   Nag. Great is Rikki-Tikki with the white teeth!

12 RIKKI-TIKKI: Bother my white teeth! Do you know where

13   she keeps her eggs?

14 DARZEE: In the melon-bed, on the end nearest the wall,

15   where the sun strikes nearly all day. She had them there

16   weeks ago.

17 RIKKI-TIKKI: And you never thought it worthwhile to tell

18   me? The end nearest the wall, you said?

19 DARZEE: *(Aghast)* Rikki-Tikki, you're not going to eat her

20   eggs?

21 RIKKI-TIKKI: Not eat, exactly, no. Darzee, if you have a

22   grain of sense you'll fly off to the stables and pretend

23   your wing is broken, and let Nagaina chase you away to

24   this bush! I must get to the melon-bed, and if I went there

25   now she'd see me.

26 DARZEE'S WIFE: Darzee, we must be sensible. We must help.

27   You know that cobras' eggs mean young cobras later on.

28   You stay here and keep our babies warm, and go on

29   singing about brave Rikki-Tikki. I'll fly to the rubbish

30   heap, and make believe my wing is broken. You're so like

31   a man in many ways! I'll go! *(DARZEE'S WIFE moves across*

32   *stage Down Right.)*

33 RIKKI-TIKKI: Thank you, thank you. I hope this works —

34   and I think it will. You know how cobras like to eat birds.

35   *(NAGAINA and DARZEE'S WIFE meet Down Right.)*

1   **DARZEE'S WIFE:** *(Fluttering)* **Oh, my wing is broken! The boy**
2   **in the house threw a stone at me and broke it!**
3   **NAGAINA:** **Hiss... hiss. You warned Rikki-Tikki when I**
4   **would have killed him. Indeed and truly, you've chosen**
5   **a bad place to be lame in.** *(Moves toward DARZEE'S WIFE.)*
6   **DARZEE'S WIFE:** *(Moving away, shrieking)* **The boy broke it**
7   **with a stone!**
8   **NAGAINA:** **Well, it may be some satisfaction to you when**
9   **you're dead to know I'll settle accounts with the boy. My**
10   **husband lies on the rubbish heap this morning, but**
11   **before night, the boy in the house will be very still. What's**
12   **the use of running away? I'm sure to catch you. Little**
13   **fool, look at me!**
14   **DARZEE'S WIFE:** **I know better than that! When a bird looks**
15   **into a cobra's eyes, he gets so frightened he can't move.**
16   **No, I won't look into your eyes!** *(NAGAINA chases*
17   *DARZEE'S WIFE around and about the stage until the bird*
18   *climbs to safety on her stool, and NAGAINA slinks away to her*
19   *seat.)*
20   **NARRATOR:** *(Entering)* **Rikki-Tikki heard them going up the**
21   **path away from the stable, and he raced for the end of**
22   **the melon-patch near the wall. There, in the warm litter**
23   **about the melons, very cunningly hidden, he found**
24   **twenty-five eggs about the size of Bantam hen eggs, but**
25   **with whitish skin instead of a shell. He bit off the tops**
26   **of the eggs as fast as he could, taking care to crush the**
27   **young cobras. At last there was only one egg left when**
28   **he heard Darzee's wife screaming:**
29   **DARZEE'S WIFE:** *(Screaming from the top of her stool)* **Rikki-**
30   **Tikki, I led Nagaina toward the house, and she went up**
31   **on the veranda, and — oh, come quickly — she means**
32   **killing! Rikki-Tikki, come help; please hurry, Rikki-**
33   **Tikki!** *(During the above, FATHER, MOTHER, and TEDDY*
34   *have moved chairs about an imaginary table to Stage Left, and*
35   *seated themselves, TEDDY to the right of the table, MOTHER*

1   *above it, and FATHER to the left of it. NAGAINA moves to*
2   *Center Stage to the right of TEDDY. The three are frozen in fear.)*
3   NAGAINA: **Son of the big man who killed my Nag, stay still.**
4   **I'm not ready yet. Wait a little. Keep very still, all you**
5   **three. If you move, I strike, and if you do not move, I**
6   **strike. Oh foolish people who killed my Nag.**
7   TEDDY: **Father . . .**
8   FATHER: **Sit still, Teddy. You mustn't move. Teddy, keep**
9   **still.** *(RIKKI-TIKKI moves to the right of NAGAINA.)*
10   RIKKI-TIKKI: *(Cries out.)* **Turn around, Nagaina, turn and**
11   **fight!**
12   NAGAINA: **All in good time. I'll settle my account with you**
13   **presently. Look at your friends, Rikki-Tikki. They're still**
14   **and white. They're afraid. They dare not move — and if**
15   **you come a step nearer I strike!**
16   RIKKI-TIKKI: **Your eggs, Nagaina, your eggs in the melon-**
17   **bed near the wall. They're all destroyed, all crushed but**
18   **this one I brought here with me.**
19   NAGAINA: *(Turning as she moves toward the mongoose)* **Ah-h!**
20   **Give it to me!**
21   RIKKI-TIKKI: *(Taunting her)* **What price for the snake's egg?**
22   **For a young cobra? For the last — for the last of your**
23   **brood! The ants are eating all the others, down by the**
24   **melon-bed!** *(She heads for RIKKI-TIKKI who ducks and runs*
25   *and circles. FATHER grabs TEDDY, pulls him past him to the*
26   *left of the table, behind the MOTHER.)* **Tricked! Tricked!**
27   **Tricked! Rikki-tck-tck!** *(Chuckling)* **The boy is safe, and it**
28   **was I — I — I that caught Nag by the hood in the**
29   **bathroom. He threw me to and fro, but he couldn't shake**
30   **me off! He was dead before the big man came to help. I**
31   **did it. Rikki-Tikki-tck-tck! Come now, Nagaina. Come and**
32   **fight with me. You shall not be a widow for long!** *(FATHER*
33   *leaves the stage, taking the MOTHER and TEDDY with him.)*
34   NAGAINA: **Give me the egg, Rikki-Tikki. Give me the last of**
35

1   my eggs, and I'll go away and never come back.
2   RIKKI-TIKKI: Yes, you'll go away, and you'll never come
3   back, for you'll go to the rubbish heap with Nag. Fight,
4   widow! The big man has gone for his stick and gun! Fight!
5   (But the cobra runs to grab her egg, and dashes about, trying to
6   escape with it. Do as much action of chasing and circling and
7   running as possible, perhaps having the two birds on their stools
8   urging RIKKI-TIKKI on, reacting to the action. Finally,
9   NAGAINA runs Off-stage, and RIKKI-TIKKI follows her.)
10   DARZEE: (Describing what is taking place) Nagaina plunged
11   into the rat hole where she and Nag used to live!
12   DARZEE'S WIFE: Yes, but Rikki-Tikki got her by the tail!
13   Oh, he's being pulled into the hole!
14   DARZEE: It's all over with Rikki-Tikki! We must sing his
15   death song. Valiant Rikki-Tikki is dead! Nagaina will
16   surely kill him underground!
17   DARZEE'S WIFE: No, Darzee! No! Rikki-Tikki is dragging
18   himself out! (RIKKI-TIKKI returns in as much disarray as
19   possible.)
20   RIKKI-TIKKI: (Brushing himself off) It's all over. The widow
21   will never come out again. Tell the garden, Darzee, that
22   Nagaina is dead! Now I'll go back to the house.
23   DARZEE: Ding-dong-tock! Nag is dead! Nagaina is dead!
24   Rikki-Tikki killed Nag! Rikki-Tikki killed Nagaina! (The
25   three humans cross to Center Stage to surround the mongoose.)
26   MOTHER: (Perhaps petting RIKKI-TIKKI) He saved our lives
27   and Teddy's life! Just think, he saved all our lives!
28   TEDDY: (Putting arm around the mongoose's shoulders) I knew
29   you would, Rikki-Tikki!
30   FATHER: Yes, he saved our lives twice.
31   RIKKI-TIKKI: (Proud of himself) Oh, it's you. What are you
32   bothering about? All the cobras are dead, and if they
33   weren't, I'm here. (All turn, backs to audience, and freeze.)
34   NARRATOR: (Come Down Right slightly) Rikki-Tikki had a
35   right to be proud of himself, but he did not grow too

1   **proud, and he kept the garden as a mongoose should**
2   **keep it, with tooth and jump and spring and bite, till**
3   **never a cobra dared show its head inside the walls.**
4   *(Curtain if there is one. If not, cast turns to face the audience*
5   *and take a bow, then exit.)*
6
7
8
9
10
11
12
13
14
15
16
17
18
19
20
21
22
23
24
25
26
27
28
29
30
31
32
33
34
35

I CAN*

by Melvin R. White, Ph.D.

Readers Theatre was used successfully in grades one and two in elementary schools on the base at Fort Carson, Colorado, to teach basic theatre practices and etiquette, and was enjoyed greatly by the children. *I Can* is one of the simple scripts they were able to perform satisfactorily with assistance by the teacher and the director, Dr. White. Four children make up the cast; one of the four must be able to whistle, designated as Number One. This brief skit may be used as a closing bit for any performance.

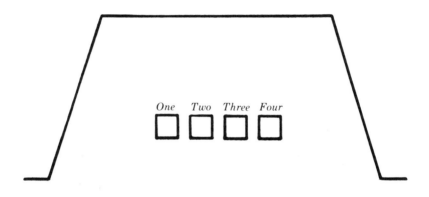

1　**SETTING:**　Four readers enter and line up Down Center.

2

3　**ONE:**　**I can stamp my right foot.** *(Does so.)*

4　**TWO, THREE, & FOUR:**　**So can we.** *(Do so.)*

5　**TWO:**　**I can stamp my left foot.** *(Does so.)*

6　**ONE, THREE, & FOUR:**　**So can we.** *(Do so.)*

7　**THREE:**　**I can count to ten.** *(Does so.)*

8　**ONE, TWO, & FOUR:**　**So can we.** *(Do so.)*

9　**ONE:**　**I can whistle.** *(Does so.)*

10　**TWO, THREE, & FOUR:**　**We can try.** *(Do so, successfully or*

11　　　*otherwise.)*

12　**ALL:**　**We can take a bow.** *(Do so, and then exit to the applause of*

13　　　*the audience.)*

14

15

16

17

18

19

20

21

22

23

24

25

26

27

28

29

30

31

32

33

34

35

The Human Spirit

THE SONG CARUSO SANG

by George P. McCallum
Adapted for Readers Theatre by the author,
assisted by Melvin R. White, Ph.D.

Mr. McCallum's short story first appeared in *The American Magazine* in May, 1955, and in its original form is basically a first-person narrative. In the ensuing script, the story materials have been extensively rewritten for Readers Theatre in dialog style, with provision for music and sound effects, if desired.

CAST OF CHARACTERS

Nine Men and two Women. The roles of the Engineer and Mr. Kamp may be read by one Man, if desired.

GIORGIO: The Narrator; a sensitive teenager, somewhat mature for his age; 15 or 16.

ENRICO CARUSO: The famous tenor; enthusiastic, filled with a love of life and people; has strong Italian accent.

THE STUDIO ENGINEER: A serious, businesslike young man.

PAPA ESPOSITO: A wise, kindly father; speaks with a slight Italian accent; middle-aged.

MAMA: A female copy of Papa; has similar accent; also middle-aged.

ANGELINA: Their sweet, attractive daughter; has a mind of her own; 19.

BEPPE: The eldest son; strongly influential in family decisions; 22.

GIOVANNI, ENRICO: The younger sons; much like Beppe but more impatient to get ahead.

DICK MANTINI: Angelina's boyfriend; ambitious but sincere and helpful; 25.

MR. KAMP: A balding little man; eccentric, impatient, weary; middle-aged.

303

The Physical Arrangement of the Scene

Throughout the script, the parenthetical directions concerning the possible positions and movements of the readers are made on the basis of the physical arrangement shown in the diagram. The readers use On-stage focus throughout, looking at and reacting to each other on the stage. The narrator, Giorgio, speaks directly to the audience at all times.

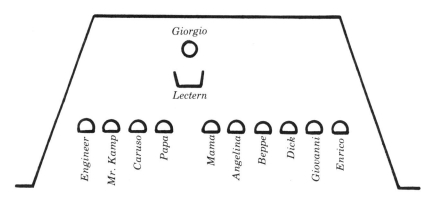

1 *(As the presentation begins, GIORGIO sits on a tall stool behind*
2 *a lectern slightly Upstage of center. If music is to be used, a*
3 *recording of Enrico Caruso's "Celeste Aïda" from the opera*
4 *"Aïda" can be heard in the background.)*
5
6 **GIORGIO:** *(To the audience)* **Hear that? Recognize it? That's**
7 **Enrico Caruso, the greatest tenor that ever lived. He's**
8 **singing "Celeste Aïda." I'm sure you've heard recordings**
9 **before of Caruso singing that great aria by Verdi. But I'll**
10 **bet you've never heard one quite like this. Let me tell**
11 **you about it. There isn't another copy of that record in**
12 **the whole world. Caruso himself gave it to my father**
13 **many years ago. What happened to the Esposito family**
14 **as a result . . . well, that's what I'd like to tell you about.**
15 **That recording was very special and it became our**
16 **proudest possession. It almost became our downfall, too.**
17 **But I'm getting ahead of the story.**
18 **Papa had known Caruso back home in Italy. That**
19 **was before Mama and Papa came to America and settled**
20 **in Brooklyn. Caruso had said that if ever Papa came to**
21 **New York to be sure to look him up. So Papa did.** *(The*
22 *music stops. PAPA rises and walks toward Downstage Right as*
23 *GIORGIO continues speaking.)* **It was at a recording studio.**
24 **Caruso was just finishing recording "Celeste Aïda," and**
25 **as the last notes died away, he looked up and saw Papa.**
26 **Immediately he called out:**
27 **CARUSO:** *(Coming from chair Down Right to left of PAPA)* **Eh,**
28 **Pasquelino! Cumme stai?**
29 **GIORGIO:** *(To audience)* **He hurried out of the studio and**
30 **embraced Papa. A few seconds later, one of the engineers**
31 **came out of the recording room.**
32 **STUDIO ENGINEER:** *(Stands, comes to left of CARUSO.)* **Excuse**
33 **me, Mr. Caruso, but I'm afraid you'll have to do the**
34 **recording over.**
35 **CARUSO: Whatta you say? Do it over? I no understand. I'm**

1   a-thinking it's-a pretty good.
2   STUDIO ENGINEER: Oh, yes, sir. It's excellent. But you see,
3   just as you finished, you called out to your friend here,
4   and — well — it got on the record. Ordinarily we could
5   eliminate something like that, but this comes
6   immediately after the last note, and I'm afraid there's
7   nothing we can do about it.
8   CARUSO: OK. You're the boss. We do it over.
9   STUDIO ENGINEER: Thank you, sir. *(Returns to his chair and*
10   *sits.)*
11   PAPA: *(Quickly, eagerly)* **Enrico** ...
12   CARUSO: Si, Pasquelino?
13   PAPA: Enrico ... I am wondering ... that record ... the one
14   you — that you spoke to me, called me by name. What
15   will happen to that one?
16   CARUSO: The engineer says it's-a-no good. So in the trash
17   can it must go.
18   PAPA: Enrico ... I ... I ...
19   CARUSO: Si, Pasquelino, my friend? What is it?
20   PAPA: Enrico ... can I have it?
21   CARUSO: You want it, Pasquelino? But what for? Did you
22   no hear the engineer? He says it is ruined. Wait. Now I
23   will make another one, a better one. I will sing it only
24   for you, my good friend.
25   PAPA: No, no, Enrico! I don't want another one. I want that
26   one ... the one in which you speak to me and call my
27   name!
28   CARUSO: Aha! Now I understand. OK, my friend! It shall be
29   yours. One autographed "Celeste Aïda" just for you!
30   PAPA: Thank you! Thank you, Enrico! *(CARUSO and PAPA*
31   *reseat themselves. GIORGIO again addresses the audience.)*
32   GIORGIO: And that is how the Esposito family came by this
33   very special recording. It was our greatest treasure. Not
34   only did Caruso give Papa his recording of "Celeste Aïda,"
35   he also helped him find a job in Sheeler's Music Store. At

1   **first it wasn't much of a job, but even if Papa was only**
2   **sweeping and mopping the floor, at least he was around**
3   **music and that was all that mattered. Mr. Sheeler took**
4   **a liking to Papa and would let him take home records on**
5   **weekends. Sunday evenings we would all sit in the parlor**
6   **while Papa played for us the great classics. When he had**
7   **played the last one, he would say:** *(All of the other members*
8   *of the Esposito family raise their heads and "come alive.")*
9   **PAPA:** *(Remaining in his seat)* **Well, my children, that is all for**
10   **tonight.**
11   **THE OTHERS:** *(Protesting)* **No, Papa! There is one more!**
12   **PAPA:**   **What? One more? But there couldn't be. Look. You**
13   **see? No, no. That is all for tonight.**
14   **ANGELINA:**   **The Caruso record, Papa!**
15   **BEPPE:**   **Yes, Papa! "Celeste Aïda." We want to hear it.**
16   **PAPA:**   **But I did not bring "Celeste Aïda" tonight. I tell you,**
17   **this is all.**
18   **ANGELINA:**   **Papa! Stop teasing us! You know the one we**
19   **mean!**
20   **MAMA:**   **Si, Pasquelino. Stop teasing the poor children. You**
21   **know very well what they want to hear.**
22   **BEPPE:**   **We want to hear** *our* **"Celeste Aïda" . . . the best one**
23   **in the world!**
24   **PAPA:**   **Oh!** *That* **"Celeste Aïda." Now, where is it? Didn't we**
25   **break it last week?**
26   *(After reacting to PAPA's line, all members of the family lower*
27   *their heads, signifying that they have "disappeared" from the*
28   *scene. GIORGIO, in his role as NARRATOR, addresses the*
29   *audience again.)*
30   **GIORGIO:**   **Sunday evenings in the parlor of the Espositos**
31   **were always like that. We would ask Papa to play the**
32   **recording Caruso had given him, and he would pretend**
33   **to know nothing about it. Then at last he would, with**
34   **great effort, recall the one we were talking about. We**
35   **would sit like statues listening to the golden notes and**

1   thrill every time when, at the end, Caruso — speaking to
2   our very own father — would call out:
3   CARUSO: *(From his seat)* **Eh, Pasquelino! Cumme stai?**
4   GIORGIO: Then Papa would remove the record from the
5   machine and carefully put it away until the following
6   Sunday. No one ever touched it but Papa.
7   The years passed. Each of the Esposito children
8   began to grow ... even I, Giorgio, the youngest of the six.
9   Beppe, the oldest, got married and moved to another part
10   of the city; but still he and his wife would come every
11   Sunday for dinner and the music in the parlor. Angelina
12   got a secretarial job with an import-export company
13   because she knew both Italian and English and was a
14   good secretary besides. One evening she brought her boss
15   home to dinner. His name was Dick Mantini, and he
16   seemed like a real nice guy. Of course, after dinner we
17   went into the parlor and listened to records from the
18   store. *(The other members of the family "come alive," as does*
19   *ANGELINA's boyfriend, DICK.)*
20 PAPA: Well, that's all for tonight, children.
21 BEPPE: Not yet, Papa. We have to hear the Caruso record.
22 ANGELINA: Yes, Papa! "Celeste Aïda."
23 PAPA: Caruso? "Celeste Aïda"? But I tell you that is all I
24   brought from the store this week.
25 MAMA: Pasquelino. Don't tease! Tonight we have a guest. He
26   will surely think the Espositos are a foolish bunch.
27 ANGELINA: You see, Dick, it's a sort of ritual. I know it must
28   sound silly but, as I told you, every Sunday the whole
29   family is together here in the parlor, and we hear records
30   Papa brings from Sheeler's. Then we insist and insist
31   until Papa plays for us his very special recording of
32   "Celeste Aïda" by Enrico Caruso.
33 DICK: Special? Why is it special?
34 ANGELINA: You'll see! Play the record for Dick, Papa.
35 PAPA: Well ... all right. But only because it is his first time.

1   You see how they pester me, young man? I don't know
2   why. Really, I don't know why they make such a fuss over
3   a record by Caruso. But every Sunday they bother me
4   until I put it on. Well, then, once more ... and that is
5   definitely all for tonight! Do I make myself clear?
6   ANGELINA: Papa! Please stop talking so much. Play the
7   record!
8   GIORGIO: *(To audience)* Dick listened politely, but it was
9   obvious he thought we were all out of our minds. Why
10   all this fuss about a record by Caruso? Then came the
11   final notes, and Caruso's words:
12   CARUSO: *(As before)* Eh, Pasquelino! Cumme stai?
13   DICK: Huh? What was that?
14   ANGELINA: That was Caruso!
15   DICK: Yeah, but what was he saying? Who was he talking to?
16   ANGELINA: He was saying, "Pasquelino! How are you?"
17   DICK: But who's Pasquelino?
18   THE OTHERS: That's Papa!
19   ANGELINA: He was talking to our very own father! Isn't it
20   wonderful? That that's why we like to hear the same
21   record every Sunday.
22   PAPA: They like to hear Caruso speak to me. Isn't it
23   ridiculous, young man?
24   ANGELINA: Papa! You love it, too!
25   DICK: *(Genuinely impressed)* Why, that *is* wonderful! And what
26   a novelty! There isn't another record like it in the world.
27   I'm sure. Enrico Caruso talking right to you, Mr. Esposito.
28   PAPA: Every time I hear the record I close my eyes and
29   imagine myself there in the studio with him. Many years
30   ago it was, but it is like yesterday.
31   DICK: You know, I'm surprised you haven't tried to sell the
32   record. You could make a lot of money with something
33   like that. It's a real gimmick. *(The members of the family*
34   *react. DICK continues.)* I've no idea what you could get for
35   such a thing, but I have a friend in the recording business.

1   I'd be glad to find out.
2 PAPA: Thank you, young man, but the record is not for sale.
3   It was given to me by my friend, Enrico Caruso. As a
4   matter of fact, I think maybe you are wrong; I doubt that
5   anyone else would have interest in it.
6 DICK: Excuse me, sir, but I think you're not looking at the
7   total picture. First of all, it's undoubtedly one of the
8   greatest recordings Caruso ever made. That alone makes
9   it valuable. But then, that little touch at the end . . . I tell
10   you, Mr. Esposito, it would sell like hot cakes.
11 PAPA: Then let the people buy hot cakes. My record is not for
12   sale! *(As GIORGIO resumes his narration, DICK and the various*
13   *members of the Esposito family lower their heads to indicate they*
14   *have "disappeared" from the scene.)*
15 GIORGIO: At this point, the others began to get funny looks
16   on their faces. It had never, in all these years, occurred
17   to us that our treasured record could be interesting for
18   anyone but the Espositos. Now here was someone who
19   was convinced it was worth money to us. We were far
20   from a rich family. We were a happy family without
21   money, but it was obvious from the looks on their faces
22   that Beppe and Giovanni and Angelina and Enrico were
23   thinking how much happier we could be *with* money.
24   Even I found myself suddenly thinking about the bicycle
25   in Nussbaum's window. Mama looked around at our faces
26   and decided the subject should be changed. *(The other*
27   *members of the family raise their heads and become "alive"*
28   *again.)*
29 MAMA: Come, everyone. We go to the kitchen and have
30   coffee. Another time you can discuss this if you think you
31   have need to.
32 PAPA: There is nothing to discuss. The record is not for sale.
33 BEPPE: But, Papa —
34 PAPA: *(Sharply)* Beppe, I said no. That's final!
35 GIORGIO: *(To audience)* It wasn't final, though. A week later,

1 after we'd had dinner and the concert and heard the
2 Caruso record, Beppe got up and made a little speech.
3 BEPPE: *(Stands.)* **Papa ... Mama ... for a long time now you**
4 **have dreamed of owning a piece of land out in Jersey**
5 **where you could have a garden and raise some grapes**
6 **and fruit trees. Both of you have worked hard, and now**
7 **it is time for you to take it easy and enjoy yourselves.**
8 **You deserve it if anyone does. Well, we have been talking —**
9 **Enrico, Angelina, Giovanni, and I. We talked to Dick again**
10 **the other night. He saw his friend from the recording**
11 **company. Papa, it looks like we could get as much as a**
12 **thousand dollars for the record. Think, Papa, what you**
13 **could do — Mama and you — with a thousand dollars!**
14 PAPA: **I said before and I say again: my record is not for sale.**
15 **Not for a thousand ... not for ten thousand dollars. We'll**
16 **talk about it no more!**
17 BEPPE: **But, Papa! Listen! You wouldn't even have to sell**
18 **your record. You could keep it. Dick's friend said the**
19 **recording company would pay you just to borrow it and**
20 **copy it. Think of it, Papa.**
21 PAPA: *(Grudgingly)* **Very well. I will think.**
22 BEPPE: *(Eagerly)* **Does that mean I can find out how to get in**
23 **touch with the man from the recording company — just**
24 **in case?**
25 PAPA: **I ... suppose.**
26 BEPPE: **Thanks, Papa! You won't be sorry.**
27 *(BEPPE reseats himself in his chair, and he and the other*
28 *members of the family lower their heads. GIORGIO resumes his*
29 *narration.)*
30 GIORGIO: **Beppe shouldn't have added those last words.**
31 **Before the week was out, Papa was sorry. Mama, too —**
32 **though she said nothing. I think even I was a little sorry.**
33 **You see, what happened was that Beppe found out that**
34 **we would probably get *more* than a thousand dollars for**
35 **the record.**

1   Suddenly our house became a completely different
2   place. Always before, it had been a happy
3   place . . . crowded and noisy and warm and everything
4   that makes a home what it is supposed to be. And now
5   it wasn't that way at all. The record by Caruso that had
6   been our greatest possession changed everything.
7   You see, what happened was this: Every one of us —
8   Beppe, Angelina, Giovanni, Enrico, and — yes, even I —
9   we got to thinking how we ought to spend all the money
10   we were going to get for the record. Giovanni thought
11   we ought to have a car. *(The members of the Esposito family*
12   *rise and play the ensuing scene in the area Down Left.)*
13 GIOVANNI: *(Crossing toward Down Left)* **Look. We've never had**
14   **a car. Think how great it would be! We could all pile in**
15   **and go for long drives on Sunday — clear up to Bear**
16   **Mountain. And in the summer we could even take**
17   **vacations to places like Grand Canyon.**
18 ANGELINA: *(Following GIOVANNI Down Left)* **No, Giovanni.**
19   **Mama wouldn't like a car. What she wants, I'm sure, is a**
20   **house. Look at all the years we've had to live in this little**
21   **apartment over the Pezzullo fruit store! Mama deserves**
22   **a nice new house.**
23 ENRICO: *(Heatedly: to ANGELINA and GIOVANNI)* **You are**
24   **both wrong, Angelina. Did it ever occur to either one of**
25   **you that Mama and Papa have had one dream since their**
26   **family has grown up and they can think a little about**
27   **themselves for a change? A trip back home to Italy! That's**
28   **what they want . . . to take all of us with them to meet**
29   **our grandparents and aunts and uncles and —**
30 ANGELINA: **Oh, sure! You say that because** *you* **want a free**
31   **trip to Italy.**
32 GIOVANNI: **And maybe there'll be a little money left over for**
33   **you to take singing lessons, Enrico.**
34 ENRICO: **What do you mean by that, Giovanni?**
35 ANGELINA: **He's right, Enrico. Just because you're named**

1   after Caruso, you think that —
2 BEPPE: Quiet! Be still, both of you! You're fighting just like
3   you did when you were in grade school. I don't know
4   where any of you get these crazy ideas. Mama and Papa
5   have talked of only one dream, and that has been a little
6   piece of farmland in Jersey. If they sell the record, that's
7   what they ought to buy with the money.
8 GIOVANNI: *(Sarcastically)* Great! Then you and Rosa could
9   take the children there for weekends. Very convenient.
10   *(The four — GIOVANNI, ANGELINA, ENRICO, and BEPPE —*
11   *ad-lib their arguing as they return to their respective chairs and*
12   *sit. As GIORGIO picks up the narration again, their voices stop;*
13   *but by the posture of their bodies and the stony-faced silence*
14   *which they maintain until they lower their heads to "disappear"*
15   *from the scene, they dramatically convey the hostilities which*
16   *have been engendered.)*
17 GIORGIO: So it went, day after day. I must admit even I had
18   dreams about how to spend the record money . . . only
19   my problem was that I changed my mind two or three
20   times a day. *(Sighs, shrugs.)* Well, things moved on. And
21   Beppe arranged for the man from the recording company
22   to come Sunday evening to hear the record. Papa would
23   not allow it out of the house.
24   By then, nobody in the Esposito family was speaking
25   to anyone. Such long faces had never before been seen
26   in our home as on that evening when we all sat around
27   the table at suppertime. Mama had insisted we all have
28   dinner together as usual. Believe me, it was far from the
29   laughing, talking, eating bunch that usually crowded
30   around the table. It was more like a wake. Just before
31   Mama brought in the soup, Papa stood up to speak. *(PAPA*
32   *stands, remaining near his chair or stepping around behind it.)*
33 PAPA: It has been two weeks now since Dick told us we
34   could get a lot of money for our Caruso record. In my
35   bones I felt this was not good. I said my record was not

1   for sale. Then we heard that we didn't have to sell — that

2   we only had to lend. It didn't seem so bad just to let them

3   copy it, so I said nothing. *(Sighs heavily, sadly.)* **But it *is***

4   **bad. Very bad. I know this now. Ever since we've thought**

5   **of selling the record, I've been watching this family, and**

6   **I see we aren't a family any more. Before ... we were**

7   **happy, and this house was filled with love and laughter.**

8   **Now there are only angry faces and sharp words. I used**

9   **to hurry home from work every night. Now I stay away.**

10   **MAMA:** *(Sniffling)* **Ay, Pasquelino! Please. The soup is getting**

11   **cold.**

12   **PAPA:** No, Mama. I will not stop. Not until I finish what I have

13   to say. The soup can be made hot again. But this

14   family ... I don't know if it can be made happy again.

15   Not with a big car ... or a house on Long Island ... a trip

16   to Italy ... or a farm in New Jersey.

17   **BEPPE:** But, Papa, we were only thinking —

18   **PAPA:** Please, Beppe. Let me finish. Why is this? I ask myself.

19   Why is it that in only a few days a family that has been

20   so happy — so very, very happy — can suddenly be so

21   sad? It is because of a record ... a record by my dear

22   friend Enrico Caruso. Now the thing that for many years

23   is happiness for Pasquelino Esposito is unhappiness. I

24   ask myself, can I buy with money this happiness once

25   again? And I find the only answer is no.

26   **BEPPE:** But, Papa, you'd still have your record and the little

27   farm in Jersey with apples and grapes ...

28   **PAPA:** Apples and grapes I can buy at the fruit store of

29   Pezzullo. A family I cannot buy in any place.

30   **GIORGIO:** *(To audience)* **With that, Papa left the table without**

31   **touching his soup and went into the parlor.** *(PAPA reseats*

32   *himself in his chair and lowers his head to signify that he is*

33   *disappearing from the scene. GIORGIO, meanwhile continues.)*

34   **Then Mama spoke to us.**

35   **MAMA:** Beppe ... Angelina ... all of you. Please. You must

1   think of all your papa has said. *(MAMA sits and lowers her*
2   *head. BEPPE rises.)*
3 BEPPE: Papa's right. And it's all my fault.
4 GIOVANNI: *(Rises, joins BEPPE.)* Your fault, Beppe?
5 BEPPE: Yes, Giovanni. I kept insisting that Papa consider
6   selling the record after he'd made it plain he didn't want
7   to.
8 GIOVANNI: Don't be stupid, Beppe! You were right to insist.
9   You were just thinking of the good of the family. Once
10   this is all over and the record is copied, Papa will see we
11   did right. He'll have his record and the money, too — like
12   you just said. *(ANGELINA rises and crosses to GIOVANNI*
13   *and BEPPE.)*
14 BEPPE: But the family? *(Worriedly)* Didn't you hear Papa
15   and see his face just now? And Mama, too? Suddenly,
16   when I looked at them, I realized we stand a chance of
17   losing more than we could buy with a few dollars.
18 ANGELINA: *(Protesting)* Beppe, this isn't like you. You've
19   always been the practical one in the family. Now you're
20   becoming a dreamer — just like Papa.
21 BEPPE: And that's so bad . . . being like Papa?
22 ANGELINA: That's isn't what I mean, and you know it.
23 GIOVANNI: Well, quit arguing, you two. Any minute now,
24   Mr. Kamp, from the record company, will be here. It's
25   too late to call and tell him not to come. At least we'll
26   have to hear what he has to say.
27 BEPPE: *(Firmly)* Anyway, we're not going to sell!
28   *(ANGELINA, GIOVANNI, and BEPPE return to their chairs,*
29   *reseat themselves, and lower their heads as GIORGIO resumes*
30   *his narration.)*
31 GIORGIO: I found myself awfully glad about what Beppe
32   had said. Suddenly the bicycle and the electric train and
33   all the other things I dreamed of buying were like nothing
34   at all. I knew now that the last thing I wanted was for
35   us to sell the Caruso record. When it went out of our

1   house, then something terribly important to the
2   Espositos would go with it ... perhaps forever. *(Pauses,*
3   *sighs.)* But ... nevertheless, at exactly seven-thirty, the
4   recording company's representative, Mr. Kamp — a
5   baldheaded little man with a very businesslike manner —
6   knocked at the door.
7   *(All of the Espositos raise their heads and "come alive." By their*
8   *facial expressions and bodily attitudes, they evidence their*
9   *feelings of excitement and uneasiness.)*
10   We all went into the parlor and sat down. The room
11   was deadly quiet, like just before a thunderstorm. Papa
12   picked up the record and placed it on the turntable. He
13   seemed nervous, and his hands were shaking as he
14   lowered the needle onto the record. Then, suddenly, he
15   stopped the machine.
16   PAPA: Excuse me, sir. I put on the wrong record. That was
17   "Vesti la Giubba." How could I have made such a stupid
18   mistake?
19   MR. KAMP: Very natural, I'm sure, Mr. Esposito. Both
20   records look exactly alike. But may I now hear "Celeste
21   Aïda"? My time *is* limited.
22   PAPA: Of course, of course. This time I have the right record.
23   GIORGIO: *(To audience)* The little man from the recording
24   company leaned forward and stared at the floor as though
25   that was where the sound was coming from. When the
26   recording finished, he nodded and asked to hear it once
27   more. Papa started the record at the beginning again.
28   Then he sat back and gazed around the room as Caruso
29   sang of his love for the beautiful Aïda. Following Papa's
30   gaze, I saw Angelina and Beppe and Enrico and
31   Giovanni — all with the same anxious expression, one
32   just like the next. They were not my brothers and sisters
33   at all, nor was this the happy time of the many other
34   Sundays. Finally, "Celeste Aïda" came to its end, and the
35   much-loved Caruso exclaimed, as always:

316

1	CARUSO: Eh, Pasquelino! Cumme stai?
2	MR. KAMP: *(Straightening in his chair)* Well, Mr. Esposito. You
3	have quite a record there. I'll admit to you frankly that
4	this is the best "Celeste Aïda" I have ever heard. Excuse
5	my immodesty, but I *am* considered one of the best
6	authorities on Caruso. So when I say this is the best, it
7	*is* the best. And that little personal touch at the
8	end...absolutely great. That alone would make it a
9	record best seller!
10	*(He laughs at his little play on the word "record"; but when the*
11	*others fail to join in, he stops and suddenly becomes serious*
12	*again.)*
13	Yes...well, I suppose you want to talk business.
14	And as I said, my time is limited. *(Clears his throat.)* Well,
15	sir, my company will pay you five thousand dollars for
16	all the rights to the use of this recording if it's what we
17	want, and I do not hesitate to assure you that it is.
18	ANGELINA: Five thousand dollars!
19	GIOVANNI: Do you hear that, Papa?
20	ENRICO: We had no idea it would be so much!
21	BEPPE: Sorry you had to come all the way out to Brooklyn
22	for nothing, Mr. Kamp. Just this afternoon we decided
23	not to sell the record or any rights to it.
24	MR. KAMP: *(Astounded)* What's that, young man?
25	ANGELINA: Beppe! What are you saying?
26	GIOVANNI: Are you out of your mind? He didn't say *one*
27	thousand —
28	ENRICO: He said *five* thousand dollars, Beppe!
29	BEPPE: I heard him. I guess the rest of you forget what we
30	agreed this afternoon. Sorry, Mr. Kamp. I repeat: the
31	record is not for sale.
32	MR. KAMP: But why? I — I don't understand.
33	BEPPE: *(Quietly)* Shall we say...for personal reasons.
34	ANGELINA: Beppe!
35	MR. KAMP: Well...I may as well tell you that my company

317

1   has authorized me to go as high as six thousand if

2   necessary to —

3   ANGELINA, GIOVANNI, ENRICO: Six thousand!

4   MR. KAMP: Yes, six thousand. But not a penny more.

5   BEPPE: Did you say . . . *six* thousand?

6   *(For a tense moment, all of the Espositos stare in stupefied silence.*

7   *Then GIORGIO again speaks to the audience, his voice charged*

8   *with emotion.)*

9   GIORGIO: As for me . . . I could not speak. And I had to turn

10   my head away because I didn't want the others to see

11   there were tears in my eyes. Through the blur I could

12   see the record where Papa had put it with the others on

13   the table. I'll never be able to explain — not even to

14   myself — how it happened. But suddenly — sobbing, "No!

15   No!" — I grabbed the record from the table and dashed

16   it to the floor, smashing it into a thousand pieces.

17   Everything in the room stopped dead still. Finally, Mr.

18   Kamp managed to speak.

19   MR. KAMP: *(Very much upset)* You're all crazy! And that's for

20   sure! *Good* night! *(He reseats himself in his chair, lowers his*

21   *head, and "disappears" from the scene as GIORGIO continues.)*

22   GIORGIO: I rushed into the kitchen, no longer able to

23   control my sobs. The others followed. *(Emotion surging into*

24   *his voice again)* It was quite a scene, what with everyone

25   crying and hugging me. To tell the truth, I was suddenly

26   embarrassed . . . but mostly I was glad . . . glad I had

27   broken the record. *(All members of the family, except BEPPE,*

28   *rise and play the ensuing scene down front near center.)*

29   PAPA: Good boy, Giorgio! This is a family again, and nothing

30   else matters.

31   GIOVANNI: You had to do it, Giorgio! It was the only way to

32   bring us to our senses.

33   ANGELINA: It took the baby of the family to make us see it.

34   Otherwise — well, I hate to think how close we came to

35   disaster.

1   **PAPA:**   Mama! We must have a celebration! Don't you have
2   something for us . . . some coffee at least? Suddenly I'm
3   hungry. I guess it's because I didn't eat any dinner this
4   evening.
5   **MAMA:**   Si, Pasquelino! I have only to heat it up. And there is
6   the cake that no one touched.
7   **ENRICO:**   Look at Mama! She's smiling for the first time in
8   two weeks! Mama, you have six children, but you had to
9   have five before you gave birth to an intelligent one.
10   **MAMA:**   I have the best children in the world . . . from the
11   oldest to the youngest.
12   **GIOVANNI:**   *(Looking around)* Hey! Speaking of the oldest —
13   where's Beppe?
14   **ANGELINA:**   I think he took Mr. Kamp to the door. *(As though*
15   *from an adjoining room, there can be heard the music and singing*
16   *of the Caruso recording.)*
17   **ENRICO:**   Listen! *(There is a short pause as all listen, their faces*
18   *filled with wonderment.)*
19   **GIOVANNI:**   It can't be!
20   **ANGELINA:**   It is! It's "Celeste Aïda"! *(BEPPE stands, a happy*
21   *smile on his face, elation in his voice.)*
22   **BEPPE:**   Yes! Papa's "Celeste Aïda."
23   **ENRICO:**   Beppe! What is it? What has happened?
24   **BEPPE:**   I guess we'll have to get a new "Vesti la Giubba." And
25   Giorgio . . . we'll also have to get you a new pair of glasses!
26   *(Laughs.)* Seems you couldn't see well enough and grabbed
27   the wrong record off the table!
28   **MAMA:**   *(Happily)* Giorgio! Giorgio has smashed the wrong
29   record!
30   *(All of the Espositos laugh, return to their respective chairs, and*
31   *reseat themselves as they listen enraptured to the strains of the*
32   *music while GIORGIO resumes his narration.)*
33   **GIORGIO:**   "Celesta Aïda!" In all the years we had listened to
34   it, it never sounded as beautiful as it did at that moment.
35   We listened as though for the first time. And when at the

1   end, Caruso called out:
2   CARUSO: Eh, Pasquelino! Cumme stai?
3   PAPA: Happy again, my friend, very happy!
4   GIORGIO: And with that answer, Papa spoke for all of us.
5   *(Moving around beside his lectern)* **Well . . . that's all there is.**
6   **We're a family again and still have the record. Maybe**
7   **someday we'll save enough money to move to that farm**
8   **in Jersey. Right now it's just something nice to dream**
9   **about. The Sunday evenings are once again as**
10   **before . . . except that Angelina has married Dick**
11   **Mantini, and now he is also with us every Sunday.** *(The*
12   *members of the family "come alive" and start listening.)* **And**
13   **every Sunday, we listen to Caruso and "Celesta Aïda," just**
14   **as if we'd never heard him say:**
15 CARUSO: Eh, Pasquelino! Cumme stai?
16 GIORGIO: Only now, Papa always answers, "Happy, my
17   friend Caruso, very happy!"
18
19
20
21
22
23
24
25
26
27
28
29
30
31
32
33
34
35

SPARRING WITH THE CHAMP

by Joan Wixen
Adapted for performance by Melvin R. White, Ph.D.

This interview with Muhammad Ali by Joan Wixen, described as "a gutsy Los Angeles-based freelancer who specializes in celebrity confrontations . . . er, interviews," provides an intriguing, different, and more human view of The Champ than is usual. Although it calls for a cast of four, it actually is a two-person script.

CAST OF CHARACTERS

ALI: Muhammad after 22 years of fighting.

REPORTER: A female "gutsy" freelancer.

ED LOMBARD: Detroit News photographer, 25-35 years old.

VOICE: One line from the imaginary crowd.

No setting is necessary. The Down Right area is Ali's farm; Down Left, the area of the ring. One piece of furniture is at center, slightly Upstage, a davenport. That's all that's needed, but in order to provide a place for the Reporter to hide, a table is placed somewhere near the davenport. As the skit opens, the Reporter enters, looks around, and gets close to the table as the opening sound effects are heard.

Sparring With the Champ from April 1977 issue of *Passages*, copyright © 1992, Joan Wixen. Used by permission. The author is presently writing two books on her life and her unique interviews with world famous celebrities. She has been a West Coast correspondent for *The Detroit News* and her work has appeared in the *L.A. Times*, *Christian Science Monitor*, *Chicago Sun Times*, *San Francisco Chronicle*, *The Washington Star* and other newspapers and magazines worldwide.

1   **SOUND:** *(Gunshots)*

2   **ALI:** *(Yell)* **Hide! Hide!** *(REPORTER dives under the table. ALI*

3   *after a pause, starts to laugh.)* **Hey, what's the matter, gal?**

4   **Nobody's after you. Don't you know we're just puttin'**

5   **you on?**

6   **REPORTER:** **Big joke. You scared the daylights out of me.**

7   *(Both laugh.)*

8   **ALI:** **OK. I'll cooperate with you now. Ask me anything you**

9   **want.** *(ALI turns back to audience as REPORTER walks Down*

10   *Center to talk to the audience.)*

11   **REPORTER:** **Muhammad Ali, once heavyweight champion**

12   **of the world, is a man of many moods. One minute he's**

13   **warm and friendly, and the next he chews you out. He's**

14   **hateful, lovable, rude, charming, self-assured — yet a**

15   **part of him comes across as someone who has no**

16   **confidence at all.** *(Transition. Cross Down Right)* **I arrived**

17   **early in the afternoon at Ali's $400,000 eighty-four acre**

18   **farm just out of Berrien Springs, Michigan. Ed Lombardo,**

19   **the Detroit News photographer, greets me and tells me**

20   **he's been with Ali all morning.**

21   **ED LOMBARDO:** **You couldn't find a more cooperative, easy-**

22   **going guy. He was like a kid out there, horseback riding**

23   **all by himself, whooping it up, screeching and yelling**

24   **and chasing all the horses in the corral.** *(ALI shadow-boxes*

25   *Down Left.)*

26   **REPORTER:** **And there is The Greatest now, in the ring,**

27   **dancing and prancing and yelling and telling jokes,**

28   **letting everyone know he's having the time of his life.**

29   **ALI:** *(To crowd)* **I'm the greatest fighter of all time. I'm the**

30   **king of all kings. Never before has there been a champion**

31   **as great as I am. Look!** *(Pointing to his face)* **I've been in**

32   **one hundred eighty-six battles and I've been fighting for**

33   **twenty-two years and I should be ugly by now, shouldn't**

34   **I? But look — look how beautiful I am. Have you ever**

35   **seen a more beautiful face?**

1   VOICE: Hey, Ali, what was your best fight?

2   ALI: Joe Frazier. It was a thriller. A chiller. But I got Joe

3   right on his vanilla. *(Laughs. Then, waving to the crowd,*

4   *crosses Down Center to the REPORTER.)*

5   REPORTER: Ali comes over, and begins berating me, loudly.

6   ALI: This is no kind of work for you. You should be at home

7   somewhere with a man and some kids, doing woman-type

8   things. *(Sudden mood change)* All right. Just come with me.

9   I'll give you a few minutes.

10   REPORTER: As I follow him into the modest living room of

11   the farmhouse, he seems uncomfortable as I sit beside

12   him on the sofa. I ask questions, but he gives perfunctory

13   answers. Finally, he explodes:

14   ALI: Look, lady, there's nothing you can ask me that hasn't

15   already been asked me twenty times before. I'm the most

16   famous human being here on this earth. I've been in sixty-

17   two countries, and wherever I go I can't step off a plane

18   without being mobbed.

19   REPORTER: *(Glaring)* So . . .

20   ALI: *(Glaring back)* So . . .

21   REPORTER: Come on now, Ali. You're just playing games

22   with me. People are interested in you, what you're like

23   when you're not "on."

24   ALI: What am I like? What am I like? *(Making snorting noises.*

25   *Walking away, mincing, hands on hips)* Well, I'll tell you

26   dearie. I'm really one of the boys, sweetie. Would you like

27   some tea? *(Laughs at himself, then turns suddenly serious*

28   *again.)* Look, I want to level with you. There's an offshoot

29   group of Muslims that want to come over now and rough

30   you up a bit.

31   REPORTER: *(Taking it in her stride)* There are a lot of

32   crackpots in the world.

33   ALI: *(Blowing a bit)* Are you saying Muslims are crackpots?

34   Muslims are the most peaceful people on earth. *(Returns*

35   *to sit by her.)* I'll bet you don't know they're taking in white

323

1	people now, too. You see, color doesn't matter to us. We
2	just want the good people of the world to unite. We love
3	all people.

4 REPORTER: *(Unbelieving)* **You mean there's no one you really**
5 **hate?! You must have some hatred for those white people**
6 **who once pushed your race down.**

7 ALI: **Don't you know those days are completely over? The**
8 **world is different now. You're trying to get me to discuss**
9 **something that happened twenty years back. I know**
10 **what I'm talking about, because I'm the first truly free**
11 **black man in America. No white man controls me in any**
12 **way. I'm the first big black man who identifies with his**
13 **own kind. I bet you've never seen a black person like me**
14 **before.**

15 REPORTER: **I have, too. There are plenty of black people**
16 **today who don't take guff from anyone.**

17 ALI: **Who're you kidding?! Don't you know those poor**
18 **"nigguhs" have been beaten down?**

19 REPORTER: **What'id you call them?**

20 ALI: **"Nigguhs." I can say "nigguhs" but you can't.**

21 REPORTER: **OK, OK. I've read how some white people have**
22 **really hurt you. How you were so affected when Emmett**
23 **Till, a kid your own age, was lynched in Mississippi. And**
24 **how a group of rich Southern men backed you in the**
25 **early stages of your career — and treated you as a piece**
26 **of property.** *(ALI tries to interrupt, but she continues, pressing*
27 *even more.)* **And how in 1960 you got the Olympic gold**
28 **medal for your country, but back in your hometown of**
29 **Louisville you were thrown out of some hamburger joint**
30 **for being black. You drove to a bridge and threw the**
31 **medal into the Ohio River. How could you do that?!**

32 ALI: *(Very serious)* **Up until that night, I thought the Olympic**
33 **medal was the most precious thing in my life. I was so**
34 **proud of it I even slept with it. But that night something**
35 **inside me broke, and somehow everything lost its magic.**

1   It was then I realized that all I had won was just a cheap
2   piece of metal attached to a shabby ribbon, and I didn't
3   want any part of it. From that moment on, I knew I had
4   to be my own kind of champion, and I wasn't going to fit
5   into some mold that the white world set for me. I wasn't
6   going to go against the best interest of my people.
7   REPORTER: When did you become a Muslim?
8   ALI: That was when I decided, and I changed my name from
9   Cassius Clay to Muhammad Ali, which means "one who
10   is worthy of praise."
11   REPORTER: *(Thoughtfully)* "Someone who is worthy of
12   praise."
13   ALI: Someday I want to go down in history as a man who
14   didn't sell his people short by becoming an Uncle Tom
15   when he got famous. *(Keep on talking)*
16   REPORTER: I understand . . .
17   ALI: *(Continuing with fervor, with tremendous conviction)* You see,
18   I am an American, only I'm part of America that isn't
19   always recognized. I am black, confident, and cocky. And
20   that is why I have to go by my own name, not a name
21   that was handed down to my family by some slave master.
22   I hope people accept me, but whether they do or not, I
23   am what I am, with or without their approval.
24   REPORTER: I think what bugs a lot of people is that you
25   refused to fight in the Vietnamese war.
26   ALI: *(Exploding again)* How could I fight in a war like that?!
27   To me it was an unjust war and I didn't want to help it
28   in any way. I used to wonder how come the people who
29   were denouncing me weren't denouncing all the
30   injustices inflicted on my people in white America.
31   REPORTER: I wonder why it is that some black people who
32   have been pushed down just stay there, while others, like
33   you, get up and try to change things.
34   ALI: *(Thoughtfully)* Life to me is like a wine cellar. It's a store-
35   house where all sorts of wines are collected, and man only

1   has to choose the wine he wishes. I feel you are what you
2   become by what wine you allow yourself to drink. And
3   the important thing is to realize the choice is within
4   yourself.
5 REPORTER: What was there in you that made you drink the
6   wine of success?
7 ALI: *(Thoughtfully, with conviction)* God himself helped me to
8   believe in myself. I feel everything has a purpose. Trees
9   have a purpose. The moon has a purpose. Rain has a
10   purpose. Anything God created has a purpose. And it is
11   the knowledge of that purpose that enables all living
12   things to fulfill themselves.
13 REPORTER: Who do you think was the most important
14   person in your life?
15 ALI: My grandfather. I'm supposed to take after him —
16   Herman, his name was. He was a proud, muscular man.
17   I remember he never spanked us, because he was so
18   strong he was afraid he might hurt us. He always got
19   across in words what he wanted to say.
20 REPORTER: What about your father?
21 ALI: My dad was a sign painter, and he was a lot like my
22   grandfather. He never raised a hand to me. He wanted
23   me to be a teacher or a lawyer, but after the first time
24   he saw me fight, he told me to keep on, that I would
25   become another Joe Louis.
26 REPORTER: And your mother?
27 ALI: My mother's a plump little woman, always cooking good
28   food. Everything always had to be perfect in her home.
29 REPORTER: I hear you have a younger brother who helps
30   with the business end of your career.
31 ALI: Yeah.
32 REPORTER: A lot of people say you're getting flabby . . . on
33   the downhill.
34 ALI: Of course I'm on the downhill. We're *all* on the downhill.
35   But I've still got some punch in me yet.

1 REPORTER: What about money? Will you have any left for
2 later on? I hear you've got a pair of Rolls-Royces, a Mark
3 V, a Greyhound Scenicruiser, boats, planes ...
4 ALI: I made over twenty-six million dollars last year. Pretty
5 good for a guy with my background, eh?
6 REPORTER: Is it true you graduated 376th in a class of 391
7 at Louisville High School?
8 ALI: Yeah ... but Louisville *Central* High School. Sure it's
9 true. I never bothered with school work. All I was
10 interested in was fighting.
11 REPORTER: When you completely stop fighting, what d'you
12 want to do?
13 ALI: Become an evangelist. I want to tell people that when
14 they mistreat others they mistreat the artist who created
15 them.
16 REPORTER: And when you're not out preaching?
17 ALI: I want to live here, ride horses, fish, exercise, and
18 enjoy life. Isn't this a great place to raise my kids?
19 REPORTER: Tell me, what attracts you to a woman?
20 ALI: I like them to be obedient, and listen carefully to what
21 I have to say. I like them to follow me; I like to lead. I
22 like them to wear long skirts and modest clothes and not
23 show their bodies. Some men think women should be
24 equal, but I'm not one of 'em.
25 REPORTER: I read that your first wife, Sonji Roi, said you
26 were impossible to live with, that you were either up or
27 down, and never made any sense. And your second wife,
28 Khalilah, also walked out on you.
29 ALI: I don't want to talk about women. You hear? You hear?
30 *(Walks away, shadow-boxing, briefly. Then laughs, and takes*
31 *Center Stage.)* I'm the greatest. I'm the greatest. Don't you
32 know that? And how can The Greatest ever know what
33 he's going to do? Nobody knows what Ali's gonna do!
34 REPORTER: Does it bother you that some people say you
35 have too big a mouth? That you're too arrogant and cocky?

1   ALI: *(Laughing)* Look, I have to be that way or else people
2   won't come to see me get beat up. It tickles me when I'm
3   out there telling everyone how great I am. Who says my
4   mouth's too big? Who says? Who says? How can someone
5   as great as me have too big a mouth? *(ALI gives her a hug.)*
6   REPORTER: At least you don't feel like poking me in the
7   nose anymore.
8   ALI: *(Shaking his head)* You know, I've been interviewed by
9   everyone, but you're something else. But I still say a
10   woman like you has no business doing this kind of work.
11   And that's enough. End of interview. *(ALI stalks off. With*
12   *a smile of satisfaction and a gesture of "ain't he something,"*
13   *REPORTER takes her leave.)*
14
15
16
17
18
19
20
21
22
23
24
25
26
27
28
29
30
31
32
33
34
35

WHERE HAVE ALL THE FLOWERS GONE?

Adapted from a newspaper column by Al Martinez

CAST OF CHARACTERS

NARRATOR: An effective storyteller, man or woman.

CHILD: Girl or boy, small.

FATHER: A good man, old enough to be the father of the child.

Stage Diagram

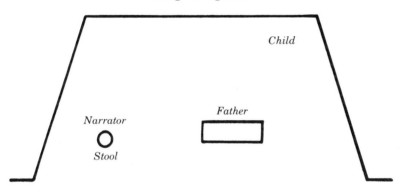

1   *(Three readers enter to take their places on stage: NARRATOR*
2   *to the stool or chair Down Right, FATHER on bench Down*
3   *Center, CHILD Up Left, standing with back to audience.*
4   *FATHER and CHILD always freeze during narration.)*
5 **NARRATOR:** *(Talking with audience)* **Once upon a time in the**
6   **year 2000 a small boy walked up to his father and asked:**
7   *(NARRATOR sits on stool Down Right after the introductory*
8   *narration; FATHER unfreezes as CHILD turns and walks*
9   *Downstage toward the bench. CHILD is referred to as "boy"*
10   *throughout, but this may be changed to "girl" and "her father,"*
11   *etc. if a girl is cast in the role.)*
12 **CHILD:** **Daddy, where did I come from?**
13 **NARRATOR:** **The man looked around frantically for his wife,**
14   **but she wasn't there, and the child persisted, so it was**
15   **up to the father.**
16 **FATHER:** **Sit down, son.** *(FATHER moves over, making room for*
17   *the CHILD.)*
18 **NARRATOR:** **The air purification unit was turned up high,**
19   **and the green lights on the door panel showed that the**
20   **house was hermetically sealed, so neither the man nor**
21   **the boy wore an oxygen mask.**
22 **FATHER:** **I guess it's time I told you about the birds and the**
23   **bees.**
24 **CHILD:** *(Puzzled)* **The what and the what?**
25 **FATHER:** *(Laughing)* **The birds and the bees. You've seen**
26   **pictures of them, I'm sure. They lived** *(Remembering)* **in**
27   **the days of clean air when such life was abundant on**
28   **earth . . . before oxygen masks and sealed homes. Before**
29   **night was heavy blackness and day a dirty twilight. In**
30   **the days when children like you played outside.**
31 **CHILD:** *(Amazed)* **Out in that?!**
32 **FATHER:** **Outside wasn't always that way, Reid. Once it was**
33   **bright yellow. Once the sun warmed the soil and flowers**
34   **grew. Once — but that wasn't what you asked, was it?**
35 **CHILD:** **I wanted to know where I came from. Was I**

1   **authorized?**

2   **FATHER:** *(Wincing)* **Oh, yes. You're officially Number A23196,**

3   **Series 24, California Unit 236, the one child allowed to**

4   **us under the Federal Birth Regulation Law of 1986.**

5   **CHILD:** **I'm the only son you'll ever have?**

6   **FATHER:** **Yes. Just you. The law forbids any others.**

7   **CHILD:** **Suppose more babies came? I'd like a brother to play**

8   **with — or even a sister.**

9   **FATHER:** **They . . . they would take them. You see, the Earth**

10   **was becoming too full of people, son. Food was becoming**

11   **a problem — there wasn't enough to eat. And our natural**

12   **resources were vanishing — oil and coal and even water**

13   **were becoming scarce. You know . . . there just plain**

14   **wasn't enough room. So the law was passed.**

15   **CHILD:** **Did you . . . plan me?**

16   **FATHER:** *(A bit amused)* **We wanted you. We wanted you very**

17   **much. I guess from that viewpoint, you were planned —**

18   **sort of.**

19   **CHILD:** **Then how did you create me?** *(They freeze, the CHILD*

20   *looking up at the FATHER, the FATHER looking down at the*

21   *CHILD.)*

22   **NARRATOR:** *(Standing)* **The father looked down at the child**

23   **tenderly. How much easier it would have been, long ago,**

24   **to use the parallel of birds and bees . . . when there were**

25   **birds and bees . . . when there were flowers, when the**

26   **clean air carried the pollen over warm fields. He wished**

27   **with all his heart he could use the parallel now . . . not**

28   **just because he liked the vision it created, but because**

29   **of his memories of warmth and light in the outdoors. But**

30   **the air purification unit hummed, the panel lights**

31   **blinked green, the day was dark with poisons.**

32   **FATHER:** **What created you?** *(Puts his arm across the CHILD's*

33   *shoulders.)* **Love created you, Reid. It's all we began with.**

34   **It's all we have left.** *(CHILD, still puzzled, walks Off-stage;*

35   *FATHER sits for a moment, brooding, and then follows CHILD.)*

1   **NARRATOR:**   And the boy went away, puzzled . . . The father
2   brooded far into the night of heavy and impure blackness.
3   *(Exits.)*
4
5
6
7
8
9
10
11
12
13
14
15
16
17
18
19
20
21
22
23
24
25
26
27
28
29
30
31
32
33
34
35

A YEAR-END DIALOGUE WITH OUTER SPACE

by John Ciardi

A compiled script from two poems, "A Year-End Dialogue with Outer Space" and "Nine Beeps for Year's End," arranged for Readers Theatre by Melvin R. White, Ph.D.

CAST OF CHARACTERS

READER ONE: Man skilled in character suggestion.

READER TWO: Man skilled in character suggestion.

The content and basic structure of the two poems, as originally written by the poet, are unchanged, and lend themselves admirably to the oral interpretive medium. Combined, they provide a powerful and highly evocative comment on the national and international scene. The author stipulated in giving permission to use his material that " 'Nine Beeps' must be produced in entirety since they are an effort to satirize *all* sacred cows and are saved from bigotry only by the fact that they satirize equally on all fronts."

The Physical Arrangement of the Scene

In a test production of this script, two lecterns were placed Down Center, side by side. Later the script was performed successfully on a bare stage. However, if desired, two stools can be provided, or a piano bench, or two tall stools on which the men can sit behind two lecterns. Focus can be either On-stage, Off-stage, or a combination of the two. The latter proved most satisfactory to the readers in a 1970 performance, and this shift from Off-stage to On-stage focus is indicated in this version. When the poems refer to the General and the President, and other officials, real names of current gentlemen in these positions should be inserted.

First published in *Saturday Review*. Reprinted by permission of the estate of Judith Ciardi.

1	*(The two readers take their positions side by side behind two*
2	*lecterns.)*
3	**READER TWO:** *(As NARRATOR)* **A year-end dialogue with**
4	**outer space.**
5	**READER ONE:** *(Off-stage focus throughout until script indicates*
6	*otherwise)* **Do you?**
7	**READER TWO:** *(Also Off-stage focus)* **Yes.**
8	**READER ONE:** **Do you what?**
9	**READER TWO:** **Whatever — to the unqualified question the**
10	**unqualified answer: I do.**
11	**READER ONE:** **Everything?**
12	**READER TWO:** **Yes.**
13	**READER ONE:** *Everything?*
14	**READER TWO:** **I do:**
15	**in the fact or in the thought of it — everything:**
16	**what is done in fact and without much thought,**
17	**what is done in fact in place of thought,**
18	**what is done premeditatively and thoughtfully in fact,**
19	**what is done in thought only — to escape fact,**
20	**or to make it bearable, or to confirm it — everything.**
21	**READER ONE:** **And do you now confess?**
22	**READER TWO:** **To myself, everything.**
23	**To the world in practical fact what is in practical fact**
24	**convenient, except that in an anger like an assault**
25	**of honesty, I do now and then not care, and do openly**
26	**admit being and having been and meaning to be everything,**
27	**and to relive it.**
28	**READER ONE:** **You have lied?**
29	**READER TWO:** **I recall that life.**
30	**READER ONE:** **Cheated?**
31	**READER TWO:** **And that one.**
32	**READER ONE:** **Stolen?**
33	**READER TWO:** **Negligently.**
34	**What has there been that would have been worth the time**
35	**it would have taken to steal it?**

1 READER ONE: But you *have*? sometimes there *was*
2   something?
3 READER TWO: At times, a trifle, and that always instantly
4   not worth keeping.
5 READER ONE: You have killed?
6 READER TWO: Always, alas, for the worst reasons.
7 READER ONE: For what reasons?
8 READER TWO: For duty. For my captain's approval.
9 READER ONE: Not for survival?
10 READER TWO: Survival lay with my captain, the controls his.
11   I killed because I could.
12 READER ONE: You were proud?
13 READER TWO: For no reason I have not survived.
14 READER ONE: Envious?
15 READER TWO: At times. But I have admired many.
16 READER ONE: Wrathful?
17 READER TWO: In bursts from the sperm center. A screeing
18   of sensation, like a Morse code I could not read
19   that was in any case drowned in a cosmic whine.
20 READER ONE: Slothful?
21 READER TWO: Yawningly, when that was my mood's
22   pleasure.
23 READER ONE: Avaricious?
24 READER TWO: No.
25 READER ONE: Gluttonous?
26 READER TWO: Hungry.
27 READER ONE: Lustful?
28 READER TWO: Gladly.
29 READER ONE: What then do you believe should be done
30   with your soul?
31 READER TWO: Erase its name and make room for another
32   experience.
33 READER ONE: Why?
34 READER TWO: First, because this one is completed and time
35   is not.

1	READER ONE:	And second?
2	READER TWO:	Because it will in any case be erased.
3	READER ONE:	And third?
4	READER TWO:	Because, though it does not matter, eternity
5		would be the one experience beyond mercy.
6	READER ONE:	And you claim mercy?
7	READER TWO:	I do.
8	READER ONE:	Why?
9	READER TWO:	Because I was born.

10 READER ONE: *(As NARRATOR, after a transition pause, speaks*
11 *to the audience)* **Thus spake John Ciardi on December 24th,**
12 **Christmas Eve, in the year of our Lord 1966.** *(Pause. Then*
13 *makes "Beep-Beep" sounds, followed by the announcement:)*
14 **Nine Beeps for Year's End.**
15 **Beep One.** *(Sound: one beep, made vocally or recorded)*

16 READER TWO: **"Stop war," he said.**
17 READER ONE: **"Fine," I said. "How?"**
18 READER TWO: **"You," he shrieked, "are the ENEMY!"**
19 READER ONE: *(Sound: two beeps)*
20 READER TWO: *(As black panelist)* **"I am your equal in every**
21 **way,"**
22 **said the educated, moderate-militant**
23 **black panelist maintaining a balance**
24 **on the *Let's Find a Subject* show.**
25 READER ONE: **"Probably," I suggested,**
26 **"I am better than you**
27 **at remembering limericks, and you**
28 **better than I at, say, math,**
29 **volleyball, and the first names**
30 **of the eternal verities, though ethno-**
31 **genetico-politically, yes,**
32 **how should we not be equal?"**
33 READER TWO: *(As black panelist)* **"So," he said. "You admit**
34 **my superiority!"** *(Slight pause; then three beeps)*
35 READER ONE: *(As Catholic layman)* **"Ecumenically moved to**

336

1   *caritas*
2   toward even the unwashed,"
3   said the genial Catholic intellectual
4   layman of new dispensations,
5   "I am ready to meet with you,
6   to listen, and to pretend
7   you are an admissable entity.
8
9   "I am even willing to think of you
10   as a decent bit of misguidance.
11
12   "Shucks, I am willing to pretend
13   you could, given a miracle,
14   make it to heaven without
15   benefit of the True Road Map.
16   Though, of course, we both know better."
17   *(Sound of four beeps)*
18   READER TWO: *(As kosher urbanist)* **"Yes, of course, the Arabs**
19   **have a right to live,"**
20   said the kosher urbanist smiling,
21   "but only the Jews are the chosen,
22   and how can there be room for two choices
23   when the right one has made the desert bloom?"
24   READER ONE: *(Makes sound of five beeps. On this, the Beep V*
25   *section, the two readers break their Off-stage focus, leave their*
26   *scripts, turn and talk directly to each other.)*
27   READER TWO: **"I love you."**
28   READER ONE: **"I adore you."**
29   READER TWO: **"I love you more."**
30   READER ONE: **"More than what?"**
31   READER TWO: **"Than you love me."**
32   READER ONE: *(Irritably)* **"Impossible."**
33   READER TWO: *(Sharply)* **"Don't argue."**
34   READER ONE: **"I was only . . ."**
35   READER TWO: *(In anger)* **"Shut up!"**

1   **READER ONE:** *(Sound of six beeps. Return to Off-stage focus.)*
2   "We need fifty thousand more men,"
3   said the General in springtime,
4   "and that will end it."
5   **READER TWO:** "It's a lot," said the President,
6   "But all right, if you're sure."
7   **READER ONE:** "I'm sure," said the General. *(Pauses, then*
8   *continues.)*
9   "We need 100,000 more men
10   and tanks, copters, planes,
11   and everything by the billion and *that*
12   will end it," said the General in winter.
13   "And, yes, I'm sure as shooting."
14   **READER TWO:** "It's a lot," said the President.
15   "Explain it to the Pentagon, please."
16   **READER ONE:** "I need 150,000 men
17   and tanks, copters, planes,
18   and some more billions and that
19   will *really* end it," said the General
20   back at the spring offensive.
21   **READER TWO:** "I've spoken to the staff," said the Pentagon,
22   "And you'll have to settle for
23   148,000 and only ninety-eight
24   percent of everything else.
25   Can you end it with that?"
26   **READER ONE:** "Hm," said the General,
27   "can you promise me
28   a million men this summer?" *(Makes sound of seven beeps.)*
29   **READER TWO:** *(As Nasser)* "I don't want to be affiliated
30   with your rotten capitalist
31   imperialist degeneracy," said Nasser.
32   "All I want is a market
33   for the oil, cash on the barrelhead,
34   plus some tourist dollars. And that
35   only until these Russian credits turn edible."

1   **READER ONE:**   *(Makes sound of eight beeps.)*
2   **READER TWO:**   *(As undergraduate)* **"Bloodsucker," said the**
3   **undergraduate**
4   **to his uncle, the customer's man,**
5   **"Don't you know we're in a war economy**
6   **and that only a vulture**
7   **would try to turn a profit in it?"**
8   **READER ONE:**   *(As the uncle)* **"So you have nothing to invest,"**
9   **said his uncle. "Maybe someday you will."**
10   **READER TWO:**   *(As associate professor)* **"Hi, Unk," said the**
11   **associate professor**
12   **Someday. "Janie just inherited**
13   **four thousand. Is that enough**
14   **to start a fund for the kids' tuition?"**
15   **READER ONE:**   *(Makes nine beep sounds.* Turns to other reader,*
16   *and uses On-stage focus.)* **"You don't rhyme."**
17   **READER TWO:**   **"What does? It's the world I'm writing about."**
18   **READER ONE:**   *(To audience)* **Thus spake John Ciardi on**
19   **December 24th, Christmas Eve, in the year of our Lord**
20   **1967.** *(Makes two loud beep sounds, if desired.)*
21
22
23   **In performance, it was found that making the beeps with the human voice*
24   *was more effective than recorded sounds. Also, in some performances the*
         readers used only a double beep ("Beep-Beep"), rather than adding an extra
25   *beep for each of the nine sections.*
26
27
28
29
30
31
32
33
34
35

ABOUT THE AUTHOR

The late Melvin "Mel" White was born ten miles east of Chug-water, Wyoming, in January of 1911. During several moves to New York, Iowa, and Wisconsin, he managed to graduate from high school in Eau Claire, Wisconsin, earn a B.A. and M.A. from the State University of Iowa, and a Ph.D. from the University of Wisconsin. With time out to serve in the Navy during World War II, he taught for 42 years before he retired from Brooklyn College, the City University of New York, in 1968. After his retirement, he was on the faculties of California State University, Hayward; California Polytechnic State University, San Luis Obispo; University of Hawaii, Hilo; Chaminade College, Honolulu; and the University of Arizona.

As a lecturer and "joke-teller," he appeared in a variety of locales, from Nihon University in Tokyo and the International Institute, Madrid, Spain, to the East-West Center, Honolulu, and the Canal Zone. He judged plays for the United States Army in Japan, Korea, Europe and the Caribbean, and conducted Readers Theatre workshops and directed plays worldwide.

Dr. White had 17 books published and 107 plays, including co-authorship of *READERS THEATRE HANDBOOK: A Dramatic Approach to Literature,* the first book on this performance art. Past President of the Army Theatre Association, past Executive Secretary of the American Educational Theatre Association, Mel was a member of the College of Fellows of the American Theatre.

341

ORDER FORM

 MERIWETHER PUBLISHING LTD.
P.O. BOX 7710
COLORADO SPRINGS, CO 80933
TELEPHONE: (719) 594-4422

Please send me the following books:

_____**Mel White's Readers Theatre Anthology #TT-B110** **$14.95**
by Melvin R. White
28 all-occasion readings for performance and storytelling

_____**Theatre Alive! #TT-B178** **$24.95**
by Dr. Norman A. Bert
An introductory anthology of world drama

_____**The Scenebook for Actors #TT-B177** **$14.95**
by Dr. Norman A. Bert
Collection of great monologs and dialogs for auditions

_____**One-Act Plays for Acting Students #TT-B159** **$14.95**
by Dr. Norman A. Bert
An anthology of complete one-act plays

_____**57 Original Auditions for Actors #TT-B181** **$8.95**
by Eddie Lawrence
A workbook of monologs for actors

_____**Theatre Games for Young Performers #TT-B188** **$10.95**
by Maria C. Novelly
Improvisations and exercises for developing acting skills

_____**Winning Monologs for Young Actors #TT-B127** **$10.95**
by Peg Kehret
Honest-to-life monologs for young actors

**These and other fine Meriwether Publishing books are available at
your local bookstore or direct from the publisher. Use the handy
order form on this page.**

NAME: _____

ORGANIZATION NAME: _____

ADDRESS: _____

CITY: _____ STATE: _____ ZIP: _____

PHONE: _____

☐ **Check Enclosed**
☐ **Visa or Mastercard #** _____
Expiration
Signature: _____ *Date:* _____
(required for Visa/Mastercard orders)

COLORADO RESIDENTS: Please add 3% sales tax.
SHIPPING: Include $2.75 for the first book and 50¢ for each additional book ordered.

☐ *Please send me a copy of your complete catalog of books and plays.*

ORDER FORM

 MERIWETHER PUBLISHING LTD.
P.O. BOX 7710
COLORADO SPRINGS, CO 80933
TELEPHONE: (719) 594-4422

Please send me the following books:

_____**Mel White's Readers Theatre Anthology #TT-B110** **$14.95**
by Melvin R. White
28 all-occasion readings for performance and storytelling

_____**Theatre Alive! #TT-B178** **$24.95**
by Dr. Norman A. Bert
An introductory anthology of world drama

_____**The Scenebook for Actors #TT-B177** **$14.95**
by Dr. Norman A. Bert
Collection of great monologs and dialogs for auditions

_____**One-Act Plays for Acting Students #TT-B159** **$14.95**
by Dr. Norman A. Bert
An anthology of complete one-act plays

_____**57 Original Auditions for Actors #TT-B181** **$8.95**
by Eddie Lawrence
A workbook of monologs for actors

_____**Theatre Games for Young Performers #TT-B188** **$10.95**
by Maria C. Novelly
Improvisations and exercises for developing acting skills

_____**Winning Monologs for Young Actors #TT-B127** **$10.95**
by Peg Kehret
Honest-to-life monologs for young actors

These and other fine Meriwether Publishing books are available at your local bookstore or direct from the publisher. Use the handy order form on this page.

NAME: _____

ORGANIZATION NAME: _____

ADDRESS: _____

CITY: _____ STATE: _____ ZIP: _____

PHONE: _____

☐ **Check Enclosed**
☐ **Visa or Mastercard #** _____

Signature: _____   *Expiration Date:* _____

(required for Visa/Mastercard orders)

COLORADO RESIDENTS: Please add 3% sales tax.
SHIPPING: Include $2.75 for the first book and 50¢ for each additional book ordered.

☐ *Please send me a copy of your complete catalog of books and plays.*